# GLOBAL EDUCATION FUTURES AGENDA

PAVEL LUKSHA,
DMITRY PESKOV

 iUniverse®

## GLOBAL EDUCATION FUTURES: AGENDA

*iUniverse books may be ordered through booksellers or by contacting:*

*iUniverse*
*1663 Liberty Drive*
*Bloomington, IN 47403*
*www.iuniverse.com*
*1-800-Authors (1-800-288-4677)*

*ISBN: 978-1-5320-2430-6 (sc)*
*ISBN: 978-1-5320-2431-3 (e)*

*Print information available on the last page.*

*iUniverse rev. date: 12/10/2019*

# GLOBAL EDUCATION FUTURES AGENDA

# TABLE OF CONTENTS

*Nothing ages as fast as the future.*
**Stanisław Lem** – Summa Technologiae

# 1. INTRODUCTION

## 1.1 THE ERA OF TRANSFORMATION

The education is witnessing an era of radical transformation. This domain for a long time could stay unsusceptible to changes experienced by the society, so that it secured its reputation as one of the most conservative areas of human activities. However, we are at the point when this situation can no longer hold. The coming decades will see an era of the most radical changes in education since the appearance of national education systems. Education-related industries such as digital technologies, medicine, and finance – and not the education system itself – will be the chief source of these changes.

Our work is an attempt to systematically describe these industries' impact on the various stages of education, primarily in the economically, technologically, and socially developed countries. Obviously, this is the first such attempt ever made (more than fifty examples of similar studies are provided at the end of the book), but it is probably one of the most systemic ones. This work is the result of more than five years of dialogues between leading experts and practitioners in education & training, high technologies, human resource management, and other related fields. It has absorbed the experience of a host of educational experiments that we were able to observe and that we either took part in or organized ourselves. Many of these experiments changed personnel training systems, reshaped practices of schools and universities, and engendered new educational startups.

Our work, however, is not intended to designate the position of a specific developers' group. We realize that 'nothing ages as fast as the future' and that our goal is not to predict how events will unfold, but rather to encourage joint action to change things. The time has come to determine what direction the global education system is moving in. This includes creating a road map to coordinate and balance the efforts of various players' who establish new rules of the game openly and honestly. Our work is an invitation to those willing, such as us, to join forces and take part in creating a new architecture, conventions, and specific solutions for the 21st century education system. It is imperative to forge an open code platform, a platform that we must forge together*. We believe that education for a new,

*\* Our group organizes a series participatory processes dedicated to this task as part of the Global Education Futures in 2015 (see www.edu2035.org).*

network-based, and post-information society can be created only upon the principles that a new society observes: open dialog, equality of standpoints, cooperation, and co-creation.

## 1.2 A GLOBAL AGENDA REPORT: WHY NOW?

The more traditional genre of reports written from global standpoints on education development (e.g., the United Nations or World Bank reports) often uses a set of assumptions such as:

- There are 'best practices' for organizing education systems that have been implemented in some of (and sometimes in the majority of) OECD countries;

- Further gradual fostering of these education systems in the future should address, first and foremost, internationalization and harmonization of education approaches, by means of institutional rankings (e.g. QS World University Rankings, The Times Higher Education World University Rankings, Webometrics Ranking, and Academic Ranking of World Universities), comparative international tests (e.g. PISA, TIMSS, Teaching And Learning International Survey (TALIS) etc.), and supranational harmonization procedures (the Bologna Process, European Higher Education Area, etc.);

- The main challenge for education systems in developing countries is to ensure the full access to primary and further to secondary education (cf. United Nations 'Millennium goals'*) and to subsequently create full-fledged systems of industrial education that follow the example of practices in the developed nations.

* http://www.un.org/ millenniumgoals/ education.shtml

Without calling into question the great significance of the work that international development institutions and harmonization tools do, we would like to point out that the countries which serve as sources of 'exemplary practices' today also find themselves at a critical juncture, a turning point. Leading OECD countries such as the United States, Great Britain, Japan, South Korea, Australia, etc., currently claim that they need to 're-assemble' their education models**. There multiple common challenges that countries' education systems face:

** In the US, it is often discussed that the education is 'broken'.

1. The development of digital technologies and telecommunications systems is changing the ways in which the knowledge is created, transferred, and stored, and in which skills are developed. Furthermore, digital technologies change the way to manage one's own development trajectory, to assess and record achievements, to administrate educational institutions, etc. These technologies are fundamentally transnational and transcultural, and can be used in any organization or family, all virtually in spite of political, ethnic, religious, and other differences. The most fundamental limitation in technology adoption rate is its cost to end user, and the Internet and digital technologies are very cheap and are affordable even for the least well-off social classes.

2. Many of the new solutions in education today come in the form of technological startups that combine digital technologies and social innovations. In the education field, new players are emerging quickly, actively taking command of new educational practices, reacting to user demands faster and with greater flexibility, all while (often) not being regulated by national educational legislation. Their position is enhanced by the fact that education in traditional school and university institutions continuously becomes more expensive (Altbach, Reisberg & Rumbley 2009), which causes governments and consumers to call for sustainable alternatives to existing education formats*. Outside the education system, a new transnational market emerges, which within a couple of decades (or even sooner) could take over the traditional educational system and introduce new standards of learning and talent management (just like Facebook sets new standards for socializing online). At the next stage, mature companies that will emerge from educational startups (and we believe that some of them may cross the bar of $100 billion capitalization within the next decade and become the new Googles or Apples of tech companies stock market) will begin to encroach on the education agenda of national governments.

* http://www.
timeshighered-
ucation.co.uk/
features/a-differ-
ent-world/2001128.
article

3. Economic progress in industrially developed countries stemming from continuing pressure of international competition, the fast shift in technologies, and increasing economic uncertainty sets the demand for new types of skills and new forms of professional education & training. On one hand, demand is on the rise for highly creative workers with as much flexibility as possible who are ready to work alone or as part of a team, and who are capable of working in various cultures and with various technological environments — implying changing requirements for basic education curriculum (so-called '21st century skills'). On the other hand, shorter preparation cycles are required for highly-focused professional skills critically needed within industries. In addition to that, the need for nonstop life-long learning models, which allow professionals to continuously refine their skills in line with the changing tasks at hand, is on the rise. These requirements necessitate the significant reorganization of professional training systems and the establishment of new requirements for school education and primary higher education. Furthermore, people are increasingly dissatisfied with existing educational institutions that are not willing to follow the altered demands of business, the public, and state, and that are focused on reproducing their practices of old.

4. Education is now literally seen as an intangible investment asset, to which all criteria of investment markets should be applied. The way this asset is created and capitalized should become transparent and easily manageable (incl. the partial 'detachment' of talent benefits from talent owners, as in stock and credit markets). There is already a multitude of financial tools for investing in one's own education or in another person's education. It is clear that a boom awaits this field in the coming years (we will discuss this issue in more detail further in this book).

5. Finally, the shifting values and preferences in industrially developed countries related to 'addressing basic needs' in the consumer society, imply that the educational system obtains a new type of 'human resource' to work with.

- On the one hand, the share of students who see no significant value in education and have no special interest in learning is on the rise. The main challenge for the education system, which acts as a space for reproducing society's activities and values, is to create motivation for such people to study. In fulfilling its objective, education is pushed into competition with mass media and new media for such students' interest and attention, which in turn forces educational programs to become more enticing and interactive (hence, in particular, the trend toward the massive gamification of education).

- On the other hand, the number of 'conscientious' students who are looking for 'their own path', understand the meaning of self-development, are willing to set their own goals to do this, and are not willing to take 'package deals' that schools and universities offer them. These are the people becoming the main users of individual education trajectories that both 'penetrate' the borders of educational institutions and combine domains of study, work, and personal development together. At the moment, no country anywhere in the world is able to provide education to such people on a mass scale.

If these challenges (and the scale of their impact) are acknowledged, they call for a new education models, the one that will efficiently use modern technological environments and that will be able to productively respond to the demands of the economy and society. Failures in education are nowadays recognized as one of the key sources of the problems in politics, society, and the economy — among them ethnic and religious conflicts, environmental over-exploitation, and corruption. Therefore, education rises to the top of agenda of leading global institutions and becomes one of the 'hottest' topics at many national and global forums.

Apart from advanced countries that face these challenges, new and strong players — namely countries with emerging economies such as BRICS countries, the Arab world, and South-East Asia — intensively participate in the global division of labor and the global political 'big game'. In order to be able to compete with other nations for markets and political agenda, these countries started to create their own education systems, often 'from scratch', by copying the models of industrialized countries. However, given the fact that the advanced countries' education systems are now themselves transforming, there is a risk that emerging nations may actually buy a 'stale good' (recipes for industrial-age educational systems) that may become obsolete in just 10 to 15 years. It would be worthwhile to spend (at least a portion of) emerging economies' billions invested into the education system in order to design the elements of their own new systems — rather than to buy again a 'new, refashioned' education system recipe in 10 years from now.

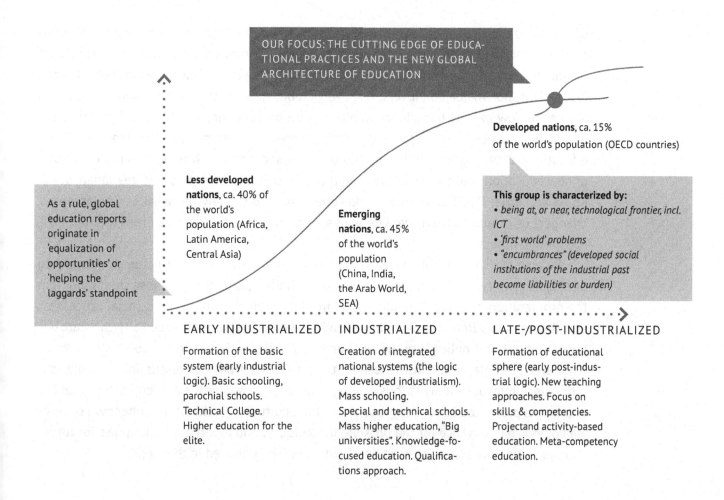

OUR FOCUS: THE CUTTING EDGE OF EDUCA-
TIONAL PRACTICES AND THE NEW GLOBAL
ARCHITECTURE OF EDUCATION

**Developed nations**, ca. 15%
of the world's population (OECD countries)

**Less developed
nations**, ca. 40% of
the world's
population (Africa,
Latin America,
Central Asia)

**Emerging
nations**, ca. 45%
of the world's
population
(China, India,
the Arab World,
SEA)

As a rule, global
education reports
originate in
'equalization of
opportunities' or
'helping the
laggards' standpoint

**This group is characterized by:**
• *being at, or near, technological frontier, incl.
ICT*
• *'first world' problems*
• *"encumbrances" (developed social
institutions of the industrial past
become liabilities or burden)*

EARLY INDUSTRIALIZED

Formation of the basic
system (early industrial
logic). Basic schooling,
parochial schools.
Technical College.
Higher education for the
elite.

INDUSTRIALIZED

Creation of integrated
national systems (the logic
of developed industrialism).
Mass schooling.
Special and technical schools.
Mass higher education, "Big
universities". Knowledge-fo-
cused education. Qualifications approach.

LATE-/POST-INDUSTRIALIZED

Formation of educational
sphere (early post-indus-
trial logic). New teaching
approaches. Focus on
skills & competencies.
Projectand activity-based
education. Meta-competency
education.

**Figure 1** The stages of development in education
systems and the Report's focus

National education systems can be (fairly conditionally) be divided into three categories
depending on the maturity of their education systems: (1) groups of developed countries
that are involved in making the transition to a new education system; (2) groups of countries with emerging economies that are already building their own education systems in
line with those in developed countries; and (3) the group of under-developed countries that
is just beginning to create modern educational institutions. The challenges faced by each
of three groups are different (see Figure 1). What is important is that all these categories
will benefit from the emergence of new education solutions. In particular, we believe that
underdeveloped countries will be able to quickly master leading technological and cultural
practices and hence leapfrog to world-class human capital using these leading educational
technologies.

For this reason, our Report focuses on determining the universal challenges and goals
for creating a new education domain. These challenges and goals will be equally applicable
to advanced countries and countries with emerging economies. A mapping of global education futures is necessary — a map of opportunities and threats that may emerge over the
next decades as new educational models unfold. Education is the point of transformation

of our civilization - after all, education is the key to building a different reality, and civilization's stability and development hinge on it. Education forges the foundation for society to be able to change its way of life. None of the existing players — neither leading educational institutions, nor major employers, not even global governance organizations — have an answer to how exactly this global sphere should be configured. But it is evident that the search for solutions should focus on cutting-edge practices exhibited by leaders of new education. Versions of the design should be discussed, first and foremost, in the real world of new education leaders that come from the United States, EU member states, Japan, South Korea and other OECD countries — and complemented by views on what can be accepted, changed, or proposed from the side of major emerging economies of China, India, Brazil, Russia, and others.

We also realize that, when discussing how this sphere will be structured, we need to distinguish two types of phenomena: the global challenges (first of all, those stemming from the proliferation of new technologies and from the global economic and social processes), and the agenda catering only to industrially developed countries, especially the Euro-Atlantic cultural and political group of countries (so-called 'first-world problems'). We tried, whenever possible, to 'cleanse' these cultural specifics from our discussion to make our rationale applicable within various country contexts. If, however, the reader believes that the arguments presented in our Report contradict the cultural practice of his or her own country, we apologize in advance for the possible inaccuracies and assert our willingness for future dialogues that will allow the refining of global vision proposed in this Report.

## 1.3 HOW WE UNDERSTAND EDUCATION

It is important to note that our understanding of education is much broader than what is universally accepted today. We see education not only as learning in formal educational institutions (they are but a small part of what we are talking about), but also as an entire process that includes upbringing, learning, and self-learning at all stages of life, from birth (or even before birth) and until death. We purposely keep the term 'education' in our discussion, because we believe that education systems of the future will have to provide solutions for all aspects of human learning and development for individuals and collectives at all stages of human life. In other words, understanding of the whole human life cycle should underpin the future design of education systems.

In the ancient times, while there were no universal schooling system, there existed many Teachers with a capital 't' — those who took an end-to-end responsibility for their students and taught them the 'art of life'. This ancient role has to be brought back into education — for education is everything that teaches a person how to live. A multitude of interested parties have an interest in a person's education throughout his entire life — such as the person himself, his family, his communities (e.g. his city or his church), his employers, the government, the business etc. Our goal is to comprehensively examine learning issues and understand how the education needed at various stages of life will develop — considering the interplay of these various stakeholders and sponsors of education.

We discuss education from the life-long learning point of view, as a nonstop process that accompanies a person from or before birth and until death (Figure 2). Several types of education over the course of a person's lifetime are more pragmatic and are meant to shape his knowledge and skills that allow for working efficiently in the economy and achieving social success. Such is the role of formal education or professional retraining. Other types of education are designed primarily for personal improvement and self-development, including working on physical and psychophysical qualities. There are also types of education that work with groups and communities, e.g. help to create teams and develop organizational skills, or to strengthen local ties within a village. We believe that a large part of one's upbringing and personal healing (including psychotherapy or fitness) should also be interpreted as education. Some types of education were well developed in ancient civilizations, but only begin to re-appear in industrially developed societies, such as the educational support of a family that undergoes transformation as it tries to adapt to the death or birth of one of its members.

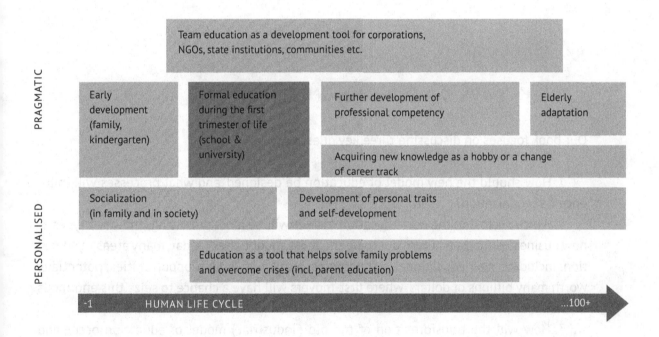

**Figure 2** Education as developmental support from birth to death

Summarizing, you could assume that education in our understanding is the institutionalized process of learning & development support throughout the human life cycle from or before birth until death. Formal institutions of education are but a small part of this phenomenon. The objective of this book is to try to examine the universal processes that affect the sphere of education in its tonality, and not only formal educational institutions.

Moreover, our book purposely avoids describing new education solutions and forms in relation to specific institutions of learning, such as schools and universities. Accordingly, specific references to K-12, colleges, or universities are only occasional. One of the key conclusions of our work is that the habitual categories of school and university education, including the association of school with one's adolescent and teenage years, and of university with the start of one's professional life, will soon undergo significant changes. Institutional forms, while preserving their exterior uniformity or naming, are rather fluid on the inside, and the university of the future will resemble modern universities no more than does Stanford University resemble a 12th century Parisian or Bologna university.

Throughout this Report we refer to the term 'industrial education' and contrast it with the 'new education,' a system of flexible, individualized, and open education that supports a person's learning demands over the course of his entire life. We took the term 'industrial education' from the work of Ken Robinson who describes it as a "manufacturing model based on linearity [of the education process] and conformity [of educational content] and batching people [into groups] for study, based primarily on their age"*. The existing system of school and university education, highly efficient in training people with standard skills but having trouble in shaping unconventional skills and in supporting individual growth, was built on these very principles.

* Ken Robinson: Bring on the Learning Revolution! http://www.ted.com/talks/sir_ken_robinson_bring_on_the_revolution.html

## 1.4 NECESSARY INTRODUCTORY REMARKS

### 1.4.1 Who Do We See As Readers of this Book?

Our book focuses on discussing three key questions:

1. How should the new model of education be designed, and what processes will influence its organization?

2. Which sectors of the new education market will be most promising, and what types of new business projects will turn out to be the most sought after? Today, many areas in education, including new educational technologies, remain as hidden opportunities, potentially worth many billions of dollars, where first-movers will have a chance to seize this enormous market.

3. How will the transformation of the old ('industrial') model of education occur, and what decisions ought to be made to manage existing educational institutions more effectively and efficiently?

We figure that the answers to these questions will interest, first and foremost, four categories of readers:

a. Investment-oriented businesses in this new sector, including the startup community and investment funds in the area of education startups, as well as medium and big businesses that invest in upgrading of professional / vocational education & training;

b. Governments/education system regulators, first and foremost those in developing countries with great economic potential (i.e. emerging economies) where systems of secondary, higher, and professional education are actively taking shape;

c. Education system administrators (school principals, university provosts, etc.) in developed countries facing the reorganization of their academic institutions.

d. Social activists that seek to make education more diverse, more human-oriented, and better serving the interests of their communities, their nation, and the world as a whole.

This book may be useful for a larger audiences of educators and learners as well. Together, we aim to discuss and attract a future that will be both desirable and advantageous for the multiple players that help shape it.

## 1.4.2 **How our Report is structured**

Our book can be seen as a narrative explaining the 'map of the future' of education that has been created through dozens of participatory sessions, with thousands of people that have participated in this process over last five years. Readers may download the full map at www.edu2030.org. This map is a multi-dimensional structure, and the stories presented in it are only one of the ways to read it.

The Report consists of the following section that subsequently unveil the map's content:

a. The first section covers the trends that drive major transformative processes in the future of education. We primarily consider technological trends, because the technology development patterns (esp. in ICT) are being widely discussed and can be easily predicted (for instance, as R&D projects prioritized by global technology companies over next decade). In addition to that, we highlight a list of the most important soft factors (political, economic, social, and cultural trends) and uncertainty factors that create the variety of global scenarios. This section discusses the effects of each technology and of the soft factors for the future of education (those who wish may skip right away over to the description of new forms of education in the next section, while using this section as a reference).

b. The second section puts forward the main 'stories of future education' that refer to main aspects inside education: globalization processes, the development of new education management tools, a shift in education formats and content, a shift in the model of cognition, and the effects the emergence of technologies that will cement the emergence of a new education model (in next 20 to 25 years). We summarize with schemes that show the organization of new education model when its infrastructure is fully established, both for the learners and for providers of learning content and experiences.

c. The third section provides a list of recommendations for some of the main groups that actively impact the development of new education: venture capital, administrators of educational institutions, and regulators.

Readers that seek practice-oriented conclusions may begin reading in the reverse order, starting with the recommendations (third section), then looking for detailed explanations for these recommendations in the 'stories of future education' (second section), and then understanding what hard and soft factors may establish this suggested future design of education systems (first section). For most readers, however, we recommend reading the book in the normal sequence, from the beginning to the end.

### 1.4.3 This Report is not a forecast, but a call for action

Any contemplation about the future belongs to the human imagination. Therefore, the language for denoting many of the visible phenomena in our imagination is often to be invented. Most of the terms used while drawing up the roadmap ought to be understood as symbols with 'images of the future' behind them, and should be interpreted in such manner. This may sound like truism, but it still worth being said: the future cannot be 'studied' (because it does not exist yet), but it can be imagined, and then transformed into an action plan through reasoning based on our logic and experience.

Creation of the 'maps of the future' is a collective work that involves a large number of stakeholders. It allows to discover the collective impressions of the most likely scenario that combines the qualities of a prediction and an action plan. Our work has brought together several thousand people from many different fields from the education community and bordering fields, and it has also generalized the key conclusions made by a host of research groups across the world.

This book makes many detailed predictions and speculates on specific dates of events from the future. We will stipulate immediately that we are not claiming to be oracles — and the predictions made are illustrative and indicative. They help to make images of the future more tangible, to shift from general arguments to specific solutions. The numbers and dates in this book act as 'markers of the future' that indicate the scale and speed of transformation. As the experience of similar foresights shows, specific predictions about hard and soft technologies come true 60 to 70% of the time, while dates are accurately predicted up to 50% of the time (Martin, 2001). Our own experience using the earlier version of education foresight (made for Russia in 2010) also showed that the many events of the future tend to become 'attracted' into present, to take place faster than forecasted*. Therefore, we call to see our ideas not so much as predictions, but rather as an invitation to take immediate action.

* This can either be attributed to the conservatism of forecasters, or to the fact that a forecast becomes an inspiration for innovators that bring new practices into life.

*Basic principles for creating 'maps of the future':*

■ The future is not set in stone. There are many possible futures — it is not determined by the past, but depends on current decisions taken by participants and stakeholders;

■ The future depends on the effort made. It can be created;

■ We can get prepared or prepare the future as we want to see it.

In accepting these principles, we realize that creating 'maps of the future' is necessary but not sufficient to develop the future model of education. Therefore, as authors of this work, we ourselves do not stop at producing 'images' - we are the 'think-and-do' tank of educational practitioners, and everything we say we also try to test on ourselves. We therefore take full responsibility for what we recommend, and we seek to embody these recommended principles. We are already creating a number of education programs based on new principles and are taking efforts to create an environment in Russia for the future education*.

The future of globalizing education is a field of huge uncertainties and enormous potential. The global education architecture — a notion that for the moment has not been apprehended nor recognized — will become one of the most important subjects on the agenda of global politics and business. The need for the global road map of the future of education has ripen. Such a roadmap ought to be created by engaging all relevant parties — everyone who is willing, and able to, act on future globalizing education. In this sense, our book is an invitation to the dialogue, a kindling for the creation of a truly global roadmap.

\* While understanding that many processes of socio-economic development in Russia have become hostages of the ongoing geopolitical dynamics, we consider our work as a non-politicized effort to develop working models of the future education that can be beneficial for our country and the world.

**Table 1**

## KEY CONCLUSIONS: THE NEW EDUCATION LANDSCAPE IN DEVELOPED COUNTRIES

| | AROUND 2017 | AROUND 2025 | AROUND 2035 |
|---|---|---|---|
| **NEW EDUCATION LANDSCAPE** (emerging formats) | • Development of educational trajectories and MOOCs<br>• Academic grades give way to achievement recognition (competency and precedent passport)<br>• New models of investment in talent and other financial / insurance tools in education for learners & investors<br>• Cognitive traction and student engagement become elements of assessment / self-assessment and evaluation procedures | • Rise of Billion-Student Universities leads to education market concentration ('educational Imperialism')<br>• Artificial tutors and mentor networks<br>• Mass market solutions allow high quality education without ever entering a school or a university<br>• Major role of gaming environments and augmented reality<br>• Objectification of education through biofeedback / neurointerfaces | • Game and teamwork are two predominating forms of education and social interaction<br>• Artificial intelligence as a mentor ('Diamond Age Primer') and a partner in research<br>• 'Live Knowledge' models and the death of 'Gutenberg Galaxy'<br>• Education in NeuroWeb-linked groups and new pedagogy |
| **OBSOLETE FORMATS** (largely recognized as ineffective given the availability of feasible formats in advanced countries) | • 'Human phonograph' industrial teaching based on standard textbooks & tests (replaced by digital technology based solutions)<br>• Standardized tests (complemented & gradually replaced by tests more focused on unique & creative abilities)<br>• End-of-semester grades (replaced by continuous result recording) | • Graduation diplomas (replaced by life-long competency diploma)<br>• Academic journals (replaced by researcher communication networks), citation indexing standards & intellectual property right management system (replaced by comprehensive digital knowledge management ontologies)<br>• Single-author textbooks<br>• Altered states of consciousness as a social deviation | • Comprehensive schools<br>• Research universities<br>• Texts (books & articles) as a predominant medium of knowledge-based communication |

# 2. KEY DRIVERS OF EDUCATION SYSTEM TRANSFORMATION

## 2.1 DRIVERS OF CHANGE – WHERE NEW EDUCATION COMES FROM

### 2.1.1 Sources of change: the external environment and internal revolutions

The transformation of education is such a comprehensive and enticing process that is becoming fixated upon individual parts of it runs the risk of absorbing our attention. This often happens when discussing the formats of future education; some commentators praise the beginning MOOC revolution in education (Harden, 2013). Without denying the enormous potential of this format's transformative role, we ought to point out that expanding MOOC is necessary but nowhere near enough (and even rather little in terms of significance) as an element of the new education architecture. What is no less important are, first and foremost, decisions related to registering achievements and using them in one's career, and that are already being incorporated into the structure of leading MOOC providers, as well as the analysis itself of the processes of online learning and of refining new education models based on them. Other commentators are predicting an era of the total virtualization and gamification of education (see Cocoran, 2010, McGonigal, 2011). We are inclined to agree that game formats and virtual universes will play a significant role in future education. Again, this is only one of the components of the new education architecture*. Yet others point to new achievements in cognitive psychology and the ability to use them for training various cognitive skills. This and a host of other findings must also be taken into account when determining future education's structure.

* Moreover, some commentators are already foretelling the death of the gamification process, claiming 'gamification is complete, what's next?' (https://medium.com/brains-minds-and-machines-1/e19198c4e4b1)

Education by nature is an extremely conservative social institution. Such is its nature as the key tool for reproducing society's knowledge and cultural base — in other words, the dominating worldview. Throughout time this institution has changed under pressures from exterior circumstances; however, these were always necessary changes that allowed for implementing the large-scale reorganization of society toward new goals.

Currently, industrially developed countries undergo a transformation stemming from assimilating a new set of technologies—first and foremost information and communication technologies—that change the nature of relationships within society, including the education sphere, towards 'network-based' societies. These technologies bring to life a plethora of change in the economic, political, public, and cultural spheres, and as a result shape new demands for education. The education sphere is bombarded with demands and innovations from a host of change-makers (see Fig. 3), including:

- New customer demands stemming from change in the business environment and lifestyle (including the demands of businesses, states, families, NGOs, etc.);

- New standards imposed by national regulators and supranational structures, that help maintain national competitiveness and international compatibility;

- New practices driven by escalating global competition between education providers (and the conversion of best practices through comparative metrics such as rankings);

- Internal systematic innovators (leading schools and higher institutes of education)

- Solutions providing alternatives to existing educational system, implemented in startups and new products of large business organizations.

By assimilating new technologies, creating new human practices based on them (ex. social networks), and changing our impressions and priorities in relation to these practices, all these players begin to shift the forms and content of education processes. For instance, the proliferation of telecommunications technologies engenders a new practice (socializing on social networks), and hence allows for peer-to-peer online education in student communities**. The rise of peer-to-peer networks forces traditional universities to take into account, for example, the fact that students often collectively solve their individual assignments in such networks (e.g. the experience of such communities in Facebook and Vkontakte).

** See http://peer-agogy.org/

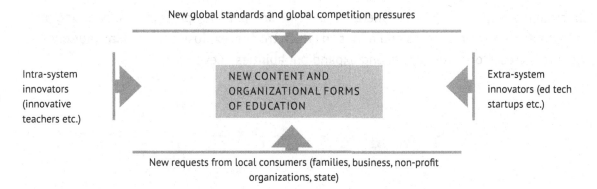

**Figure 3** Main sources of transformation pressures on education systems

We will stipulate right away that we are not aspiring to idealize information and communications technologies or yet again declare a technological revolution in education: this has been done many times before us and without us. Information and communications technologies also have their own dark side. In particular, they often tend to replace educational content with form, which distorts education and inter-human communications as a whole. For example, the culture of reading and understanding long texts, such as this Report, is being quickly lost right before our eyes — while strategic decisions that have consequences for thousands and millions of human lives are often made based on 5 to 10 PowerPoint slides. We apparently are losing more than just the practice of reading. We are losing the ability to shape and support complex and disciplined thinking. The challenge of building a new education is not to take down preceding practices, but to breathe new life into them, through finding and rethinking the jewels of education approaches coming from Indian ashrams, Jesuit schools, scholastic universities or research and development groups that existed in the beginning of the 20th century.

## 2.1.2 Three infrastructure spheres that have the greatest impact on the transformation of education

The three spheres engendering new technologies and practices that influence the education process itself and the system of perceptions of education (Table 2) are the socio-economic sectors that have basic, infrastructural features:

- 'Infrastructure of exchange': the sphere of information and communications technologies that influences all processes of creating and transferring information;

- 'Production and consumption infrastructure': the financial and investment sphere that sets the common rules of interaction in the economic system and — in line with the increase in interconnection between production and education — for the educational system;

■ 'Infrastructure of physicality': the sphere of medicine and popular sports (fitness) working (in a grassroots sense) with bodies and minds, in which there is explosive growth in solutions meant to increase our productivity and expand our abilities in everyday life.

**Table 2**
## THE IMPACT OF THREE KEY SPHERES ON EDUCATION

| INDUSTRY | USING PRODUCTS IN THE EDUCATION INDUSTRY | USING KEY CONCEPTS AND PERCEPTIONS |
|---|---|---|
| ICT | • Technological solutions (soft and hard) that impact obtaining and conveying knowledge and skills | • Open professional training and certification program (including a transparent competence model • Project work and startup work practice. |
| FINANCE | • Education as an investment object (loans, investing in employee training, the Upstart model, etc.) • Education insurance model (protection from 'wrong' knowledge, rewards for 'properly used' knowledge) | • Return on investment in education (efficiency monitoring) • Learning as a venture investment (insuring risks) |
| HEALTHCARE AND FITNESS | • Integral psychophysiological training systems • Psychophysiological simulators • Active substances for increasing mental / creative productivity | • Systems of training • Competition, rankings, and award systems (as principal motivation) |

Greater detail on technologies and social practices that occur based on them are considered below in sections 2.2 and 2.3.

### 2.1.3 Why we focus the most attention on technologies

There are several reasons why we focus so much attention on technologies when discussing future education:

a. Timely created and/or successfully assimilated technologies have a radical impact on social structures, and on society's priorities and competitiveness. There are a number of such examples, from the wheel and gunpowder to the rubber and antibiotics, when specific technologies have completely changed civilization and redefined world leadership*.

* See example. http://www.geniusstuff.com/blog/list/10-inventions-changed-world/

b. Technologies are often indifferent ('Teflon'-like) by nature in relation to social, economic, and cultural differences. Technological standards pervade over cultural: Angolan and Norwegian children use tablets the same way, while the United States, Iran, and Mongolia have the same servers and drive the same cars. The main thing the divides technology users is the cost of access to these technologies. If technology turns out to be very cheap, then it truly becomes unifying, popularizing, transnational, and transcultural. Modern telecommunications technologies in particular can easily be associated with these types of technologies: they are relatively inexpensive for the individual user, which ensures a high penetration rate in developed countries and emerging economies.

c. The main challenge in a mass education system is to present new approaches and solutions that allow the education system to overcome the challenges facing it without a dramatic drop in quality. It is insufficient to create new learning methods if the diffusion of such methods is constrained by the lengthy preparation or the special selection of their bearers. Therefore, many revolutionary approaches in education, whether it be the Dewey approach or the Montessori method, serve as a source of inspiration but are very slowly replicated. In contrast, cheap technologies that allow unbundling content from its holders are able to quickly and efficiently penetrate the education process and become rapidly large-scale. This the primary reason why the education earlier used printed textbooks as a tool for knowledge transfer, even without a direct access to its author. Therefore, technologies meant for the mainstream user (and the large-scale solutions created with such technologies) need to be discussed first and foremost.

d. Regulating the education system is a subject of special interest. Since creating and conveying modern technologies by nature is a transnational process, they set new requirements for the architecture of education systems that in the future also must be determined globally. The initial movement towards this type of architecture can already been seen: the standardization of academic contracts and requirements for qualifications, teaching and writing research articles in 'the language of international communication,' and standardizing levels of training (Bologna process, PhD level, etc.). Even so, the broad proliferation of new technologies — and moreover, the general shift in the social structure thanks to assimilating new production and distribution technologies (see section 2.3.1) — will establish the aggregate of borderline conditions for a new architecture. Discussing the ideas for a new global architecture is a challenge that future versions of this Report may address.

---

Legend, page 21

| | | | |
|---|---|---|---|
| TREND | HARD TECHNOLOGY | EVENT | POLICY |
| SUBTREND | SOFT TECHNOLOGY | THREAT | SCENARIO Y-JUNCTION |

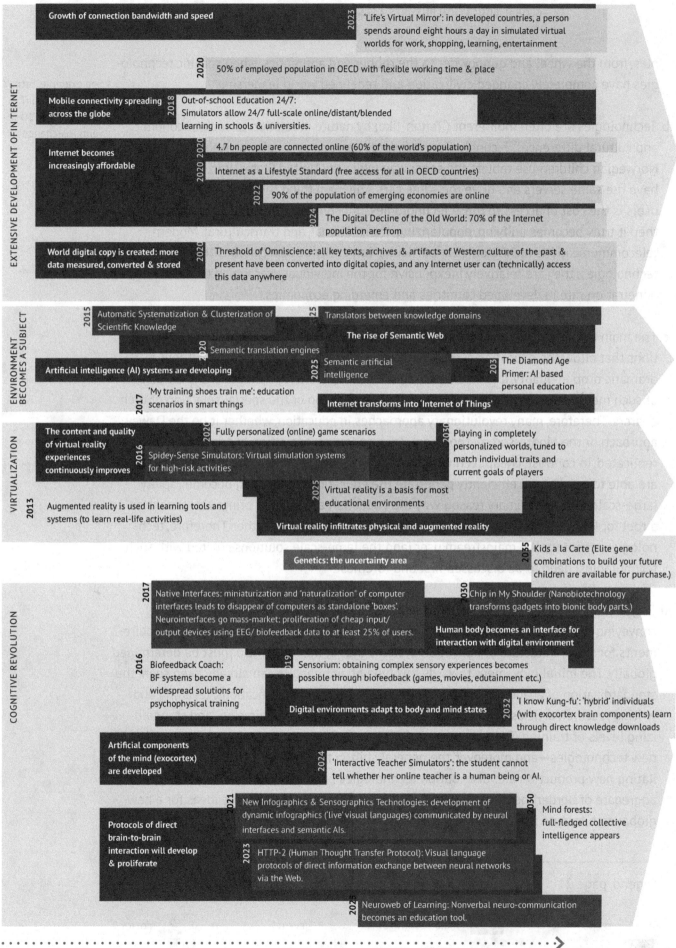

**EXTENSIVE DEVELOPMENT OF INTERNET**

Growth of connection bandwidth and speed

2023 'Life's Virtual Mirror': in developed countries, a person spends around eight hours a day in simulated virtual worlds for work, shopping, learning, entertainment

2020 50% of employed population in OECD with flexible working time & place

Mobile connectivity spreading across the globe

2018 Out-of-school Education 24/7: Simulators allow 24/7 full-scale online/distant/blended learning in schools & universities.

Internet becomes increasingly affordable

2020 4.7 bn people are connected online (60% of the world's population)

Internet as a Lifestyle Standard (free access for all in OECD countries)

2022 90% of the population of emerging economies are online

2024 The Digital Decline of the Old World: 70% of the Internet population are from

World digital copy is created: more data measured, converted & stored

2020 Threshold of Omniscience: all key texts, archives & artifacts of Western culture of the past & present have been converted into digital copies, and any Internet user can (technically) access this data anywhere

**ENVIRONMENT BECOMES A SUBJECT**

2015 Automatic Systematization & Clusterization of Scientific Knowledge

25 Translators between knowledge domains

The rise of Semantic Web

2020 Semantic translation engines

Artificial intelligence (AI) systems are developing

2025 Semantic artificial intelligence

203 The Diamond Age Primer: AI based personal education

2017 'My training shoes train me': education scenarios in smart things

Internet transforms into 'Internet of Things'

**VIRTUALIZATION**

The content and quality of virtual reality experiences continuously improves

2020 Fully personalized (online) game scenarios

2030 Playing in completely personalized worlds, tuned to match individual traits and current goals of players

2016 Spidey-Sense Simulators: Virtual simulation systems for high-risk activities

2025 Virtual reality is a basis for most educational environments

2013 Augmented reality is used in learning tools and systems (to learn real-life activities)

Virtual reality infiltrates physical and augmented reality

2035 Kids a la Carte (Elite gene combinations to build your future children are available for purchase.)

Genetics: the uncertainty area

**COGNITIVE REVOLUTION**

2017 Native Interfaces: miniaturization and 'naturalization' of computer interfaces leads to disappear of computers as standalone 'boxes'. Neurointerfaces go mass-market: proliferation of cheap input/output devices using EEG/ biofeedback data to at least 25% of users.

2030 Chip in My Shoulder (Nanobiotechnology transforms gadgets into bionic body parts.)

Human body becomes an interface for interaction with digital environment

2016 Biofeedback Coach: BF systems become a widespread solutions for psychophysical training

2019 Sensorium: obtaining complex sensory experiences becomes possible through biofeedback (games, movies, edutainment etc.)

2032 'I know Kung-fu': 'hybrid' individuals (with exocortex brain components) learn through direct knowledge downloads

Digital environments adapt to body and mind states

Artificial components of the mind (exocortex) are developed

2024 'Interactive Teacher Simulators': the student cannot tell whether her online teacher is a human being or AI.

2021 New Infographics & Sensographics Technologies: development of dynamic infographics ('live' visual languages) communicated by neural interfaces and semantic AIs.

2030 Mind forests: full-fledged collective intelligence appears

Protocols of direct brain-to-brain interaction will develop & proliferate

2023 HTTP-2 (Human Thought Transfer Protocol): Visual language protocols of direct information exchange between neural networks via the Web.

2023 Neuroweb of Learning: Nonverbal neuro-communication becomes an education tool.

2013     2020     2025     2030

## 2.2 NEW TECHNOLOGIES THAT WE HAVE TO LIVE WITH

*I can state flatly that heavier than air flying machines are impossible*
**Lord Kelvin**, British mathematician and physicist, President of the British Royal Society, 1895

Technologies and social practices are inseparable. From antiquity to the present, the shift in the type of material culture has impacted social practices, while these very social practices in turn have influenced how people think and act. It is now important for us to understand which technologies 'within' the education system will affect the basic processes in the education system, such as transferring and acquiring knowledge and skills, registering achievements, assessing education quality, and creating motivation and cognition itself. Many of technologies described below exist even today, others are expected to be created within the coming decade. Sceptics implying that the world will remain unchanged should remember how often other sceptics were wrong in the past — say, Lord Kelvin denied the possibility of airplanes only ten years before the Wright brothers flight.

### 2.2.1 The extensive development of the Internet

Some of the trends in the development of the digital environment are extensive: they will continue the processes that have been going on for the past 15 to 20 years. We believe that there are no objective reasons for these processes to stop. Here are some of the most important trends:

1. Channel capacity is increasing and data-transfer speed is on the rise. New opportunities (the transfer of high-quality video, audio, etc.) for any additional information allow making the online participation experience all the closer to offline interaction. We presume that by 2025 specialized virtual worlds with the participation effect will become just as habitual an environment in developed countries for learning, work, and entertainment as schools, offices, and malls.

2. The Internet is becoming mobile. Developing wireless access, miniaturizing access devices (smartphones, tablets, etc.), decreasing how much energy these devices use, and creating solutions for automizing their energy supply (ex. bodily energy collection models) all support mobility technologically. The presumption is made that by 2020 computers and telephones will transform into universal portable devices integrated between themselves with our clothing and accessories*.

This means that the user is less and less attached to specific 'access points' and is more easily able to integrate 'instant information access' into the patterns of his social activeness. For example, it is already common for many users to receive background information during a business meeting, to fact-check speakers' words during a lecture and at the same time discuss the lecture's content with their social network. Mobility and a flexible work schedule

* Ex. see the road map for the European research project WearIT@Work http://www.wearitatwork.com/fileadmin/user_upload/Documentation/Talk1_Road_Map_2020.pdf

are already the work standard for at least 50% of employees in industrially developed countries (Wolff 2009). Moreover, mobility sets a new standard for Internet communication, where users use mainly mobile apps and not browsers for visiting various websites. In other words, a transition is taking place from a 'single Internet' to an 'Internet as a set of apps.'

In the future, mobility will allow students to be absent from a specially assigned, physical space (ex. from the classroom), but at the same time they will be able to constantly remain within the learning process and in contact with their group or mentor. We presume that the first full-fledged schools operating 24/7 could emerge around 2015 to 2017; however, leading educational institutions have already significantly expanded their undertakings for ensuring mobility. Mobility is very important for new education platforms (including MOOC platforms), as a significant number of their users are adults who find it convenient to study while on the road and not at random.

3. The Internet is becoming more and more accessible. Around the time of the completion of this book (mid-2014), the world already has roughly 2.7 billion Internet users, and this number is growing fast. Approximately 80% of the population has access to the Internet in industrially developed countries*, while some have already reached higher than 90%**. Penetration is actively taking place in quickly developing countries. Mobile Internet and the broad use of smartphones provide Internet access for virtually everyone no matter what age or financial standing. Network World*** estimates that by 2020 the number of Internet users will rise to 4.7 billion (or more than two-thirds of the Earth's population). What is significant is that the majority of the increase will come from China, India, South-East Asia, Latin America, and Asia. By 2025, over 70% of users will not come from OECD countries. New Internet users will demand cultural content they can relate to and they will create such content. Therefore, the Internet content landscape will change drastically in the coming decade.

4. The reality surrounding us is being actively digitized. A modern management model is impossible without have digital workflow management, accounting and oversight systems in the financial sphere, industry, trade, and state administration. Digital modeling and engineering are the operating standard in the high-technology industry. Projects to digitize accumulated research and technical knowledge and cultural heritage are actively being carried out in archives and libraries. More and more data on the everyday world around us will be digitized, and the Internet will accumulate more and more data in cloud storage data distribution centers; infrastructure and technological solutions are being actively developed for this process. The following forecast illustrates the dynamics of this process: if the volume of data created on the Internet in 2013 was 4.4 zettabytes, then in 2025 Virgin Media Business predicts that this volume could reach 100 zettabytes.*1

Given the two preceding trends and the digitization trend, the presumption can be made that in the near future the goal will purposely be set to create a full-fledged digital copy of the world, including video and photograph recording, geodata, information about an object's material components shown in real time, and various obscure dependencies that describe the empirical dependencies of the surrounding world. The trend of processing

* http://www.itu.int/en/ITU-D/Statistics/Documents/facts/ICTFactsFigures2013.pdf

** http://data.worldbank.org/indicator/IT.NET.USER.P2

*** http://www.networkworld.com/news/2010/010410-outlook-vision-predictions.html

*1 http://www.virginmediabusiness.co.uk/News-and-events/News/News-archives/2012/Avatars-super-crowdsourcing-printing-your-own-medication-and-the-death-of-the-office-are-you-ready-for-Generation-IP-2025/

large volumes of data (Big Data) is the first step to reaching such a world, while the real time collection and processing of data (BigLiveData), constant synchronization of 'reality' and its digital copy are the second step. It is clear that the majority of libraries, archives, technical documents, and museum repositories will be digitized within 10 to 15 years in developed countries. The process is moving toward the situation where a digital copy of the world will be created, any knowledge from the past and present will be accessible (given the appropriate access keys), and this knowledge will be accessible virtually anywhere in the world; a situation where anyone on Earth can have potential omniscience and omni-knowledge on the knowledge horizon (we metaphorically call this the 'point of omniscience'). The onset of the 'point of omniscience' depends on the distribution of data-collection technologies emerging within Big Data and on the development of artificial intelligence that will be able to process these data. This, however, is most likely mainly an engineering challenge.

As far as education is concerned, this means that the teacher's role as the 'keeper of knowledge' (or reproducer of knowledge) will vanish in the coming years, and whoever can show how to handle this knowledge will take their place. Knowledge will be shaped and skills verified at the same time as practical goals are taken on. The size of a person's knowledge base will not be a competitive advantage by itself, but it will be important as a condition for being successful at one's job. It is clear that meta-skills that took shape through memorizing and resolving standard challenges in the past will not lose their significance; however, we can see that other means will be needed to shape them. Moreover, libraries (which are already turning into co-working centers with paper books as interior decorations (Peterson, 2013)) and museums (which will more and more be turning into research centers, while they will be visited more and more often through virtual reality) will see their purpose change.

Here we should mention right away two limitations on the path to using the broadening possibilities of the Internet in education:

a. The potential access to information does not mean the possibility to use it. As studies of neurophysiological mechanisms responsible for a successful search show, in order to obtain knowledge from the Internet, you need to have a rough idea of what the potential result will look like (Small et al., 2009). Putting it differently, you need to have a basic worldview with a small hole that information found on the Internet fills. If you do not have a worldview, then this knowledge will be virtually useless since it is not clear what it should be attached to. Therefore, the purpose of a basic education, in which a worldview is shaped, cannot be substituted by free access to a digital library; however, this does not mean that previous methods for assimilating a worldview (for example, learning facts from history, biology, and geography) will yield their place to more modern methods such as 'long games' in learning game universes or simulators.

b. Excess information and turnkey solutions on the Internet cause people to be cognitively dependent, to develop the 'culture of copying.' This can be deduced from taking Facebook users as an example: the majority of their posts are not their original work, but rather links to other people's texts that often have not even been read in full, while other users' reactions to these texts boil down mainly to 'liking' them and typical responses. The degeneration of the culture of reading and writing, as well as accessibility of fraud in standard knowledge and qualifications verification systems, are both the repercussions felt from the spread of the 'culture of copying.' For example, the share of plagiarism in theses papers and dissertations defended in the Western European universities reaches 30% (according to Stefan Weber's 'The Google-Copy-Paste-Syndrome' study (Maurer et al., 2007), which defines this phenomenon as 'text culture without brains').

Both limitations indicate the need to create additional education solutions that deal directly with these threats. In particularly, it is already clear that the Internet easily hacks the existing education models (as opposed to the real-life teacher, 'the Internet is all-knowing'), but Internet education does not substitute for their intended result (ex. shaping a worldview). Therefore, finding new ways to shape a complete worldview (and only this will let humans consciously use the Internet for self-development) is critical.

## 2.2.2 The digital environment as an agent

The trends in this group have to do with a qualitative change in the digital environment: constantly transfer complex intellectual functions to it that are inherent to man, and at the same time have it gain quasi-subjectiveness, where the digital environment can play the role of 'younger partner' in many common and work processes.

1. The Internet is becoming semantic. It is expected that in the coming decade the problem of digital systems' lack of capability to understand meanings and handle them will be resolved. A number of research centers, in following Tim Berners-Lee's proposal (Berners-Lee et al., 2001), set the goal of creating a semantically structured Internet or a semantic web. Compiling a 'dictionary of meanings' that is developed for semantic machine translation by MIT Media Lab, Microsoft Systran, ABBYY, etc., could be one of the possible foundations for such technology (Currently used automatic translators translate according to statistical language models, which makes them suitable for technical translation but not for literary translation). The first such commercial system, ABBYY Compreno, was released in early 2014.* The large-scale use of semantic translation systems, expected by 2020, could create an environment where the overwhelming number of texts, audio and video recordings are easily and accurately translated into other languages. When developing this type of technology in the more distant future, we can also expect that there will be translators between professional domains of knowledge (ex. a system that explains a highly professional text to uniformed readers). When this occurs, the majority of obstacles that limit the accessibility of knowledge from one culture to another will vanish rather quickly (within 15 to 20 years). Although the ability to implement semantic translation technology has still not been proven, the likelihood that it will be created is fairly high (there are working prototypes). Therefore, our prediction has been made given the possibility that this technology will emerge.

* http://www.
abbyy-developers.
eu/en:tech:linguistic:

2. Artificial intelligence systems are being developed. The process of automating routine intellectual operations in a certain sense is the main subject matter in the evolution of IT systems. Artificial intelligence systems as recommendation services and decision-making support systems, game environments that imitate complex behavior, and systems for analyzing big data masses have already increased rapidly in use. It is evident that the process of 'rearranging the routine' into a digital environment will continue, and a significant portion of routine human activity, such as bookkeeping or writing program codes, could be rendered obsolete in the coming 10 to 15 years (Manyika et al., 2013). This concerns even fields that traditionally are considered to be creative, such as journalism. The automation process is likely even to accelerate, since the way in which routine operations are automized is a potentially automizable routine (analyzing behavior patterns, turning them into an algorithm, and programming the algorithm).

The emergence of solutions in semantic translation and the semantic Internet allow expecting a qualitative leap in the development of artificial intelligence systems. It is now the inability to handle meanings that is one of the stumbling points in implementing accomplishing high-level (human-like) artificial intelligence.* Furthermore, it is worth noting that even probabilistic artificial intelligence achieves impressive success in fields we are accustomed to: IBM's Deep Blue defeated the chess world champion in 1997, and IBM's Watson beat the record holders on the game show Jeopardy! in 2012 (it is important to stress that this game requires uncommon linguistic reasoning). The emergence of human-like artificial intelligence will clearly have an impact on all spheres of human life, including on education and cognition. In the near future, artificial intelligence could be used for putting together academic assignments for students while taking into account their current achievements, education trajectory, and learning style. With time, artificial intelligence could be transformed into a full-fledged individual mentor that accounts for all of an individual's particularities in life. We call such systems 'The Diamond Primer' as per the Letter Book from Neal Stephenson's science fiction book 'The Diamond Age: Or, A Young Lady's Illustrated Primer' (this topic will be discussed in greater detail in section 3.2).

* http://www. aeonmagazine. com/being-human/ david-deutsch-artificial-intelligence/

3. The Internet is turning into the Internet of things. The world around us is becoming all the more intellectual. We can report the quality of intellectualness to any one of the subjects in the space thanks to built-in sensors and a processor, 'smart materials' that can change their features depending on the situation, the connectivity of all these things to the Internet, and their being synchronized between themselves. They can turn from passive interior elements into actives ones. The Internet of things penetration rates are very high: in 2013 approximately 10 billion Internet connections (roughly half of all connections) related to various technical objects, sensors, and devices, while by 2020 it is expected that more than 50 billion various devices will be connected to Internet.**

** http://www. ericsson.com/res/ docs/whitepapers/ wp-50-billions.pdf

The Internet of things will penetrate various spaces. A transition to Industry 4.0 is being discussed as part of the new European integration paradigm. The technological environment is not only fully robotized production, but this production knows how to independently adapt to optimal operational modes, and then how to independently learn how to optimize or reconstruct production (Nikolaus, 2013). Consumer robotechnics will become a significant part of the Internet of things: the number of consumer robots in cities is doubling every nine months (it is expected that by 2030 there will be more robots than people on Earth). It is in recent years that the explosive growth in robotechnics began because of the drastic drop in prices for components and spare parts (thanks to the spread of composite materials, 3D printing, and other modern material technologies). Robots and other objects of the Internet of things will become an important part of learning spaces, especially in scenarios for educating small children and school kids.

Another application is in an urban environment, where smart power networks adjust themselves to energy consumption levels in individual homes and apartments, and provide the possibility for those who installed a wind generator or solar battery at their home to sell the energy to their neighbors. Smart lighting adjusts to the number of people on the street or in a room, to the work they are doing, and even to individual preferences for the level of lighting. Smart transportation establishes routes through the city by itself while taking into account the predicted traffic problems, road construction, or unexpected situations. The household environment inside a smart home not only sets up health and thrifty living conditions (including keeping track of water and energy saving), but also washes clothes, does the dishes, cleans up the apartment, orders and even prepares food. Smart clothing reports the level of activity during the day or the need to be washed. The possibilities for the joint development of the urban environment and the Internet of things are virtually unlimited.*

* http://www.iot-i.eu/public/public-deliverables/d2.1/

The Internet of things will allow for creating fundamentally new scenarios for man to interact with the world. For example, there will be a host of opportunities for monitoring your healthy lifestyle: a person can keep track in real time of his level of physical activity and what types, his diet and how such diet impacts his health. Insurance companies could sell this very same system as part of an insurance plan. Employers and the state could have access to such insurance and use the system of economic incentives to motivate people to lead a healthy lifestyle (below we will discuss the factors of systems of reputational capital (section 2.3.4) and the gamification of everyday life (section 3.4.3) that could impact the rapid development of these types of arrangements). For all intents and purposes, we are talking about systems for educating adults, where their surrounding habitat is the educator. This provides education with new challenges and new possibilities (see Box 'How Could Learning Look with the Internet of Things').

## Box 1
### How Could Learning Look with the Internet of Things

Imagine this picture from the not-so-distant future: a person gets out of bed in the night and goes to the kitchen to open the fridge and cut himself a piece of cheese. He cannot get to the cheese, however, since his tennis shoes sent a signal to the fridge that he had not ran the five kilometers today that he was supposed to. Therefore, the environment can be programmed in a specific way depending on the objectives: get thin, athletic, hard-working, smart, etc. It can be programmed so that it will help you concentrate on your studies or work by shutting off all the distracting factors or by stimulating you to work, with 'bonuses' for any given local achievement. In other words, the environment trains the person to have a specific behavior.

What could also be another, more humane scenario is teaching a child at the playground, where a smart sandbox or a slide not only looks after the child's safety, but also offers kids games to develop their logical thinking or to help socialize among themselves.

The Internet of everything is the culmination of the Internet of things. Now, the Internet of everything is described as a network that unites people, processes, data, and things; however, first, the 'human part' of the Internet with time will become more profound as interfaces and the content of data being transferred develops (see sections 2.2.4 and 3.6.1 on NeuroWeb below); second, other living organisms will be connected to the Internet as well, beginning with pets, then wild animals, plants, and many of them will have the chance to master communications practices (and what is extremely likely is this will allow them to enter a new stage of biological evolution and begin their own cultural evolution). With time (it is entirely possible in hundreds of years) and prosperous development, the Internet could become a universal environment that encompasses the entire planet and that unites the geosphere, atmosphere, hydrosphere, biosphere, and noosphere into a single whole, thus turning them into a real 'intelligent planet.'

## 2.2.3 **Virtualization**

These trends have to do with the development of the digital reality that may not have direct counterparts in the physical reality, while at the same time could become a significant part of people's daily experience.

1. The content and quality of experience in virtual reality improve together. Science fiction novels and movies, beginning at the end of the 1970s, predicted that virtual environments would become widely used, but we are yet to be living in the worlds of TRON and Johnny Mnemonic. At the same time, the video game industry, the main driver of virtualization, has been confidently and increasingly developing over the past 30 years, and now several prerequisites have taken shape that make the 'triumph of virtuality' likely in the coming decade:

- Expanding channel size: as a result, visual, and audio (and later kinesthetic) experiences will become all the more diverse and 'real';

- Worlds are becoming all the more interactive. Their physical reality is increasing, as is players' ability to interact with objects and with each other, worlds 'memorize changes that players make (if five years ago this was presented as a huge achievement, then now this is becoming the game standard);

- Artificial intelligence is demonstrating more and more complex behavior. Non-game characters are capable of handling complex independent strategies (military, economic, and even social).

Given the dynamic described above in the development of artificial intelligence, its application as a 'director' and 'designer' in the coming seven to 10 years will allow for living out completely individualized game scenarios (developers have been programming in scenarios with a large number of forks in the road and a diversity of endings for more than 10 years already, and a constant search is going on for how to make the game structure and ending as open as possible). The chance will emerge in the coming 15 to 20 years for genuine individual game universes that are fully adapted to the player's current goals and particularities.

As far as learning is concerned, the game industry's potential is drastically underestimated. Virtual games are built so that the player is never bored: he is given tasks that he is capable of carrying out and that fits his psychophysical profile, while on the other hand they give him bonus points and new skills. The same model can be used in the educational process as well by building it so that it is interesting for the 'player' to move onto new levels. In this sense, people's lives today have just a faint likeness with just how interesting they could in fact become by using game moves. Moreover, the game reality can be reproduced not only during the learning process, but also during work and other things, and elements of the virtual interface will be everywhere.

Virtual worlds in education could be very broadly applied and would affect professional training, learning social skills, shaping worldviews, rectifying deviating behavior, etc. Virtual worlds, serving as the technology for developing simulators and training systems, could become the foundation for most educational environments in the coming 10 to 15 years (we discuss this subject in greater detail in section 3.4).

2. Virtual reality is penetrating the physical (augmented reality). Given the growth in mobility and increase in channel space, augmented reality technology could become ubiquitous in the coming five to 10 years, and this will be helped by the broad development of 'wearable' technologies (such as Google Glass) and by the miniaturization of 'wearable' devices (ex. there has been initial success in creating 'wearable' contact lens monitors.)*

* http://www.technologyreview.com/news/515666/contact-lens-computer-like-google-glass-without-the-glasses/

What makes augmented reality special is that it allows saturating any physical space by turning it into highly specialized spaces for games, learning, research, or joint creativity, all the while with fairly little investment in equipment and without any radical physical changes. In particularly, augmented reality will soon be able to transform the process for developing new products (technology businessman Elon Musk is looking to create new digital engineering environments based on Oculus Rift glasses.)** Augmented reality on the shop floor can easily provide employees with training in production processes (such as, for example, in the ARMAR project,)*** or in industrial safety. Any home or backyard in the city can be transformed into a museum whose exponents will be visible only for people who put on these special glasses. You can also add virtual guides, virtual theatrical shows, and much more. The possibilities are emerging to create urban educational games, such as specialized educational quests for children and adults that combine virtual and live interaction. Teaching children and adults to behave safely in the city (dangerous situation simulators based on augmented reality that we expect to become available in 2015-2016) could become one of its important applications. The scenario of the ubiquitous use of augmented reality for education is described in Vernor Vinge's great book 'End of the Rainbow (Vinge, 2006)

** http://singularityhub.com/2013/09/08/musk-tests-oculus-rift-leap-motion-controller-to-design-3d-printed-rocket-parts/

*** http://graphics.cs.columbia.edu/projects/armar/

## 2.2.4 **The cognitive revolution**

These trends have to do with the beginning of the daily use of neuropsychological technologies that are directly targeted at working with our body and mind. When these technologies become widely used, the technical environment begins to 'know' more about us than we do about ourselves, and we are given the chance to interact with the technical environment, between ourselves, and with ourselves using methods that knew no equals in the past. Since the majority of these technologies' approach is related to the achievements of cognitive sciences, and we call this phenomenon 'the cognitive revolution.'

   1. **The body becomes an interface for interacting with the digital environment.** Existing interfaces for interaction between a person and a computer/network are extremely non-physiological. We are forced to spend many hours in stationary and not the most physiological poses, virtually motionless, in closed-off spaces, constantly focusing on a narrow rectangle with a display measuring several dozen centimeters. The advent of computers has engendered an entire host of new civilizational illnesses, the least of which is the early-stage spreading of near-sightedness, back problems, and an increase in obesity stemming from the lack of movement and physical exercise. The other side of the coin is that our body is a part of our mind, and we are intended to think and speak with our body (Varela et al., 1992). By not having the chance to use the majority of our body for creativity and games, we lose a significant part of our potential.

   A lot of movement has taken place in the past five to seven years toward creating natural and physiological interfaces that engage the entire body's potential. First, various scanners of the body's position and facial expresses (ex. Kinect, LeapMotion, MYO, etc.), and visual direction (ex. Eye Tribe, etc.) are extensive in the game industry and in corporate marketing. Second, instantaneous health status controllers (pulse, blood pressure, etc.) and physical activity monitors (ex. Fitbit, Jawbone, etc.) are widely used in the fields of medicine and fitness.

   Finally, devices started to become popular that allow directly recording brain activity and turning encephalogram into managing signals for a game, sending messages, etc. — neurointerfaces (ex Emotiv and more). These devices are already comparatively inexpensive.* It can be expected that inexpensive neurointerfaces (at the price of a good computer mouse) will be everywhere within five to seven years as mandatory input-output components — when a fairly efficient 'driver' will be created between data on the brain's electric activity and operational system. What is important is that these devices are fundamentally changing the model of interaction with the computer. In a certain sense, 'the thought is becoming material' (since the perceived action is in control, not the actual movement or speech).

   Such devices in the foreseeable future will be miniaturized, built-in as elements of clothing, decorations, tattoos, or the simplest of implants (or, in cases with body scanners, they will become a part of the 'smart environment' of the home, street, or public space). By the end of the 2020s, devices that interact with the technological environment can begin to be implanted as parts of the body or internal organs as both nano- and biotechnologies develop and converge (it is entirely possible that at this time the slogan 'Intel inside' will used in relation to people and not computers).

* The new interface Emotiv Insight at pre-sale sells for 229$. The release of new interfaces for $100 is expected by the end of 2014.

The development of such interfaces combined with the broad penetration of augmented reality will cause a rather drastic change in the accustomed environment for working, learning, playing sports, and vacationing. Working and creating will be possible in any space and on any surface by using gestures and voice commands to create videos, displays, three-dimensional objects, or texts, roughly in the same way that a sculptor or fashion designer work now. We will stress yet again that interaction interfaces will change, and rather radically, to the point where today's computer in the next generation will look just as archaic as the telephone from the end of the 19th century looks to us.

### 2. The digital environment is adapting to the states of the body and mind.

Monitoring a person's objective psychophysiological parameters allows for under-standing just how much a person at any given time is active, engaged in a process, and understands what is being told to him. The corporate world is already realizing and using these possibilities: the developing field of neuromarketing is tied to the intentional hard-ware-specific observation of the states of the body/mind and of the adaption to them (ex. advertisements) in order to scan information on consumer preferences or propose goods appropriate to the state (Żurawicki, 2010). Using similar technologies in the work environ-ment allows for assessing operators' willingness to work (including in the intellectual work environment. Ex. market traders in specific conditions can risk more, which increase the likelihood of losses*), recommend breaks or adapt the work space to the worker's individual state, which allows for increasing the productivity of complex labor (Sutarto et al., 2010).

Biological Feedback (BF) returns monitoring one's state to the user himself, giving the person a signal about what his current state is (ex. his stress level or concentration level are somewhat high), how it changes from moment to moment, and through this creates the opportunity to regulate his state. Using biomonitoring and BF of the connection in educa-tion is already providing large opportunities. First, monitoring states allows determining what time of day and what environment are most effective for each specific person to learn, and customizes individual learning plans. Second, the chance emerges to teach a person how to self-manage his health (to relax, to concentrate, etc.); the BF principle serves as the basis for a number of rather successful devices for learning states (ex. Wild Divine, Melon, etc.). In a certain sense, learning resource states is more important than learning knowl-edge, because the right state is a prerequisite for assimilating knowledge, and virtually no one teaches this anymore (although the increasing popularity in the practice of meditation for self-regulation in the corporate world ought to be pointed out). We believe that users' increasing acceptance of biomonitoring and BF devices will make training simulators a common occurrence at the least in professional and administrative education in the coming five to 10 years.

BF possibilities could be used to create deep immersion virtual worlds where not only visual and audio experiences are simulated, but so are tactile experiences, and all are adjusted to fit the user. We can expect similar such production ('sensoria') to be released by the end of the 2010s.

* http://www.wired.co.uk/magazine/archive/2013/01/features/why-men-risk-it-all

### 3. Artificial psychological components will be developed (exocortex)

The digital environment is already beginning to play the role of the 'external' psyche (exocortex, namely the brain's 'external' crust), taking a number of customary functions away from people. The 'removed memory' in our mobile devices (when you do not need to remember the names, numbers, or addresses of your friends, or memorize plans and theses from meetings) or the virtually atrophied ability of mental arithmetic are the most typical of these displays. Automating and developing the artificial intelligence systems that we addressed in section 2.2.2 will constantly provide the opportunities for to remove many burdening, routine actions. As a result, in the next 5 to 7 years we can expect the emergence in the digital environment of subpersonalities (avatars) that act in their owner's interests in specific situations. In particularly, an avatar can fulfill the role of personal concierge (pay bills, choose a vacation or entertainment, act as a personal secretary, etc.). Furthermore, an avatar is able to support its owner's activity in a research group (such as tracking and processing news), social networks (placing and promoting material about a person), etc. What is significant is that an avatar can 'be born' not only through directly teaching a program your personal preferences, but also as a 'mold' of a person's activities. For example, artificial intelligence can analyze a regularly repeated activity and then replicate it based on the patterns found.

Applying avatars in learning could entirely begin by the 2020s to free professors and teachers of a routine burden. In particular, an avatar that has taken a 'mold' of a teacher is able in the teacher's place to conduct classes, draw up test assignments, and grade them. Moreover, this 'virtual teacher' will be available 24/7. Here, the teacher turns from a performer into a customizer of his own avatar and into a 'complex case specialist.'

In the more distant future, avatarization technology becomes even more productive, if the exocortex is able to be completely synchronized with the live part, and based on this giving a person increased opportunities (human enhancement systems). Such 'hybrid personalities' that bring together artificial and natural components within the nervous system with artificial components (including cloud components) could emerge within 15 to 20 years (if the development of the neurosciences does not encounter insurmountable obstacles). It is evident that the idea itself of learning for such hybrid personalities is fundamentally changing. For example, there is the chance to quickly download a skill or piece of knowledge into the 'artificial part,' and they then become accessible to the 'natural part' (it could be that such mechanisms could be behind the actual implementation of high-speed learning from the famous film 'The Matrix').

### 4. Interaction protocols of the nervous systems will be developed 'directly'.

The listed trends are important prerequisites for the 'cognitive revolution'; however, the most notable changes will take place when neurotechnologies begin to operate directly with the nervous system while skipping the receptor and effector system. The neurointerfaces already described are the first sign, of course, but future systems must functionally be much broader.

Neurointerface limitations stem, first and foremost, from their low signal reading accuracy. High accuracy in reading data from neurons or neuron groups is currently possible only invasively ('electrodes into the brain'), while non-invasive solutions (popular 'entertaining' interfaces, such as Emotiv) provide a fairly inaccurate picture. As a result, non-invasive interfaces can be used to carry out simple tasks, such as controlling a video game character's movement, but more complex solutions have yet to be created. Furthermore, non-invasive interfaces allow for reading signals, but not for transferring them, namely you cannot create a sensation, much less 'download' any significant patterns into the brain. At the same time, it is clear that there is a tenacious psychological barrier among users to establishing an invasive interface: individual experimenters such as Ken Warwick may be willing to do this, but it is unlikely that the average gamer or design engineer would agree to this. There are, however, several solutions that could potentially circumvent this limitation, in particularly, neuroninterfaces could be based upon nanorobots that are injected into the blood and station themselves on the neurons.* Optogenetics' developments, which allow accurately reading and changing the state of neurons through gene-focused modification and optics, have very promising potential (Pastrana, 2010). Finally, developments in stimulating the nerve tissue through focused ultrasound (FUS), which allow for a fundamentally non-invasive effect, have a lot of potential.

Whatever the case, working through direct interaction with the nervous system promises a lot of potential and will be continued. It is significant that this work is not limited to strengthening an individual brain-computer interface (BCI); they are intended for directly connecting two (or more) brains through a network (brain-brain interface, BBI). Successful BBI experiments are taking place right before our very eyes, such as in fall 2012, when Harvard researchers conducted a successful experiment involving a person controlling the movements of a rat's tail through a non-invasive neurointerface (Yoo et al. 2013). At approximately the same time, an experiment with an invasive interface was conducted involving one rat teaching another from a distance how to correctly interact with a feeder.**

By all accounts, these technologies are suitable for simple (motor) skills, but in the case of complex cognitive skills, they require significant refinement. In particular, intermediaries are required for complex communication in management and creativity, namely new information exchange and structuring protocols. This includes artificial languages capable of recording meanings created when two or more subjects interact. We believe that within 10 years there will be an operating (suitable for popular use) technological solution using neurointerfaces to exchange images and ideas between people, which is what we conditionally call HTTP-2: Human Thought Transfer Protocol (see the Box 'Possible solutions in HTTP-2').

* http://techland.time.com/2012/05/09/robot-that-connects-to-neurons-could-provide-key-to-understanding-the-human-brain/

** http://www.nature.com/srep/2013/130228/srep01319/full/srep01319.html

Box 2
*Possible Solutions in HTTP-2*

HTTP-2 pre-alpha is a basic solution to the issue of transferring the brain's electrical activity to traditional types of data (text, image, cursor control, etc.) and subsequently transferring them according to standard protocols. There are currently a number of projects for decoding conceivable human images and 'reading' motor commands 'from the brain.'

A complete HTTP-2 is a protocol that allows transferring ideas and notions of differing clarity, including notions of formal thinking, non-verbal messages, emotions, etc. It is not registering patters that correspond to 'words and pictures' that become the neurointerface's goal, but rather registering ideas, meta-structures of a message and subsequently transferring along the special 'semantic' protocols. What is likely here is that the HTTP protocol interfaces will be implemented into a sensor language of dynamic pictures whose structure corresponds to an idea at a specific time (roughly as abstractionist art-house cartoons).

The emergence of technologies for the direct transfer of meanings, images, and feelings could fundamentally alter the approaches to learning, including the learning speed, methods for packaging and passing on knowledge and skills, and new opportunities for both joint and mutual learning. We believe that the first groups using HTTP-2 possibilities will emerge within three to five years after this protocol is released, namely by the middle of the 2020s. As such groups assimilate the possibilities of joint existence in the neuro-network, they will start to have new mental phenomena, and by the middle of the 2030s it will be likely to expect the phenomenon that we call the 'forest of consciousnesses,' namely of full-fledged collective intellect.

In some sense, it is becoming pointless to address pedagogy in its current meaning given the emergence of the direct loading of experience into the nervous system, of 'hybrid personalities,' 'forests of consciousnesses,' and other phenomena. Therefore, we believe the 'cognitive revolution' and its culmination to be NeuroWeb (next-generation Internet based on neurointerfaces) technologies that 'round out' the development of the current cycle of high-technological pedagogy. Detailed discussions of the possibilities of pedagogy related to these 'rounding out' technologies are presented in section 3.7; however, it should be noted that it is impossible to make the transition to the 'pedagogical Internet' without assimilating all the practices of 'network pedagogy' that are now actively being developed in online education, virtual worlds, and other technological solutions of the near and mid-term future.

## 2.2.5 Genetics: a zone of uncertainty

1. Controlling inherent potential. Possibilities created by genetics, as far as both determining people's potential and the possibility for influencing this potential are concerned, have caused heated arguments ever since the beginning of the 20th century. The main issue here, of course, is that they come into direct conflict with the values systems of Western liberalism and humanism, which have at their core the fundamental equality of each and every person's rights and opportunities. It needs to be said that resting upon the thesis of human equality has led to enormous shifts in the field of education, from the transition to the joint teaching of men and women in the early 20th century to blind & deaf students having exclusive education and receiving higher education.

A fundamental question related to the application of genetics is whether these capabilities to learn (and especially to be implemented in specific spheres) are genetically prescribed. At present, there are two opposed points of view on this:

- the deterministic view assumes that genes virtually program a person's fate by determining the possibilities for his being successful in any given professional or social sphere by setting out a combination of cognitive capabilities, temperament, resistance to stress, physical makeup, inherited diseases, etc. (modern sports medicine meant to 'create supermen' with prescribed mental qualities are built in the same logic (Hakimi et al. 2007);

* In 2014, one of the authors of this Report has coordinated the launch of the Foundation for Deaf-Blind, a project to recreate a school of rehabilitative pedagogy (http://so-edinenie.org/en). The Foundation's goal is not only to completely restore the archives of the Meshcheryakov group, but also to create new pedagogical practices based on the developments from the 1970s using modern IT and neurological technologies.

** http://www.toqon-line.com/blog/the-coming-chinese-superstate/

*** http://www.economist.com/blogs/economist-explains/2013/04/economist-explains-why-gene-patents-controversial

▪ the adaptive view points out that the human body, including the nerve tissue, is a highly plastic structure, and that a large portion of inherited limitations could be prolonged when doing certain exercises (in particularly, in the 1960s and 1970s Soviet Union, a group led by Alexander Meshcheryakov conducted extremely successful experiments on higher education for blind-deaf people, some of which led a full-fledged scientific career (Meshcheryakov, 1974; Meshcheryakov, 1979; Bakhurst & Padden, 1991)).*

In a certain sense, both schools are right, and the example with blind and deaf children shows this (the limitations are objective, but surmountable). The question is what 'line' is the process for using the achievements of genetics moving along. For example, China sets its immediate goals for 'positive eugenics' and raising a 'generation of supermen.'** There is demand for 'programming children' (this could concern not only gender, but physical and mental characteristics as well). Coupled with the developing subject on patenting genes,*** this could in the coming 15 to 20 years lead to creating a large market for 'made-to-order children' with obvious social repercussions coming from the rebirth of a cast system along genetic lines (an image of a world such as this can be found in many works, from Huxley's 'Brave New World' to the film 'Gattaca'). On the other hand, the development of neurophysiological solutions such as exoskeletons and artificial organs (and, in the future, additional upgrades of the nervous system) allows surmounting many of the genetic limitations, and U.S. and E.U. researchers are going down this exact road.

2. Impact on life expectancy. There is yet one more sphere whose ethics are much more rarely subject to doubt: the possibility of genetics influencing life expectancy and the quality of one's final years of life. It is extremely likely (this is for the moment one of the scientific hypotheses) that aging and age-related illnesses (including cancer and Alzheimer's disease) are 'programmed' into our genes. If this is so, then the reason is in the mechanisms of biological evolution. Namely, individuals must age and die in biological populations so that the genotype of the population can be updated (since selection takes place not among individual organisms, but among populations and species as a whole (Millstein, 2006)). In the case of humans, however, this mechanism begins to produce a problem in that we evolve to a much greater extent through our culture, through accumulating and transferring knowledge and experience, and therefore death (especially the death of great people of the arts, scientists, businessmen, politicians, etc.) is a much greater problem for our species. Options for increasing life expectancy lie in different spheres, including the sphere of cyberization, although studies in the field of genetics are some of the most promising (at least to the point that geneticists have managed to significantly increase life expectancy for a number of experimental organisms (Curtsinger 2007)). This means that it is highly likely that life expectancy in industrially developed countries will increase (a period of 120 to 140 years is currently considered realistic), while the active period of life will continue to increase as well. Given that the birth rate is in decline in industrially developed countries, we are coming into a situation where the makeup of the population is rebalancing in favor of the elderly, and it is this group that could become one of the main customers for various types of education (see also section 2.3.3)

## 2.2.6 A list of education solutions based on new technologies

When the ICT possibilities for education are discussed, people often think 'from the past', referring to low-quality educational videos on YouTube. One needs to think 'from the future' instead, imagining something like personalized educational extravaganzas that may look like Cirque du Soleil performances, created by the artificial intelligence, adopted to the psychological profile of a student, and controlled at his desire. ICT is one of the most actively growing spheres that is absorbing all the more industries and fields, and there is no reason to assume that this process will stop in the coming 15 to 20 years (although such an option is theoretically possible if the industry comes to a point where it is physically impossible to support any given type of Moore's law; Gordon Moore, for whom the law is named after, spoke of this possibility several years ago*). Even existing technologies, however, when correctly applied (and given a certain drop in price) allow revolutionizing learning models by making them more flexible, practical, student-oriented, you name it.

* http://news.tech-world.com/operating-systems/3477/moores-law-is-dead-says-gordon-moore/

Below (see Table 3) is a description of a cloud of education solutions shaped directly on the basis of the list of technologies provided below; however, before presenting this list, we will discuss the general trends of new technologies' influence on the processes of learning, mentoring, and assessment.

### 1. Learning and upbringing processes
The following are the principal processes that can be referred to in the development of learning and mentoring:

a. Technologies reduce the access price to the 'education standard.' In this sense, the 'education machine' that was the industry standard in the education system gradually replaces human components (ex. 'teacher reproducers,' developers, and graders of standard tests and trainers with a standard program) for more inexpensive automatic components.

b. As a result, the learning process becomes all the more widespread and complete, since access to automatic 'mentors' in all areas of life (given the distribution of popular technologies) costs less than access to live teachers and tutors.

c. The ability to keep track of and account for individual particularities and student demands is one of the advantages of automatic systems. As a result, learning and mentoring are becoming truly individualized (we will discuss this in greater detail in section 3.2).

d. Automatic solutions are well adjusted for conveying standard and structured experience and knowledge; however, structuring this experience is the starting point of their work. As a result, gurus (highly qualified bearers of benchmark knowledge/experience) are turning out to be the resource that education systems have a deficit of. Through automization that frees bearers of knowledge and experience from the ritual of repetition (ex. from repeatedly reading standard lectures), they get the chance to focus on the main unique quality that involves (a) the unique thought structure of such people, (b) their ability to have 'liberating' and 'empowering' influence on their students, and (c) the all-around physiological communications related to it between the 'guru' and his students. The 'gurus' of the future at the center of the processes of the education system, in a certain sense return to the status and position of their predecessors from the traditional system of training of Brahman: teachers mentoring students in self-development given their particular personal path and their unique personality structure.

e. Although the position of individual gurus looks attractive for a number of reasons (among them being the constantly growing complexity of the surrounding world and an enormous diversity of skills necessary for a productive and healthy life in this world), it is more likely that, along with outstanding individual gurus, the majority of gurus will be distributed collective agents — that is, learning happens through access to collective competences of the community. Most likely, individual gurus will be persona brands for the appropriate schools or communities that provide collective learning. As we will discuss in section 3.3, a notable part of new education is already taking place and will continue to take place in communities of practice, in groups that as part of their activities implement a system of unique knowledge and skills. Moreover, since a significant number of students will be adults, they will also be able to act as gurus for other students, which will help increase mutual exchange models in communities.

Therefore, one can point to the consequences of new technologies adoption in the education system:

1. It is highly likely that future learning could become even more stratified. Dividing into strata will be determined by the possibilities of 'live' access (including by the cost of this access) to unique bearers of skills: gurus and communities of practice.

2. Widespread knowledge and skills will be passed on, first and foremost, through automized solutions (through hybrid online/offline formats, such as in blended learning, at the initial stages, and then in working with fully automized mentor systems).

3. 'Live' learning will be relatively more expensive and, as a result, be more of a bonus, and in most cases will be organized not as lengthy joint learning, but as short intensive sessions. This learning's content will be focused not on conveying publicly available information and working out routine exercises, but on developing complex general skills having to do with creative thinking and supporting its psychophysical 'attitude.' Working with values and limiting ideas should also be an important part of this live learning. Moreover, adult education will be organized 'horizontally' to a great extent through the mutual exchange of knowledge.

4. On the other hand, technologies allow not only for making learning elite, but also for democratizing it. Namely, technologies can act as the instrument that provides a host of people with equal access to obtaining knowledge and skills, including from gurus and communities. Ensuring equal access regardless of race, ethnicity, gender, age, financial standing, or other indicators is a very important process that inspires many teachers of the past and present, and there are no particular technological barriers to creating such an environment where each student is provided equal rights and opportunities. In this sense, a lot will depend on the values systems that will be held together when designing future education systems.

2. **Assessment and motivation processes**

Registering achievements and assessment are a critical component of the education process. One can point to several trends in the development of assessment systems:

a. Providing feedback to a student over to what extent and how well he has mastered a subject is the primary purpose of assessment, and only then does the goal emerge of signaling to the outside world about the quality of his knowledge. As a result, there is a trend toward cutting the 'assessment cycle' (ex. giving a grade not on the results of a six-month learning period, but as a weekly progress test) and increasing the assessment's comprehensiveness (ex. grading the original thinking and not the ability to give the right answer).

b. Assessment has a social purpose as a tool of social differentiation based on the capabilities manifested. In this sense, grading can be directly all the more tied to objective social stimuli, such as social status or well-being and not to the results of education, but rather directly during the education process.

c. Moreover, grading can be used as an instrument to assess the economic efficiency of education (including when making decisions on investments in education for the students themselves, parents, employers, or sponsors). In this sense, not only the student's knowledge and skills should be the subject matter to be assessed, but also course thoroughness, professor skills, the quality of the education environment, etc.

d. External assessment has a number of limitations since it is based on the perceptions of other people about what is 'right' and what is 'wrong,' and because all too often it results from past experience and not from future tasks. Therefore, any external assessment must be supplemented by a self-assessment, and not only should the achievements be assessed, but so should the entire process (which is a part of the student's life, and in this sense must be assessed as far as quality of life is concerned!).

e. Assessment using tests (tests of knowledge or on demonstrating projects) can be supplemented or even replaced by monitoring during the education process, and not only on evident achievements (ex. completed assignments), but also on secondary data. For example, a student's behavioral pattern (preferential school schedule, timely completed assignments, etc.) and even objective parameters of the body and nervous system could be subject matter to be graded.

f. Given everything said above, it is very important that assessment must support the learning process, not block the student's independence, creative and cognitive activity because of a drop in motivation. In particular, having assessment that is too often and too harsh (including assessment that the student's long-term future could depend on) will most likely block rather than help the student's development.

Consequences for the development of new educational technologies:

1. The assessment system goes far beyond the education system (which is only an individual case of such system). It is becoming possible in society to transition to an 'economy of merit' as to a universal system for assessing the achievements of every individual. In this system, reputation becomes reputational capital that allows obtaining access to knowledge and resources (for more detail see section 2.3.4). Their integration with similar systems of achievement is the natural development of an assessment system.

2. Achievement assessment systems (both inside and outside education) could be built as a continuous assessment process in a game-like dynamic (roughly as is done in MMORPG, where a player obtains points for each game move and in total earns levels and bonus points that come with them). Such a system built within the logic of quests and achievements, and built into augmented reality, could accompany a person throughout the entire day: you can earn points for a healthy lifestyle, proper social behavior ('help an elderly woman across the road'), etc. When combining the learning process, education turns into a 'personal quest to prime one's persona' when a student, in acting as a player, develops himself according to the recommended scenario.

3. The transition takes place from a hierarchical assessment system (when teachers assess students or bosses assess their subordinates) to an all-around assessment (everybody assesses everybody). As far as the educational process is concerned, the final assessment of each person is formed out of the assessments of everyone with whom the student interacted with during the educational process (ex. implementing an educational project), and this gives a much more complete picture of both the student's current qualities and 'development zones.' Furthermore, not only are the students assessed, but so are both the educational content and the education space, and this assessment allows for co-customizing the components of the education process much faster and more productively.

4. It is not so much important to assess achievements as it is to assess the capability to achieve as such, namely assess skill: an achievement is a one-time result, while a skill shows the ability to repeat such achievement. In this sense, one-time assessments of achievements can be gathered into a 'skills profile' that, in gradually expanding as a person develops, is able to accompany a person his entire life, from his very first years to the end. Human education,

his social activeness (including informal), and his professional activities are linked between each other through this profile, because they all are reflected in this profile. This allows for giving more complete assessments of each individual by being based not only on academic successes. Let us say that a school bully in this case could be not an outsider of the academic process, but rather a person with high communicative and organizational skills.

5. Assessing results is not the only indicator of the quality of a student and studies. What is no less important is assessing how the learning process itself is going. Leaders of the academic process are able to discuss the individual learning style, the student's engagement, work rate on assignments, etc. This 'assessment in process' opportunity has already been implemented in some MOOC platforms, in particularly in Coursera (see section 3.1.2). The student is able to talk about how interesting, full, understandable, and developing the learning process is. These parameters can be assessed, including through the student's objective psychophysiological parameters (using neurointerfaces and biomonitors in real time). Assessing the process allows for controlling the 'instantaneous state' in education (Shernoff, 2002): reaching a fine balance between 'too simple' and 'too difficult,' when learning seemingly takes place 'by itself.' As a result, intellectual and emotional engagement emerges (cognitive traction and engagement) in the learning process.

**Table 3**

# NEW EDUCATION TOOLS BASED ON NEW TECHNOLOGIES

| | CORE EDUCATIONAL PROCESSES | TRADITIONAL SOLUTIONS | NEW SOLUTIONS |
|---|---|---|---|
| **1** | **PASSING DOWN A STANDARD EXPERIENCE OR PRACTICE FROM TEACHER OR EXPERT** | | |
| 1.1 | Teaching or learning of verbal knowledge | Lecture or textbook | Online multimedia libraries, massive online courses etc. |
| 1.2 | Teaching of nonverbal knowledge through communication with its holder | Lecture or personal tutorial | Virtual tutors (artificial intelligence, AI), wearable devices for biofeedback learning |
| 1.3 | Teaching of nonverbal knowledge through skill training | Personal tutorial & mentorship or apprenticeship | Wearable devices or virtual simulators |
| **2** | **INDEPENDENT ACQUISITION OF EXPERIENCE, INDIVIDUALLY OR IN A GROUP** | | |
| 2.1 | Quest or challenge | Sports competitions, adventure camping etc. | Gaming environments and 'sensoriums', urban quests using augmented reality etc. |
| 2.2 | Research or experiment | Work in a laboratory, discussions in a research group | Distributed, distance and virtual labs and research teams, also with AIs as a team members |
| 2.3 | Creative (individual or team) project | Group work (planning, discussions, experiments, etc.) | Distributed group work in social networks, work in virtual environments (incl. gaming) |
| **3** | **ASSESSMENT AND RECORDING OF ACHIEVEMENTS** | | |
| 3.1 | Selecting students for the course / program | Entrance exam, interview | Gene testing; forecast of education and career trajectory based on achievement profile and comparative big data analysis |
| 3.2 | Interim evaluation of achievements and feedback | Interim task evaluation | Comprehensive continuous monitoring (incl. gaming-based behavior monitoring inside augmented reality / Internet of things games) |
| 3.3 | Final examination | Final work (diploma or chef d'œuvre) | Personal competence profile, personal virtual portfolio, virtual environment game, creation and stress testing of a virtual world / digital model |
| **4** | **MOTIVATION FOR EDUCATION** | | |
| 4.1 | Competitive motivation | Contests or competitions | Gamification: competitive gaming models |
| 4.2 | Achievement motivation | Evaluation & grading systems | Gamification, reputational & financial capital management systems |
| 4.3 | Social pressure | Admonitions or threats from teachers, parents, etc. | Preventive management of educational results (systems for achievement prediction) |
| 4.4 | Pleasure from the educational process | Teacher's personal charisma, use of entertaining components (e.g. movies) | Adjustable gaming models, Biofeedback systems (tracking the intensity of experiences in the learning process) |

## WAVES OF TECHNOLOGICAL INNOVATIONS

**2014 Start in Web.** Online startup accelerators and team fairs.

**2015 Green & Lean.** Eco-thinking in production & urban life becomes one of the core subjects in schools & universities

**System engineering** (incl. CDIO) at the core of professional lifelong learning in technologies

**2020 Multi-Bio-DIY-Cooker.** Domestic appliances (e.g. 3D printer) allow to produce wide range of food and pharma products at home.

**2030 NBIC convergence dominates product markets**

**2025 Era of Self-organization.** Hybrid / network structures become dominant in advanced economies

## NEW MODELS OF BUSINESS ORGANIZATION AND COOR-DINATION

**2035 'Ideology Collapse'** (real economies mix of 'plannedliberal-capital-anarchocommunism')

## SHIFT IN EMPLOYMENT PATTERNS AND LIFESTYLES

**2025 On the Sidelines!** A significant share of population start losing their professions to automation and are unable to adapt to changing conditions.

**The New Spare**

**2016 Gerbil on a Treadmill.** Involving socially marginalized people into employment & personal development through alternate reality games.

**2014 Web-based Sandboxes.** DIY and science clubs for school kids and students go online.

**Fab Labs** become mass educational solution for OECD universities.

**DIY-models Exchanges.** Emergence of online platforms to trade and exchange blueprints for 3D-printing.

**2020 Bio-DIY-Labs.** Mobile labs producing biomedical products.

**Spread of DIY culture**

**2023 WorkPlay.** Online and virtual gamers are engaged on the mass-scale to help solve reallife tasks.

**2018 From gaming generation to Homo Ludens:** gaming becomes a life norm

**Gaming Achievement Logic** Used in Education for real-time monitoring of individual current educational trajectory and learning achievements.

**2030 Attempt Culture.** Game culture becomes an integral element of work and everyday urban life.

**2014 Education** becomes a means of overcoming personal existential crises — midlife crisis, ageing crisis etc.

**Increasing demand for authenticity & self-actualization**

## NEW FINANCIAL ARCHITECTURE & REPUTATION ECONOMY

**2013 Development of Independent Digital Currencies.** Amid the crisis of national economies, independent digital currencies become real alternatives to national currencies

**Search for new models of global financial architecture**

**2025 Collapse of Bismarckian Pension Systems.** Due to economic complications, OECD countries are forced to adopt post-Soviet pension model (minimum subsistence level for the majority of pensioners).

**2014 States Strike Back.** States lead fight with transnational corporations: campaigns for "deoffshorization", transaction transparency, increased financial control, control over digital financial communication.

**Development of the Reputation Economics**

**2017 Family Universities.** Lifelong learning for families: images of family future, family competencies & family teams

**2013 Mixed-Age Education.** Peer- and cross-age tutoring (in & between families) is a means of family reintegration.

**School in the Womb.** Prenatal study programs: acquisition of knowledge and skils in the womb.

## SHIFT IN PATTERNS OF FAMILY ORGANIZATION & CHILDHOOD

**2020 Modern families in search for identity**

**Family Universities.** Lifelong learning for families: images of family future, family competencies & family teams

**Mixed-Age Education.** Peer— and cross-age tutoring (in & between families) is a means of family reintegration.

**School in the Womb.** Prenatal study programs: acquisition of knowledge and skils in the womb.

**New family education: competent parents and cross-generational integration**

**New childhood model: Early maturing kids**

**2018 Mickey-Mouse-Club-Law.** Introduction of legislation regulating early-age intellectual labor (10+).

**2025 A Captain at Fifteen.** Mixed-age education substitutes physical age for social.

**2021 T-9 Dislexia.** The culture of written text changes dramatically or begins to die out due to reliance on and heavy use of predictive texting.

**'New Mowglis':** A generation of children raised by computers

**2030 Generation with Shaky Values,** whose members grew in gaming environments (augmented reality with game-achievement logic) has contorted or unstable values

2013          2020          2035

## 2.3 MACROFACTORS THAT SET THE CONTEXT FOR THE TRANSFORMATION OF EDUCATION

*'What does all this have to do with education?!'*
A representative of the Russian Ministry of Education and Science at the presentation of the first edition of this Report in May 2013

Macrofactors are the chief political, economic, social, and cultural factors of society's global transformation that will have an impact on the field of education in terms of content, training formats, and the very place of education in public life. The demographic dynamics and influence of technologies on public life, first and foremost, cause these macrofactors. Below (Tables 4 and 5) we explain how it is any given macrofactors that will impact the processes and content in education systems. If to answer in a general sense the question that the representative of the Russian Ministry of Education asked us: education is always a 'shot into the future' (the target, namely economic performance, is located on the horizon from several years to several decades from today's time of learning). We must understand what kind of world awaits that we are preparing ourselves and our children for.

### 2.3.1 New technological structure

1. **The flourishing of new industries.** The advent of a 'package' of new industries and the gradual restructuring of the economy's technological base in industrially developed countries is the most important economic process. An accepted point on economic transformation presumed that the transition taking place to a post-industrial society would mean the gradually displacement of production to countries with low labor costs and low environmental requirements, while industrially developed countries would hold onto the development and distribution of the end product (Cock et al., 2005). The process of active outsourcing, however, slowed down by the middle of the 2000s, and by the end of the 2000s there came to be the widespread understanding that a transfer of production to other countries simultaneously means the loss of technological skill in developing and supporting a product (Szirmai et al., 2013). Now we have the era of re-industrialization, the rebirth of industrial production in developed countries that, nonetheless, will be built upon a different technological foundation than the production of the previous structure (Hall, 2010). Moreover, it is evident that the differences between 'leading' and 'traditional' industries (both may see the rapid

Legend, page 45

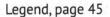 TREND

 SUBTREND

 HARD TECHNOLOGY

SOFT TECHNOLOGY

 EVENT

THREAT

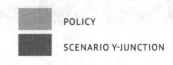 POLICY

SCENARIO Y-JUNCTION

change in technologies, and the assimilation of leading practices) will be effaced in the process of re-industrialization, just as will traditional perceptions about industry borders. Therefore, the issue of technologies that direct change is more important. Two main trends that will determine neo-industrial production are intellectualization and greening, and they are related to the increasing requirements for the habitat quality from principal consumers: urban residents in developed and rapidly developing countries.* As a result, the following is a list of technological sectors that are the most likely to grow in the coming 10 to 15 years:**

- New materials (composites, 'smart materials' and biological materials used in transport, construction, small-goods production, medicine, etc.) and locally produced related new technologies (3D printing of household goods, organs and medicinal drugs, food, etc.)

- Smart environment and Internet of things technologies (smart utilities sensors, smart electrical circuits, smart lighting, smart transport, etc.), household robotechnics (with robot vacuum cleaners and multicookers, robot pets, robot resident tutors, robot attendants, and robot sex dolls being the first examples) and new smart industry (ex. Industry 4.0 model of cyberphysical production systems (Nikolaus, 2013)).

- Genetic technology-based biotechnologies are not only genetically modified macro-organisms (plants and animals) that tackle the food production issue close to places where food is consumed (ex. in vertical greenhouses or home 'integrated catering facilities' (Despommier, 2009)), but also micro-organisms for all different kinds of household purposes (food and medicinal drug production, trash processing, fuel production, water and air purification) (Brand, 2010).

- New energy production technologies: nuclear technologies, renewable sources (sun, wind, etc.) and biological sources (biofuel and biogas) are the most likely energy mix of new energy for the coming decade. Breakthroughs in electric transportation (ex. Tesla Motors) and the production of third-generation, algae-based biofuel and fourth-generation biofuel (with genetically modified bacteria) capable of making big changes to the current consumption of hydrocarbons, first and foremost oil, should especially be stressed (Frost & Sullivan, 2010).

Removing spatial limitations is one of the most important features of a new industry. It become ultra-local: any necessary goods will be produced for an individual home or group of households by 3D-printing and biotechnologies, whereas exchange happens in the domain of information flows, with 3D printer digital models, personal preferences information, media products, etc. becoming objects of exchange.

It should be noted in addition that, although the features of the new economic structure are beginning to take shape, its advent will be gradual, and will stem from a cycle of the replacement of old infrastructure with new infrastructure (including in the energy and extraction industries), shifting people from one industry to another and shaping new habits in production and consumption. For all intents and purposes, truly shaping a new techno-

* http://ec.europa. eu/environment/ life/publications/ lifepublications/ lifefocus/documents/ urban_lr.pdf

** According to a number of studies based on the Technology Radar method, such as http://thoughtworks. fileburst.com/assets/ technology-radar-may-2013.pdf

logical structure in industrially developed countries is a process that will last until 2050 (so, for example, South Korea plans to be one of the first countries to transition completely to 'smart' energy networks by 2030, but E.U. countries and the United States both are implementing similar plans and in similar time frames, which means that the restructuring of their energy infrastructure will take place around 2035-2040). We will see a multi-layered process where industrial production is not liquidated, but rather drastically reconsidered through the logic of post-industrial models (ex. the mentioned Industry 4.0). This process could be accelerated, if breakthrough results in creating new energy sources will be made (ex. low-energy nuclear synthesis, which at present is considered impossible).

2. **Greening of the economy.** Green technologies at the heart of the majority of the listed industries are a demand of the time (it is hard to overestimate the consequences of human activities polluting the environment (IPCC, 2013)) and act at the same time as a new public ideology and new locomotive of economic growth. That very same goal of victory over 'the plastic threat' (Ackerman, 2010) (including over the giant floating plastic trash island in the Pacific Ocean that is disrupting the balance in plankton reproduction and the entire food chain of fish and marine animals) is likely not less ambitious, but more ambitious than the goal of victory in the Cold War. Green technology at the end of the 20th century was usually more expensive and less productive than non-green methods of production and consumption. Now, in the 21st century, the main bet is being placed on simultaneous environmental friendliness and cost effectiveness, on having green technologies that are superior to their non-green competitors in economic performance. 'Lean' methodology, Toyota production system, 6-sigma and similar methods of mass-scale industrial production optimization have challenged the traditional assumption that it is impossible to simultaneously improve the quality and reduce the cost of a product. Similarly, lean & green methods and technologies challenge the assumption that greener solutions cannot be more beneficial economically.

We believe that skills related to this 'lean & green' thinking will make up a significant part of the educational content in the coming years. This should include, for example, the entire system of the perceptions of modern systemic engineering promoted by the CDIO standard.* This is, first and foremost, the perception of product and technology management through the entire life cycle, including disposal and re-use. Moreover, habitat management and adjusting the habitat to one's own needs (the same bio-DYI development that, for example, Freeman Dyson writes about (Dyson, 1999)) will gradually become a part of the daily skills for residents of new cities. Other such 'household' skills in all likelihood will include design and programming skills (see the IFTF's full-scale report 'When everything is programmable').**

It is worth pointing out that 'green thinking' as a model for treating nature responsibly is an individual case of responsible 'global thinking,' where a person tries to weigh not only the environmental consequences of his actions, but also the social and cultural consequences. In essence, people in industrially developed countries go through perceptions of being responsible to the natural environment to get to the perception of the environmental friendliness of their own actions as a whole, and subsequently go through this to start managing ecology of their minds (a topic prophetically brought up in the

* http://www.cdio.org

** http://www.iftf.org/our-work/people-technology/technology-horizons/when-everything-is-programmable/

works of Gregory Bateson (Bateson, 1972)). Teaching mind ecology — that is, mindfulness in all aspects of one's life, — would call for a radical revision of curriculum, beginning with pre-school and early school levels. However, if we seek to restore the balance between the human civilization and the planet Earth, to achieve the true sustainability of communities, nations, and humanity as a whole* — then we should take all necessary efforts to implement such programs on the mass education.

* http://www. triplepundit. com/2011/10/ systemic-sustain- ability/

3. **The wave of startups.** The economy will not be restructured instantaneously, making the launch of a wave of technological startups (taking place right now in most OECD countries and in many developing countries) the most important part in the transition process. Education plays an extremely important role in supporting a popular startup culture. As 'cultivating' and 'accelerating' startups is becoming the leading investment practice, startup accelerators are playing more and more of a role as 'startup production factories,' and the education process of teaching skills for doing business, project-based learning, and mentoring all lie in the heart of accelerators' activities.

Although the neo-industry will have great significance as far as providing for the demands of residents of developed countries is concerned, it will not be able to ensure a sufficient number of jobs, as the trend of driving people out of the industrial production sphere has gone nowhere (just as the trend of driving people out of the routine intellectual labor sphere that we addressed above). At the same time, new, service-related spheres are growing fast, where labor productivity growth is supported by a large number of employees. These are 'people-oriented' industries such as security, healthcare, entertainment, and education. Essentially, Daniel Bell documented this process more than 40 years ago (Bell, 1973), but it again becomes relevant with industry beginning to be rebuilt. It is important to note at this time that education and self-development could become one of the backbone industries for the new economy not only as far as ensuring the transition to a new technological (and social) structure is concerned, but also as an independent employment sector whose demand for various services with time will only grow.

## 2.3.2 Changing the business and management organization models in industries

1. **Evolution toward flexibility.** 'Flexibility' is the defining notion of a new system of organizing production and distribution. The global economy is becoming increasingly complex and uncertain, while the rate of change is constantly growing. Therefore, business organizations are making the transition from rigorously organized hierarchical structures to an adaptive network structure that is capable of self-redesigining in the face of transformations and crises. What is significant is that these structures are hybrids that would have been hard to conceive some 30 to 40 years ago. For example, R&D alliances between competitors in a highly competitive market, or networks of independent small businesses that interact together in growing their sales and investment policies, or systems where groups of product users design innovations

The model of 'learning organization' sits at the center of these changes, as suggested by Chris Argyris and Peter Senge (Argyris & Schon, 1978; Senge, 1990). What makes learning organizations stand out is that they encourage employees, teams, divisions, and organizations as a whole to learn constantly through creating an atmosphere of trust, free discussion, experimenting, sharing experiences, constantly improving; they allocate their resources for these purposes. Willingness to constant renovation and engendering of innovative management practices is the defining feature of modern businesses (Hamel, 2007). In other words, learning organizations are able to change their action models 'as a whole', through processes of 'self-education'.

The first established trend is the transition to models of open management in one of the most critical areas of business operation: the creation of new products. The model of open innovations that Henry Chesbrough (2003) described presumes that an organization is forced to assign a significant portion of the development process outside its walls and to an innovative ecosystem. Meanwhile, not one company, but a 'cloud' of interconnected companies becomes the technology title holder (and the holder of access to the corresponding market). We would add that major organizations even encourage such hybridization by shaping new technologies by way of independent startups at their own corporate incubators or by spinning off development.

2. **Digitizing value creation links.** A similar co-development process would not be technologically possible (or at least would be extremely difficult), if it were not for the digital revolution at the end of the 1990s and beginning of the 2000s, which handed over all work on R&D projects to specialized digital environments. At the same time, the majority of industries became unified, the set of standard basic solutions (modules), whose foundation was used to design and assemble specific products, was gradually coordinated. Digitization and the transition to modularity have allowed carrying out the joint, simultaneous development of new products in groups of dozens and hundreds of interconnected (but at the same time independent) companies that implement the same production preparation process at the same time. It is not just one R&D division that is behind a cutting-edge, high technology product such as the Apple iPhone or Boeing Dreamliner, but a host of development groups that, nonetheless, work together more flexibly, rapidly, and efficiently than their predecessors working within just one organization (Enkel, Gassmann, Chesbrough, 2009). What is significant is that special engineers called ontologists, who describe the 'basic vocabulary' for designing and producing a new product given its future use, are the coordinators of these activities*. In some sense, it is ontologists who prescribe the basic user features of solutions and devices, and who are the 'grey cardinals' of the new technological reality. This implies that education & training systems should prepare people to new working conditions, such as horizontally organized and flexible organization, intrapreneurship and worker empowerment, high level of uncertainty etc. This should be done by re-creating these new and emerging working conditions in educational contexts — e.g. replacing teaching as process in which a holder of 'sacred knowledge' shares it with ignorant students — by collective exploration of subjects that are unknown to both teachers and students and therefore require creative experimentation, teamwork, and sharing of insights.

* http://15926.org/

3. **The rise of hybrid forms of organization.** Developments are not the first practice to go through 'networkization': the production and sales organization system had earlier gone through the same process, first in consumer industries, and then in the raw-materials sectors (although highly integrated companies still remain in many sectors). Developing network technologies allows presuming that this process will continue, and in the next 10 to 15 years hybrid forms of economic organization (systems of independent small and medium-sized organizations incorporated by an internal network and quasi-market) will become a widely and, possibly, dominating type of production organization. Given the production revolution described above (section 2.3.1), production will make the transition to highly local forms, and most importantly, will keep organizations together: these are common ideas, meanings, and sets of technologies. In this sense, brands are not corporate property, but collective property, acting as the markets of company and development group networks (approximately as is happening now with the Linux brand).

More radical production organization options are possible as well, such as a company that is completely built on the self-organization and self-determination of its employees. What is interesting here is the experience of software company Valve, a well-known developer of computer games that has employees without specifically defined responsibilities or allegiance to a project or team (all the way up to the point where all they have to do is shift their table and computer to transition to a new project), and teams determine for themselves which promising programs they believe should be worked on. In other words, the transition in such companies takes place from formal hierarchical organizational models to network horizontal modals that are more similar to communities where members share, first and foremost, intents and values.

4. **The collapse of the political economy.** In the distant future, around the 2030s and beyond, we can presume that the main problem that will have engendered the industrial economy—the problem of limited key resources and the necessity to concentrate them for efficient production—will be gradually surmounted by new production organization systems. If you are to separate yourself from the possibilities that the potential of new production technologies using nanorobots promise (since none of these potentially possible technologies exist as a prototype), even 3D-printing based production (should it become cheaper in the future) and small-scale energy co-smart grids will have a revolutionary effect in most industrial sectors, namely the transition from major production centers to local ones. This is an economy where material goods are available to everyone in the necessary and sufficient quantity, and at a price that is close to nothing; at the same time, there are prices, and both financial settlements and very complex forms of capital turnover are preserved. This is an economy where virtually total anarchy rules, because it is made up of a host of small, independent manufacturers. At the same time, this economy is rather strictly controlled, with elements of a dictatorship and even total control à la '1984.' In it we can find the triumph of communism as Marx predicted, and the triumph of the free market as Hayek predicted; but this is neither a communist paradise nor a liberal utopia. In this sense, in the coming 20-25 years, over the course of one generation, the world will clash with the final irrelevance and collapse of ideologies that have directed society's development in the industrial

world over the past 150 years. The first signs of this emerging order are experiments that resemble socialist communes of 19th century, that began spreading after 2008 crisis as a sharing economy*. The speed of the changes taking place is such that the descriptions of network activities are going out of date faster than society can assimilate them. We cannot describe the society of tomorrow, but we can predict the society of the day after tomorrow. Therefore, a new social theory must be built not upon the analysis of existing trends, but upon extending them from the future to the present (ex. built upon the trend of gradually shaping a 'point of omniscience' or 'Internet of everything') — and this understanding (and some of the practices that result from it) should even now be included into the school and vocational education curriculum.

### 2.3.3 Changing the employment and lifestyle structure

1. **'Extra people' and post-industrial skills.** The development of new technologies, including the automization of routine intellectual labor, has caused a lot of enthusiasm in industrially developed countries; however, the realization has come about over recent years that the arrival of new technologies presents a serious threat for many habitual professions. Robotization is capable of displacing us from the manual labor sphere, initially from routine manual labor, and then from rather complex manual labor. The same thing is happening in the sphere of intellectual labor and even creativity,** provided that the displacement speed could be much greater than the economy's ability to create appropriate substitutes in new sectors, including the services sector (which traditionally absorbs workers from the industrial sector as machines replace them).

Should we really be afraid of machines that will completely replace us and strip us of our means of subsistence? This question has emerged repeatedly since the beginning of the Industrial Revolution, leading not only to the rise of the Luddite movement in the 19th century, but also to constant protests against the latest round of automization throughout the 20th century. German Sociologist F. Jünger discussed this threat of uncontrolled automization profoundly in the middle of the 20th century (Jünger 1949). He showed in his work that every time more jobs would emerge around the industrial sphere than automization would displace, because automization allowed having a more profound division of labor in spheres that before had been perceived as wholes, such as in intellectual or creative work.

We can expect roughly the same movement if a new set of sectors is unfurled; however, as the experience of large economic reorganization has shown—such as the market launch in the economies of the former socialist camp or the reorganization of industries in Great Britain and Germany—the transition is not automatic, does not happen instantaneously, and the social poignancy of it can be completely random. For example, the populations in the countries once part of the former Soviet Union were virtually 'thrown in cold water' and adapted to a new economic market reality in an environment close to that of wartime or of the Great Depression. People's transition to the new rules of the game could be ensured to a large extent, if education plays its role (as a social buffer) by providing the opportunity to obtain new, sought-after skills, development expertise in self-employment, and even just

* http://www.huffingtonpost.com/steven-strauss/welcome-to-the-sharing-economy_b_4516707.html

** http://www.technologyreview.com/featured-story/515926/how-technology-is-destroying-jobs/

'sit it out' for several years during an economic recession (in particularly, the last behavior model is very popular in business education, which in terms of a demand model is counter-cyclical.)*

When reorganizing an economy (section 2.3.1), developing new administrative models (section 2.3.2) and a new financial architecture (section 2.3.42.3.4), the emergence of a large number of 'extra' people who have not been adapted enough and who have not found a place in new sectors is inevitable in the coming decade. It is natural that governments in industrially developed countries, even when gradually moving away from the welfare state model (see ex. speech by the King of the Netherlands William-Alexander in September 2013),** do not want to create superfluous social tension in their countries. As a result, a 'new order' can be expected for education to resolve the problem of adapting and transition people to new socio-economic circumstances.

A fair amount of solutions here could be proposed, but we can point to only the potential of some moves: First—and movement here has already begun—reorganizing educational content is necessary, taking into account the expertise that is sought after in the future. The Partnership for 21st century skills is one of the most notable programs here. This program has brought the leading software and equipment manufacturers together with producers of new educational methods and with experimenter schools in the United States and several OECD countries. Second, education spaces, in which new skills can be shaped, academic projects can be elaborated on, etc., are necessary. In addition to traditional (and not very popular) forms of professional advancement courses, virtual worlds (including specialized ones) that act as spaces to 'overexpose' and retrain 'extra' people (we will talk about this again in section 3.4) could be such spaces in the foreseeable future (by 2020-2025).

2. **Destroying the tyranny of specialists: from specialized production to the DIY culture.**
The restructuring of the economy discussed earlier is typified by, among other things, the advent of new technologies that ensure the decentralization of the production of goods and services, first and foremost of mass 3D printing and technologies of the Internet of Th ings (ex. 'smart grids').

Today's cultural orientation on self-sufficiency, craft, and manual production is closely tied to an entire number of subcultures that are incorporated by the common idea of anti-corporatism, anti-consumerism (and often connected to anti-globalism). Within these subcultures, independent production (do-it-yourself, DIY) is the standard of counter cultural life (in particularly, the famous Whole Earth Catalogue, a 1970s cult magazine, was meant first and foremost to support the DIY culture by connecting producers and consumers of DIY solutions to each other). DIY culture is geared toward authenticity, developing a person's individual and creative energy, and restoring the feeling of personal uniqueness and inde-pendence, which is closely tied to restoring lively relationships between people that have not been tainted by commercial gain.

Long chains for creating a material product in the new economy are being downsized into mini-factories (network connected 3D printers, and possibly in the future molecular micro- and nanofactories), where production chains are capable of making any idea come to life that has been drawn up as a sketch or program for such device, while instructing manu-

* http://www.gmac.com/~/media/Files/gmac/Research/Geographic%20 Trends/n-america-geo-trend-ty2011.pdf

** King's speech to parliament heralds end of Dutch welfare state http://www.ft.com/cms/s/0/934952a6-1fad-11e3-aa36-00144feab7de.html

facturing complexes becomes the object of exchange. Separate individuals or small groups, using fast prototyping systems, 3D printers, cell printers, and portable chemical synthesizers, are able to create products whose production used to require the coordinated efforts of large corporations. Individualization or targeting is helping spread the DIY culture. This is a trend indicating the unprecedented customization of products where the user has greater and greater participation, and in the end leading to the independent creation of products and the world around oneself using high technology tools.

This draws the user closer to the possibility to directly transform his own ideas into a product, and at the same time create the opportunities for the ubiquitous rebirth of the DIY culture, or 'new craftsmanship.' The new production model will most likely be closer to the network structures of communities of 'new craftsmen' (section 2.3.2) described above, which by their size could nonetheless turn out to be just as big as traditional corporations. Such communities will aspire to an image of a shop floor culture, namely a dynamic mosaic of small groups with unique, all the more refined specializations, goals, and expertise. In a certain sense, 'new craftsmanship' on a new technological foundation rethinks the issue of the division of labor: a profound specialization in the sphere of material production is likely secondary or absent in general, but there is a profound specialization in the sphere of intellectual and creative labor that is based on the unique and authentic supply of a product from the producer (roughly just like how now—given the author's style—artists' works are coveted).

Incidentally, such a 'new craftsmanship' model is in no way discarding the proliferation of globalism and, to the contrary, is its continuation. The same goes for how the IKEA store model presumes that the user will take part in a good's assembly: the model of the conditional ModelStore will presume local production at home. The market of manufacturers of the digital models of things that are used as a base for making objects will include both major players (IKEA or Home Depot will be able to sell not turnkey sets, but rather digital models and expendable supplies) and a host of small developers.

The chief barrier on the path to proliferating new craftsmanship sits first and foremost in the virtually lost culture of customized material production. This is approximately the case with how modern man delegated doctors the responsibility for his health, teachers the responsibility for his skills, and material-goods suppliers the responsibility for his self-sustainment. Hence, the question arises over the mass capability to restore control over our lives, including in self-dependence (and self-development at that) at a time when all the technological prerequisites are at our fingertips. As a result, it is education, including non-systemic education, which can tip the scales in favor of either the mass division or assimilation of DIY practices. In the long term, assimilating the DIY culture could both help the destruction of the 'tyranny of specialists' who control domains of knowledge, and the authentic democratization of technologies; at the same time, it could help the transition to a horizontally, rather than vertically, connected community of control and learning.

**3. From kidults to homo ludens: playing as a norm of life and standard of activities.** The change in the location of playing is yet another important shift taking place in modern culture. We will discuss this subject in more detail in section 3.4, but here we would like to make several early remarks.

First, playing is a necessary component of life for the majority of higher animals, whether they are dolphins, dogs, or chimpanzees. Animals are capable of playing through their entire life, and playing's purposes in their lives are extremely multifaceted: playing serves learning, sexual courtship, relaxing, or the ritualized struggle. The fact that playing does not happen 'for real,' namely that there is always a second chance, is the most important peculiarity of playing. People inherited playing behavior from the animal world, and playing since the most ancient of times has served also as a tool for resolving many different social problems.

Second, (continuing this logic) culture remained extremely playing-oriented in pre-industrial societies: the spirit of playing pierces all aspects of human behavior (Johan Huizinga wrote about this extensively in his book Homo Ludens). Playing was pushed from the cultural center to the periphery, such as to professional sport, art, and entertainment). And to the contrary, the lack of an evident playing component in the majority of types of human activities, such as economics, state administration, war, etc. (despite that it is game theory that is the modern paradigm describing these types of activities!), has not deprived social life of its inevitable conventionality, but has forced talking about it as about 'a game that has forgotten its playing nature.'

Third, by the end of the 20th century, the predominant satisfaction of the basic needs of the majority of the population in developed countries has led to a situation where the 'harsh truth of life' does not require becoming an adult immediately (see also section 2.3.5). A subgroup has emerged of kidults (adultescents), and heightened interest in games (real-life and virtual) is one of the typical characteristics of adult life (Summerskill, 2000). If psychologists have predominantly interpreted the behavior of such people as the 'Peter Pan Syndrome), then we believe that a natural human demand for restoring playing's natural role in society is expressed in their behavior.

To a certain extent, in the 2000s this demand had already been heard: gamification has started to be all the more widely practiced in education, social communications, R&D, and other 'serious' types of activities. We presume that this trend is not situational, but rather one of the strongest in new culture that will become all the more game-based as man leaves the physical and intellectual routine. Proliferating virtual worlds and augmented reality, and transforming them into a part of daily life, will help the prevalence of game models, the onset of the 'game totality' era. We will return to this topic below.

4. **'New old' people: increasing the duration of active life.\*** Above (Section 2.2.5) we discussed the possible impact of genetics on the increase in the average life expectancy. In adding to the potential that new developments in genetic medicine create, there are other systemic measures as well that lead to an increase in life expectancy and a rise in the quality of one's final years of life. In particularly, changing urban living conditions: increasing water and air quality from liquidating toxic agents, augmenting the amount of recreational space, decreasing stress at work and in urban areas, making sports and preventive treatment more popular, and proliferating new models of medicine (preventive and predictive medicine). All this can lengthen one's life by 30 to 40 years at the least (and starting at 80+ years in industrially developed countries). With people in society aged 120, we will come upon a situation where it will be realistic to have four, and even five, generations in one family living together.

* This section is to a large extent based on the theses of Sergei Gradirovsky 'The 120-year-old man as an anthopo-project'

When changing the structure of labor employment from physical labor to intellectual and creative labor, the period of active working life is entirely possible until 80 to 90 years of age (we now see this in the research sphere, where some researchers continue their career until they are around 100 years old).* This means that, in particularly, that there is the possibility of meaningful employment in a large number of professional fields, opening up for complete, professional recognition and for implementing a large number of one's own 'lengthy' projects. The perception of old age as one of 'a time to take it easy' is vanishing. This to a large extent is also a politically justified move, since with a significant increase in life expectancy, supporting the 'Bismarckian' pension model is impossible without radically increasing base retirement age.

It is significant for us to establish that a new group of consumers with a specific demand is already emerging (and will grow quickly) in education. First, this is a group that is showing a demand for adapting to the changing world ('adaption of extra people' as is described above). Second, this is a group that is allowing for a certain experiment with their lives, when a 'mandatory program' (related to a social norm: having children, building a career, accumulating wealth, etc.) is implemented, but there is the chance to assimilate an activity to one's liking, to take part in volunteer projects, etc. We concede that it is this group that can fill the ranks of DIY culture and 'new craftsmanship' followers. Third, this group is engaged not so much in 'vertical' models of education, in obtaining knowledge from 'gurus,' as much in horizontal models, in exchanging knowledge with younger people and among themselves.

5. **The shift in the paradigm of needs: from downshifters to self-actualizing people.** Another important cultural shift is also tied to the infusion of basic needs in consumer society. In particularly, the United States, disappointment with the promises of consumer society, reflected by the famous proverb 'money doesn't buy happiness' (Howe & Strauss, 1991) followed the rise of the baby-boomer generation. The choice of generation X toward downshifting—the widespread rejection of a career after securing one's 'basic needs' and the fundamental admission that it is impossible to follow the previous rules when it is impossible to change the surrounding reality—was the first social reaction. In the following generations (generation Y and especially generation Z**), however, we see the increasing understanding of the value of creative self-fulfillment and the willingness to demand the necessary conditions for this. Of course, the external circumstances for this (business and the state's prime concern with 'innovation') must dovetail with the internal circumstances.

It can be considered, however, that this process is an entirely logical 'movement up along the Maslow hierarchy of needs,*** when self-actualization stops being the valued prerogative of the elite and becomes a value of the majority (in other words, the 'Maslow hierarchy' or its more accurate counterparts describe not the individual hierarchy of values, but rather the statistical patterns in society). Moreover, the presumption can be made that enslaving people with the process of consumption is not the profound goal of the 'surplus economy' (Diamandis & Kotler, 2012), that the superfluous focus on material consumption acts as public dysfunction (including dysfunction linked to the attempt of obsolete corporate forms to reproduce themselves), and their aspiration from consumerism to self-realiza-

* Ex. Ronald Coase, a Nobel Prize winner in economics who died in 2013 at the age of 103, continued to publish and take part in research discussions even during the last years of his life.

** Classification of generations – e.g. http://www.socialmarketing.org/newsletter/features/generation3.htm

*** Strictly speaking, Abraham Maslow himself did not implement the Maslow hierarchy of needs, a methodical system of human needs, but rather his adherents did. Given that the Maslow model has been repeatedly criticized over the decades that have passed since it was created (ex. Wahba, Bridwell, 1976), what is more important for us is the very perception of a hierarchical nature of needs and the existence of a certain hierarchy that corresponds to the standard cultural values.

tion is a normal process of social improvement. The first signs of this trend come from the increasing attention to authenticity in all spheres, including the sphere of one's own professional self-realization. We believe that this cohort in the future will become one of the key consumers of individualized education (more details on this in section 3.2).

## 2.3.4 The new financial architecture and 'reputational capital'

1. **The demand for a new financial hierarchy.** The demand for new models of financial organization inevitably accompanies the process of global economic development every time a crisis hits (which, essentially, is a symptom of dysfunction in the existing models). Discussions about a 'new financial architecture' have been taking place since the 2008 global financial and economic crisis hit, and although it is likely that intermediate solutions will be found, we presume that the coming 10 to 15 years will be an era of turbulence. Two chief reasons for this have to do with the inevitable restructuring of the global 'rules of the game:'*

* See http://www. weforum.org/issues/ new-financial-archi- tecture

- First, a significant restructuring of the economy toward new technologies (accompanied by the large-scale flow over of capital and the re-assessment of values, and thus both the inevitable areas of instability and bubbles;

- Second, the reorganization of state finances that stems from states' decreasing ability to support the welfare state (including the pension system, state system for supporting the unemployed, migrants, etc.) and from the gradual transfer of state duties to private operators or communities.

Three specific factors related to the current state of the financial system itself are super-imposed upon this:

- The complexity and opaqueness of the existing architecture (offshorization and smudging property rights, the developed financial derivatives system, blurring regulators' risk and loss control over systemic risks) is often labeled the main reason for the 2008 financial crisis. Despite regulators and financial institutions' active work on this subject, the situation is far from resolved.

- The dependence of the global financial system on the state of the 'leading economy' (at the moment, the U.S. economy) that is perceived as a threat to global stability (since the leading economy always has the impetus to control the global situation in its domestic interests, and not in the interests of the system as a whole). As a result, there is the need to create new values (and alternative issue centers, including those that are independent of specific states that ensure these values) as a way to increase stability.

- The lack of accounting for new values in the traditional financial and monetary system (ex. the value of reputation, creative work, etc.). The result is the inappropriate perception of segments of the new economy in the financial sector, and the lack of productivity of currency forms of interaction for the new economy.

In this sense, the demand for the financial architecture taking shape is to ensure systematic reliability and the necessary level of trust for the global economic system (aggregate of world economies) in order to avoid the game of 'the few versus the many.' Many experiments are being conducted in this field that are, in particular, related to the emergence of new currencies independent of national states and even private operators, a sort of 'new gold' (in particularly, crypto-currencies such as Bitcoin).* Friedrich Hayek expressed the idea in the middle of the 1970s (Hayek, 1976) that the privatization of issuing money can bring about a more efficient organization of currency circulation, and it has been gaining popularity ever since.

* http://bitcoin.org/en/faq

Transformation of the financial system has several serious implications for education. One of them (maybe minor yet still important) is the requirment of ubiquitous financial literacy, that should be a general skill of any adult in developed countries, similar to the skill of writing, calculating, and using computer software. Other implication is that the financial system will look for new investment tools to replace markets with decreased profitability (e.g. derivatives) — and one of those markets will be the direct investment into talents (this possibility will be considered in detail in 3.2.3).

2. **Time and reputational capital: from volunteering to a 'transparent society.'** Time banks are one of the possible models that overcome the limitations of the existing financial system. Edgar Cahn, the creator of the first time bank model, proposed it as a way to resolve the problems of social mutual assistance as the efficiency of government social programs decreases. Time banks work on the principle that each person has valuable qualities, some of these qualities are priceless, and people can help one another through mutual respect and mutual assistance.** Time banks give people the chance to exchange social services, and a significant part of these services deal directly with issues of education (working with children, learning skills, mentorship, etc.)*** A model similar to time banks is being successfully used as well for stimulating 'learning networks' within school education (see Box 'SABER Brazilian system').

** http://timebanks.org/about

*** http://besttime-bank.org/Links/Time%20Dollar/Education.htm

Besides time banks, there are models close to them that are meant to assess each participant's investment in the community, and for each participant to receive the corresponding reputational capital (in essence, the amount of time invested in a community is approximately a reflection of this investment). Reputation since antiquity has been an inconspicuous

Box 3
*SABER Brazilian system*

Brazil implemented the SABER voucher system meant for increasing the number of students able to afford a higher education, and to develop the system of mutual assistance between school children. SABER does not have any value and can be used only to pay for one's education in a higher institute of education. Vouchers are given to young school children to pay for mentor services on the condition that the student has chosen a mentor a class ahead to help catch up in his weak subjects. Then, SABER switches over to older grades, and so on and so forth, until it reaches a school child in an older grade. After this, a 17-year-old student is able to pay part of his higher education tuition using accumulate SABER currency.

but important economic value, for it often impacts social status and provides access to the majority of resources (including material resources, human capital, etc.). Individual communities already have the chance to objectivize reputation (ex. reputation in science correlates with the author citation rate, namely their impact on the current scientific process).

Reputation for most people can be objectivized within social networks, and a number of startup companies are now working on finding models of 'digital' reputation, such as reflecting a community's recognition of an individual's merits (ex. TrustCloud, TrustRank, Legit, WhyTrusted, etc.). There are a number of problems as these models evolve, with celebrity bias being one of them: people who are able to control the public's attention, and not those who are most useful for society, are promoted (as a result, pornography stars will have higher status than scientists and engineers). A full-fledged 'merit consideration' system must reflect not so much media success, as must a person's actual contribution to the lives of others through creating new meanings, passing along knowledge, volunteering, and other 'people-for-people' actions. Merit assessment systems must develop not from media formats, but from community practices where certain practices assess the contribution of others and penalize for their insignificance or lack of unethical nature of behavior (ex. this is how the Russian sites of the community of IT specialists Habrahabr, designers Lepra, and their international counterparts (such as IT community StackOverflow, specialized community of products Microsoft Technet, or question-and-answer community Ask) are organized.

In the future, reputational capital assessment systems must integrate online and offline reputations. If an online reputation can fully be built in real time depending on a person's every action in the online communities, then his offline actions (in work, living, communicating with friends, etc.) are entirely capable of shaping this reputation as well. When most residents of developed countries are online 24 hours a day, when an intelligent environment of the Internet of Things, augmented reality, and biomonitoring devices surround each of us, then there is the chance both to have continuous behavior (self)-monitoring using technological solutions and continuous cross assessment, and to transform assessments into a complete reputation indicator. In this sense, we are entering a The Transparent Society (this is rather profoundly described in David Brin's book by the same title (Brin, 1998). Although The Transparent Society is rather uncomfortable when interpreting it through the perceptions of privacy from the past (including uncomfortable for people who have something to hide), it provides a host of advantages for 'honest citizens.' The advent of a 'transparent society' bolsters the trends described above that has to do with the search for authenticity, because external honesty stimulates internal honesty and vice-versa.

The spread of integrated reputation capital models may have a significant impact on our abilities to learn and build a career. This is based on the logic where reputational capital is one of the significant investments, while education and career decisions take into account the expected influence on the level of reputational capital. It is highly likely that in a society with financial security problems that have been for the most part resolved (we talked above about the technological possibilities of building such a society in the coming decades), it is reputational currencies that will determine people's access to resources that are significant to them, such as knowledge and the attention of others (Hunt, 2009). Moreover, we believe that the emergence of online markets can be expected in the near future, where a combination of reputational and time capital will be used to pay for all different types of online education services (already up-and-running foreign language learning online education resources, such as MyLanugageExchange, Italki, Polyglot, etc., can be considered the first such examples). In the future, a universal 'education currency' that brings together various mutual-learning networks could also well emerge based on these markets.

## 2.3.5 The new family and a shift in the childhood model

1. **The modernist family: searching for a new identity.** The changes taking place in the structure of basic public institutions are bound to affect the family organization model. The perceptions of the family norm have been reconsidered repeatedly over the past decades, as we have observed explosive growth in all different types of family organization: communities, guest families, same-sex marriages, unions for jointly raising children, neo-tribes, etc. (Budgeon, Roseneil, 2004).

The reasons for the drawn-out family crisis are completely understandable. The family's original and traditional function (first and foremost as an institution within the agrarian and early industrial society) was the ability to survive and reproduce together, including the conveying of culture and experience between generations. Marriage as a social institution also had meaning in the context of joint ownership and disposal of property. In a modern city, all these tasks can now be taken care of without a partner in the modern city, especially given the rise of new technologies. Any function can be outsourced (including taking care of daily activities, raising children, caring for the ill and the elderly), virtually any type of sexual relationship can be arranged, and one's own network of interaction can be built according to one's own interests. All this 'tears up' the family structure and puts the need for joint existence in doubt. It is clear that with the emergence of human-like robots in everyday life in the coming 10 to 15 years that are capable of replacing a partner or family members in most of these functions, the family crisis will become even more exacerbated.

In some sense, the family is searching for its identity and the meaning of its existence. Modern psychology of family relations offers a new model based on the family being not a place for comfort and survival, but rather a place for developing together. In other words, the family's realizing the meaning of joint existence is the family's main identity: its image of a joint future where each is able to grow together with others and with other's help. We presume that there is virtually no education for families that is meant to find the meanings of joint existence, while the need for it is colossal. As a result, we expect to see the expansion of 'family universities' begin in the coming 10 to 15 years. These will be universities where families, in relying on their own 'image of the future,' are able to jointly obtain the skills they need for existing and growing together (including through participating in joint creative projects for the entire family), and mutually teach each other useful skills (just as, for example, the Canadian Family University Foundation* or U.S. projects such as Elmbrook Family University,** etc., do this).

* http://www.familyuniversity.org/about.html

** http://www.elmbrookschools.org/community/family-university/index.aspx

2. **New internal family education: competent parenting and intergenerational integration.** A separate issue in this logic concerns the passing along of intergenerational experience, namely adolescent and adult relationships. Parents' behavior predominantly follows the patterns vested within the family or cultural surroundings. As opposed to professional teachers, educators and psychologists, parents do not feel that their actions are substantiated enough, and often they do think about whether their actions could be detrimental or obstructive for their children's development. It is evident that in a family where each person has the chance to grow, additional attention must be paid to the children's development as beings with special qualities and special needs. If adults are able to take responsibility upon themselves for their own development, then they also are responsible to a large extent for their children's development as well. Hence, the question arises of how to raise a child properly (including through the use of all the possibilities that the market of developmental games, education services, etc., is able to offer him). As a result, more responsible parents demand 'parental guidance,' education and tutoring services that allow raising more well rounded, healthier, and developed child. We believe that competent parenting programs, including through the 'family universities' already mentioned above, will de-facto become the standard for training future parents as this demand is recognized. Fostering competent parenting could help reconsider the attitude toward pregnancy in that it could be well possible to talk about children's early development stage before they are born. Prenatal pedagogy, pun intended, is in the embryonic state, although we fully concede there will be experimental solutions in the coming decade of the 'school in the womb' format (ex. Amazon and Toys R Us sell devices, such as BabyPlus Prenatal Education System* that permit making contact with the child through music).

* http://www.baby-plus.com/

Another important function of internal-family education is to pass on intergenerational experience related to a family's life, its own personal history. 20th century psychology dedicated a lot of effort into how the importance of the 'family fingerprint' in a person's life, first and foremost the mother and father's experience (oftentimes passed on non-verbally, through the very structure of family communications), but also the experience of previous generations. The family identity crisis is 'tearing apart' the family not only between partners (ex. mother and father), but also between generations. As a result, generations do not 'hear' each other. Generations' unique experience is lost as 'irrelevant,' which is traumatic for both the older and younger generations. Education can play an extremely important role as a family reintegrator by offering learning and creative activities that several generations can be engaged in at once, from the oldest to the youngest generations. Furthermore, this reconstruction of family history (in formats of documenting the recollections of older family members) is a very important step, for which there is already demand but virtually no supply (not counting websites that analyze genealogy and search archives). The way we see it, there is extremely high demand in this sector, its possibilities are only starting to be recognized, and all kinds of educational and entertaining solutions, including in virtual worlds and augmented reality (and various live interest groups as well) could be highly sought after as non-systemic education grows.

3. **A new action model: the group of early independent children.** Not just parents, but also children can act as the initiators of change in the family. The childhood model has gone

through several significant changes over recent centuries. For example the idea of 'childhood' as a special period in a person's life up to a certain time did not exist, and a child was seen as a 'little person' (therefore, during Dickens' time, a notable number of children were forced to work starting at five or six years of age).* Now, it is highly likely that we are at the point of yet another significant change. Most of the 20th century was dedicated to 'giving children a childhood,' including the fight against the exploitation of child labor. Indeed, child labor is a big problem in underdeveloped countries, where children are engaged in complex and dangerous labor; however, the situation is different in developed countries, where children are able to turn their 'child-like' interest into an activity that provides economic revenue. The first children designers and child programmers, who are starting to make money on the Internet in amounts comparable to what adults make, are already emerging.** Just last year saw the first nine-year-old millionaire, English artist Kieron Williamson, who made this money selling his paintings.

The emergence of this group of children (albeit for the moment sparse, but growing fairly quickly) raises a number of questions: is this child labor legal (and what is keeping it from being considered legal, including being recognized and promoted by international organizations such as the ILO)? To what extent does a child have the right to dispose of the results of his labor? To what extent can a child become a legally competent member of the family (and can a child make decisions over the family's property)? Can a child, in becoming early independent, make the decision to live separately, and starting at what age (applicable legislation partially answers these questions, but whether these answers are suitable is another question)?

Furthermore, an important question is to what extent overall does the concept of biological age remain 'applicable' for regulating children's rights. How fast a personality evolves (ex. according to Erik Erickson) depends to a large extent on the person's abilities and the traits of the developing environment. New education is capable of adjusting these speeds and allowing some students to reach not only intellectual maturity significantly earlier than is now accepted, but also emotional and social maturity as well. The 'automized initiative for reaching the needed age' model can be substituted by the 'initiatives when completing in advance a specific level of personal achievements' model, and in the future by an achievements profile that opens the doors to an ever expanding range of activities (education, business and political activities, sexual activity, right to access pharmacological 'cognitive intensifiers', etc.). Here the risks of social de-adaptation, which are typical for a significant number of infant prodigies who show early success only to deflate when entering adult age because of not being psychological ready, need to be kept in mind. As a result, such 'achievement profiles' must be sufficiently complete to take into account the psychological readiness for the next stage in becoming an adult. In other words, all-age, total education could replace physical age with social age as the early coming-of-age model spreads.

4. **'New Mowglis': the generation of children taught with tablets.** The proliferation of new technologies in the education space for children can have not only positive effects, but also negative repercussions. Gadgets and virtual game environments for a modern child make up their accustomed habitat, while for parents it is simpler to just give a child a tablet

* http://www.victorianweb.org/history/hist8.html

** See http://www.dailymail.co.uk/news/article-2061653/iPad-app-developer-Thomas-Suarez-aged-TWELVE-gives-amazing-talk-TEDxManhattan-Beach.html

than think about how to teach or entertain him. Many of these children, who began using electronic tablets from the cradle, often even use finger gestures to try and control their parents or objects.

The 'tablet children' generation is a sort of 'new Mowglis' who have at the very least a portion of their patterns shaped by educational and entertainment applications. The following potential problems of perception that children (who are already starting school and around 2025 will enter university) could have are being widely discussed (Small & Vorgan, 2008):

- Poor sensorial experience. Compared with the regular world, tablets provided a restricted perception of experience, including non-distinct textures, less compre-hensive sounds, a lack of tactical contact and bodily sensations (which establishes a simplified 'map of reality');

- Periodic difficulties with differentiating between the virtual and real worlds. These problems are observed even in adult users, although they will be the most distinct in 'new Mowglis' by going beyond not only 'the reality of virtual friends,' but also the prioritization of the imagined and the played compared with reality;

- The habit of compacting events together that is established from actively using appli-cations and browsers. Since the number of events in virtual reality is notably higher, offline reality for children turns out to be too 'slow' and 'boring' (which in addition exacerbates distracted attention problems when learning).

We will stipulate right away that these are the problems of today and the interfaces that exist now. The growth of the child industry is not following the path of migration to tablets or any other detached system, but rather the path of integration of kinesthesis and audio with new media. In this sense, the 'tablet threat' is not systemic: the rapid development of technologies at the next step will permit integrating all of a child's surroundings (be it his own room, playroom at kindergarten, or entertainment center at a mall) into a model of the world where reality, virtuality, and augmented reality compliment each other organically. It is in this world of 'indiscriminate' reality that adults will spend their lives (see section 2.2.1 and 2.2.3), and therefore children must enter this 'indiscriminate' world amicably, through the developmental and game environment surrounding them.

In the future, however, we can expect several currently underestimated, but more serious problems that have to do with the proliferation of new technologies in relation to shaping complex mental structures:

- 'New dyslexia': In an environment where a full-fledged search or choice turns out to be a rather complex cognitive act (see section 2.2.1), it is easier for the user, especially for a child, to choose by relying upon various non-binding services. As a result, there is essentially the risk that the capability to construct a complex cognitive skill will waste away. The decreasing capability to write competently is one way in which this is manifested: when writing on a smartphone or tablet, there is no longer any need to be able to write the entire world; all you have to do is know the first several letters, and the tablet will propose its own suggestion for the word (as well as fix incorrect spelling). An automized activity does not develop in a child's conscience and therefore is not assimilated, which brings about a deficit in the appropriate functions, or 'dyslexia' in a broad sense. In other words, we get people who are not capable of complex cognitive activities as adults, because the 'assisting' IT solutions did not permit the corresponding skills to take shape.

■ 'A floating worldview': In a situation where virtual worlds become the chief structuring and developmental environment for a child, while the main motivation system is based on obtaining game exploits, what results is a generation with an extremely unstable and distorted (as far as the present day is concerned) system of perceptions of the world, including the perception of morals and ethics. In a world where each person observes their stratum of reality shaped in real time by teacher programmers or, even more so, created indefinably large groups of people according to their own laws through the crowdsourcing principle, it becomes much harder to talk about what is real and what is not. Virtual worlds with arbitrarily constructed physical and ethical laws and rules* undermine the conventional worldview and dominating values systems in society. Education, meanwhile, built upon these laws and beginning at preschool age, interrupts the traditional path of adults passing on values systems to children. It is not the blurring of the field of values, but rather the possibility that the 'floating worldview' contradicts the goals for the development of an individual and society.

* For example, the Fallout videogame series has the game determine a player's level of 'good/evil' by making ethically tainted decisions that influence the player's standing in the game. Grand Theft Auto or Postal, on the other had, oftentimes do not make it possible to go through the game using ethical methods.

These problems can be viewed as challenges or borderline conditions when designing new educational environments. In particularly, non-binding services on smartphones, tablets, and other devices could be supplemented with a special development module for children that not only corrects errors, but also gives feedback and teaches how to do something correctly. By the same token, if game environments will work with the intention of shaping children's productive perceptions of the world (including ethics systems), then the 'floating worldview' problem will be rectified. Implementing such a process technically is relatively easy, for ethics can be written out as a set of codes coordinated through an open, democratic process and woven into various game models (including the reputation game models that we describe in section 3.4.3); By the same account, digital models of the scientific worldview (which we describe in section 3.5.3) can be passed on directly to educational game environments.

This, however, is not the point. The listed threats point to the fundamental difficulty that new education is confronting already. New technologies do not take into account (or take into account as a last resort) the goals related to developing individuals and human communities. It is evident that in the logic of market development, corporations follow demand and developers following market specialists; however, as far as children's products are concerned, producers have ethical responsibility as well, because these products inevitably have a developmental and educational component to them. Furthermore, when we speak of products that directly intrude upon our processes of communication and our way of life, be it tablets or biomonitors with BF, then adults have the same responsibility as well.

The catastrophic repercussions of new technologies for the new generation's mind have not onset yet, but the responsibility for them not have yet occurred is with the producers of new program solutions and virtual worlds. The programming community needs the support of standards and norms for working efficiently with children's minds. This means, among other things, shaping specific rules for interfaces meant for use by different ages of children (and not only in terms of shielding children from gore and violence). In the extreme case, it is necessary to pass on a developmental paradigm in the architecture of software as the key paradigm.

**Table 4**

# THE IMPACT OF SOCIAL MACROTRENDS ON EDUCATION SYSTEMS

| | MACRO TREND | NEW EDUCATIONAL CONTENT (curriculum components or principles of program design) | NEW EDUCATIONAL FORMATS (teaching, assessment, motivation etc.) |
|---|---|---|---|
| 1 | New wave of technological innovations & global greening of cities and industries | • Skills & knowledge for emerging industries<br>• Systems thinking (also: systems engineering)<br>• In the more distant future: ecology of the mind (as system of principles guiding educational program design for managers & businesspeople, engineers, and social workers) | • Startup accelerators with educational component as a vehicle for economic modernization |
| 2 | Shift in models of business organization and industry management | • Skills & knowledge for new models of business management (e.g. distributed community-based production)<br>• Meta-competencies for modelling & manipulating ontologies | • Webs of learning / communities of practice as the key educational environment (also: corporate universities reloaded) |
| 3 | Shift in employment patterns and lifestyles | • DIY competencies (return of the do-it-yourself & craftsmanship culture)<br>• Re-training / re-education programs for the 'new aged'<br>• Programs aimed to facilitate & support personal self-actualization | • Domination of gaming formats<br>• Virtual worlds to help buffer the social tension through retraining of new unemployed<br>• New talent investment models |
| 4 | New financial architecture & reputation economy | N/A | • Reputation capital as a (cross-institutional) model of assessment<br>• Models of reciprocal teaching & learning (supported by non-monetary exchanges)<br>• Transparency principle in educational process organization, tracking of intermediary results and recording of achievements |
| 5 | Shift in patterns of family organization & childhood | • Rehabilitation education for the 'new dislexics'<br>• Skills for competent parenting<br>• Programs to help discover family shared values | • 'Child-friendly cities'<br>• 'Gateways' to provide professional education for early-maturing children<br>• Cross-generational universities |

# 2.4 FACTORS OF UNCERTAINTY

*'We do not know enough about how the present will lead into the future'*
**Gregory Bateson**, Steps to an Ecology of Mind

## 2.4.1 **Factors of uncertainty: the fate of globalization**

1. **Variations for the development of the global economy.** The future political and economic landscape is the subject of numerous discussions (ex. National Intelligence Council 2010, 2012, Walker 2010, etc.),* and there is no point in reproducing these discussions within our Report; nonetheless, taking into account that globalization is one of the most important processes in the sphere of education and science (see section 3.1), and that scientific and education globalization is closely tied to globalization in economics, culture, and politics, we believe that it is important to discuss the possible routes that the global economy could take in the coming 15 to 20 years.

A crisis is usually a symptom of rebuilding and a time when new grounds for growth take shape. Above we showed how the landscape of the economic, social, political, and cultural changes, in accumulating, are leading to a collapse of the existing 'rules of the game' and to the shaping of new such rules. A crisis to a large extent is the consequence of technological reorganization (section 2.3.1), of the change in administrative models (section 2.3.2) and finances (section 2.3.4) in the economy, of change in demographics and lifestyle (section 2.3.3).

Fundamental questions about the future of globalization:

- Will one or several globalization models develop, and who will control the process of creating and proliferating standards as globalization unfolds? It is already evident that the vigorous growth of the 'new champions,' including China and other Asian countries, will not allow the E.U. and United States to retain full control over the transnational agenda (e.g. it is expected that China will overtake the United States in the 2020s as the top economic superpower (National Intelligence Council, 2012)). At the same time, the new players can support 'common protocols' of globalization, including preserving specific positions for the United States (or U.S.-E.U. alliance) in global financial and economic markets in the interests of maintaining global economic and political stability. Another scenario is that Asian countries within 10 to 15 years will aspire to revisit the organization of their economies by focusing, first and foremost, on the Asian macro-region, and in the future offer itself as the new 'standards leader.' This means, among other things, that international standards and innovative solutions in education could be spread at different speeds.

- How intense will the next global economic crises be and how many of them will there be? It is hard to say for certain 'how deep the rabbit hole is' and what potential sources

* http://reports.weforum.org/outlook-2013/the-future-of-globalization- http://www.wfs.org/blogs/ian-bremmer/top-geopolitical-risks-2013http://oilprice.com/Geo-Politics/International/Changing-the-Balance-of-Power-16-Geopolitical-Megatrends-Affecting-Every-Aspect-of-your-Life.html

of instability there are in the architecture of the global economy. Back in in the middle of 2008, a significant number of forecasts were that an economic crisis unfurling in the next several months was 'unlikely' (Colander et al., 2009). Based on several dozen discussions with leading international economists, we believe that the shaping of a new global financial and economic architecture is far from complete, and at least one more significant swing in the economic crisis awaits us before the end of the 2010s.* Given that Asia's largest economies recognize this threat as well, it is increasing their interest in 'regionalization.'

* Predicting global financial crises is a very thankless job. Therefore, we are not contending to indicate when and under what circumstances such a new crisis could begin. The only thing that is clear is that the reasons that caused the crisis in 2008 to a significant extent continue to remain in place. Moreover, there are several systemic sources of financial instability such as the U.S. national debt that could 'implode' either in the near future or in several decades; the repercussions of their 'implosion' are unpredictable.

■ To what extent will global transformation be ensured? During crises in the past, leading countries that lost strong economic standings often became the initiators of small or large 'triumphant' wars. Peripheral countries are usually the victims, although the tragic experience of WWI and WWII, and of civil wars in the former Soviet Union and Yugoslavia after their collapse, shows that even industrially developed countries are capable given certain conditions of going from amicability to extreme belligerence within just a few years. In case of the scenario when economically and politically significant countries (e.g. US, China, Russia or any other large countries) are involved into direct military conflict, it will inevitably and significantly slow down the human-centered education, including the processes of its globalization.

Whatever the case, we presume that the process of globalization is natural for humanity (evidence of this comes from the aspiration 'to unite peoples under one sky' that can be found in the crusades of Alexander the Great, in the dream of Genghis Khan, and in the triumphs of Napoleon), and the existing technological base in telecommunications and transportation makes it much more stable than ever before. Furthermore—and this is the most important argument—the interdependence of the largest economies is now higher than ever: with the exception of the United States and China, virtually no country is capable of producing even one complex technological product by itself (and supporting the current level of well-being in industrially developed countries, and growing it in developing countries depend on having and proliferating complex technologies). First and foremost, technological, scientific, cultural and social cooperation — and not politicians' promises — will keep the world together and increase its connectedness.

### Additional commentary (August 2014):

The material for our Report was written mostly in the fall of 2013. Unfortunately, the events of Spring & Summer 2014 involving Russia and Ukraine have shown just how fragile the consensus that the modern global administrative model hangs on is. At present, Russia is being quickly isolated from the global agenda and from the global structures that are developing this agenda (G7, World Bank, Parliamentary Assembly of the EU, international programs of scientific and technical cooperation, etc.). This isolation is being supported by Cold War rhetoric not only within the country itself, but also in most developed countries, including the EU and United States. It is difficult to say how far this isolation could go. What is clear, however, is that 100 years ago, in early 1914, it seemed that European countries' economic interdependence makes any serious wars impossible; however, in just a matter of months, the antagonistic rhetoric led to the bloodiest conflict that humanity had ever seen. It is therefore institutions supporting peace around the world (peacekeeping processes and those who organize them) that are important as never before. Peace, however, is the duty not only of professional peacekeepers, but also the duty and responsibility of each conscious citizen who is capable of stopping the antagonistic attitude within himself, realizing that the very chance to continue dialog is more important than proving one's own righteousness. In using the words of the recently deceased great Russian philosopher Grigory Pomeranets, 'the devil begins with the foam on the lips of an angel fighting for the just cause'.

2. **The reaction of national governments to the proliferation of global content through networks.** The increase in the penetration of modern technologies and the content that they encompass is one of the most important processes in developing countries, including in the context of discussing future education. Although the world may be heading in the direction of increased connectedness, the free circulation of intellectual and cultural products from other countries is seen by many national governments as a threat (and sometimes a completely justified threat). As a result, the governments of these countries are striving to restrict public access to Internet content, usually under the pretext of protecting against 'terrorists, drug dealers, pedophiles, and organized crime' (well-known as 'the four horsemen of the Infocalypse'*). A host of major countries, including China, the UAE, Iran, Pakistan, North Korea, etc. have imposed strict restrictions on access to Internet content (see the Box 4 'Filtering and Monitoring Internet Access'). In the future, other states concerned with preserving their 'national identity' (or with maintaining the stability of their own political regimes) could follow the same decision). Eduard Snowden's public revelations

Box 4
## Filtering and Monitoring Internet Access

A 2013 Reporters Without Borders report writes that a third of Internet users do not have unencumbered access to the Internet where filtering is not used or there are no access restrictions. The strictest system of content control was created in North Korea: the public does not have access to the worldwide web. The country has its own closed-off Internet, while the head of state personally approves the list of people and institutions that are given access to the worldwide web. The UAE imposes strict control over traffic content, with the country's only provider filtering politically hazardous content and information that undermine the country's moral values; Twitter access is granted via passport. China also has a system of control over Internet content, with the Internet being monitored by the 'Golden Shield' system and the public not having access to sites (including leading global resources such as Google, Facebook, Twitter, etc.) that the government agencies have not approved. Russia also has introduced restrictions on Internet access, while options for creating an 'island' Internet for children are also being discussed (and, with the unfolding conflict of 2014, of 'detaching' national networks altogether). In the United States, where the Internet officially is free, the National Security Agency has created PRISM, the world's largest and most technologically advanced user surveillance system.

* http://en.wikipedia.org/wiki/Four_Horsemen_of_the_Infocalypse

about the PRISM extensive American Internet monitoring system and the U.S. systems for surveying the governments of allied countries, provides an additional shot in the arm for the governments of many countries to develop projects to isolate Internet communications, including at the individual level.*

* Ex. The BRICs Cable project announced by a South African group of developers http://www.brics-cable.com/

Since educational content as far as a number of traditional countries is concerned is one of the possible threats to their intellectual and spiritual security (we will discuss this in detail below, in section 3.1), it is entirely likely that there will be censorship meant directly to regulate educational content provided over the Internet. In particularly, it is entirely likely that the governments of a number of countries, such as China, the UAE, and Russia, will impose restrictions and licensing on virtual worlds with educational components, MOOC courses, and other educational content.

The imposing of a universal Internet identifier for accessing the web (similar to a social security or passport number) is another extremely likely event that is right on our doorsteps that could decrease Internet freedoms and possibilities. Essentially, there is already a host of universal, benign identifiers, such as Google Accounts, on the Internet as it is, with identifiers being developed at the same time for access to 'electronic government' websites that permit obtaining various state services over the Internet, and effectively shaping national standards for Internet user identification. State regulators are engaged not only in ensuring the public easy access to government services, but also in being more efficient in carrying out the duties of state security online, with the capability of identifying a user being the principal features of such security. Indirect identification and monitoring systems (ex. PRISM in the United States and SORM in Russia) could be replaced by direct state identifiers as a whole in a number of counties, most likely by the end of the 2010s. Internet identifiers are being discussed supranationally as well to make them their own sort of standards for Internet access.** It goes without saying that these restrictions could create additional difficulties for circulating information between users, including in the sphere of education.

** http://www.worl-de-idcongress.com/

## 2.4.2 Factor of uncertainty: Asia's new role

Discussing issues of future education often gravitates to 'Euro-Atlantism': discussions about how European and American educational institutions and projects will develop, and how standards forged in the E.U. and United States will be conveyed to the rest of the world. This approach has its own indisputable grounds: it is the Euro-Atlantic world that became the leader of the industrial revolution, it is there that modern approaches to organizing education systems were engendered, and it was through assimilating European and American administrative models that several countries of the South (such as Japan, South Korea, and Singapore) have been able to join the club of economically developed countries.

It is well known, however, that the human history is similar to a relay race, where one group of leaders passes on its knowledge and practices to another group of leaders to retreat into the background (and often to disappear). The majority of human history that we are aware of features Asia, especially India, China, and the Middle East, as the main world cultural and economic center, a source of innovation and development. Asia's role had to do with a high rate of fertile lands and a favorable climate, which allowed attaining a high population density, increasing cultural solidity, and intensifying cultural exchanges (including through constantly being mixed together in local wars) (Lockard, 2012). From the 18th century to the middle of the 20th century, Asia was mired in subordination, following the path of Europe, and since this period dovetailed with the time of forging national systems of industrial education, a certain European centrism remains in discussions of the future of education systems. At the beginning of the 21st century, however, it is already evident that the global center of economic activity is migrating to the Pacific Ocean region, and that this shift will have an inevitable impact on priorities in organizing education systems (Barber et al., 2012).

We believe that the role of cultural heritage and possible comprehensive innovations from Asian countries at present is underestimated, and that Asia's new role in the global economy and culture could have an unexpected impact on the future of education. In some sense, the Asian vogue's triumph on the global podiums, the broad popularity of anime and costume play, Taiwanese smartphones in the pockets of European users, and the singer Psy's 'most viral' video Gangam Style* are only the sprouts of a process that is just beginning. Asia's stance is to inevitably change for the following reasons:

First, fast urbanization is taking place in densely populated Asian states (China, India, Indonesia, Pakistan, Bangladesh, etc.). This urbanization has to do with these countries being actively included in the global division of labor. The U.N. predicts that approximately 800 million people (roughly 500 million in China and India) will be added to the urban population of the Asian region from 2011 to 2030 (UN-Habitat, 2012). China's construction boom is a reflection of this process: the creation of entire new cities with several million people actively populating them as they are completed, which has even given rise to the legend of ghost cities that are built to support the Chinese economy.**

Cities by nature are inherently a significantly more densely populated organization of the processes of the division of labor and communication. They always act as the regional economic and cultural centers, as sources of new technologies and social practices. New and fast growing cities, where 'effervescence' is engendering new practices and traditions, are especially active in this role. Asian cities will inevitably become the centers of new urban culture that actively contend to take their spot in the global urban landscape. The urban culture of such centers usually takes shape at the junction of traditional local culture and global trends, and the meanings behind them. Hence, we inevitably will see a change in the global cultural space through interventions of Asian cultural content and practices engendered by the Asian urban population. We can presently give only a very limited prediction of what kind of content this will be. What is already evident is that this intervention of new 'Asian urban culture' is beginning through global networks of communications. The Internet is quickly ceasing to be Euro-centric both as far as content and user practices are concerned. In the coming 10 years, we can fully expect that it is Asian users who will start to determine the new standards of Internet communication.***

The second important issue is Asian countries' quest for a new place in the global division of labor and their willingness to offer their own agenda. In some sense, the 'Asian tigers,' especially South Korea (which started with low-level production, in essence selling

* http://www.scientificamerican.com/article/graphic-science-how-gangnam-style-went-viral/

** http://www.forbes.com/sites/greatspeculations/2013/07/16/china-may-have-ghost-cities-but-rapid-growth-is-no-apparition/

*** http://www.slideshare.net/yiibu/the-emerging-global-web

cheap manual labor) have already gone down this path and they in just several decades now manufacture high technologies; they are the global technology leaders in a number of sectors (consumer electronics, energy, ship building, etc.). As far as large Asian countries are concerned, however, it is not enough to just reproduce the 'tigers" experience, because the capacity of their economies is potentially much greater, and therefore they must look for new recipes, including the offering of their own model for global economic development.

This especially concerns China. After having begun its path as the 'world's factory,' China has quickly assimilated skills necessary for organizing complex manufacturing, and simultaneously cultivated the potential of the numerous members of the middle class. Now, China presents several challenges for the world. The first such challenge is the ambitions in signature industries such as the space industry. For example, the Chinese space program is planned before the year 2100 and includes building its own Chinese lunar and Mars bases.* Although practical space exploration before a breakthrough in technology to send people to orbit is rather difficult, the symbolic meaning of such plans is hard to overestimate: they are showing the ambition of a true space power that is challenging the world to a new (global) space race. The second challenge is China's proposed discussion of a new meaning for the consumer society, for a 'new dream.'** The quest for the 'Chinese dream,' which differs from the 'American dream,' about a society where a productive balance of personal and public interests is complied with, could be not only political rhetoric, but also a sort of 'cultural program' of the new Chinese elite. Even though at the moment it is hard to say whether this dream can come true, whether it can be attractive not only within Chinese society, but also outside of it, the very cultural ambition in terms of the proposal of new meanings for industrial civilization is extremely important.

Moreover, Asian countries' search for a new place under the sun is forcing them to quickly assimilate the knowledge and practices of leading economic and technological countries. This has required Asian countries to develop education systems — comparable by institutional density with European counterparts (namely adjusted for the amount of the population) — that are capable of taking on tens of millions of people, more than in all industrially developed countries.*** It is evident that the social burden of supporting such large-scale systems of industrial education is extremely high, and therefore the demand is very high for a new generation of education solutions that allows for meeting the challenge of human capital development at a faster and cheaper rate.

This is not the most important issue, however, as far as education is concerned. The culture of Asian countries—first and foremost Chinese and Indian culture—is based on other conceptual grounds than Euro-Atlantic culture. Egyptian practitioners of hieratic education, the ancient Greek culture of critical thinking and dialog, the search for truth in Christian monastic communities, and the culture of liberal medieval universities are the 'spiritual ancestors' of the European education system. The Indian and Chinese civilizations developed along similar paths, but these were their own paths: the philosophical systems of Taoism, Confucianism, Chan Buddhism, Vajrayana Buddhist psychology, and the schools of Vedanta and Jainism are powerful intellectual traditions that are based on world views that are largely different from European perceptions. Their own approaches to learning and education have been engendered within these traditions, and they are in many ways more

* http://www.afp.com/en/news/topstories/china-prepares-grow-vegetables-mars

** http://edition.cnn.com/2013/05/26/world/asia/chinese-dream-xi-jinping/index.html

*** http://www.britishcouncil.org/sites/britishcouncil.uk2/files/the_shape_of_things_to_come_-_higher_education_global_trends_and_emerging_opportunities_to_2020.pdf

holistic than their European counterparts. Many principles of harmonic education have been forged within the traditions Vedanta and Confucianism for adults, and European researchers of 'life-long education' are only now rediscovering these principles.

Hence, we come upon the most important question: can China, India, and countries linked to them culturally, within their educational and scientific institutions, found new schools of thought that draw upon the ancient traditions of these countries, and nonetheless that correspond to the present day's challenges, and that can overcome the limitations of the European model of thought (and possibly provide their way to transcend the Aristotelian logic that has defined the development of European philosophy science for more than two thousand years)? The answer to this question is not very trivial: one can point to the examples of South Korea, during the period of the country's modernization, as it integrated elements of Protestantism into its national culture, and through this developed a quality of its own human capital (McCleary, 2013); or of Singapore and Hong Kong, whose rapid development was related to the assimilation of British administrative practices. We believe, however, that Asian intellectual traditions have a lot of resources hiding within them, and that through dialog about the practical challenges of civilized development (such as the architecture of global education or new communication environments of the NeuroWeb) at the junction of European and Asian cultures will new synthetic schools of thought take shape.

## 2.4.3 The place of religions and spiritual traditions in society of the future

Industrialization, the rise of the natural sciences and the liberal-humanistic worldview from the middle of the 19th century to the end of the 20th century, led to a significant fall in the role of religion in public life, at least as a public institution 'responsible' for the worldview and for supporting dominate values. At the same time, beginning in the 1970s, disenchantment with 'secular' projects grew in society, in many ways because science was unable to present its own version of value-conscious and conception values for human life and the existence of humanity (Capra, 1982);* however, a number of authors, such as Albert Schweitzer (Schweitzer, 1987), made the attempt to create a version for such grounds, a 'humanistic project.' As a result, many countries (especially where society did not modernize very profoundly, including a large percentage of rural residents or a small percentage of people with a higher education) saw the beginning of the rebirth of traditional religions, their being all the more involved in public life and in educational content. What probably looks the most impressive is the rebirth of Islamic traditions (ex. the number of Muslims completing the hajj: if in 1920 roughly 70 thousand pilgrims visited Mecca, then in 2012 there were more than 3 million of them).** In some instances, the rebirth of a religion can have a political underlining, as a government aspires to control the population (for example, as in the case with the 'alliance' in the 1990s and 2000s between the Russian government and the Russian Orthodox Church, which was meant to replace communism with Russian Orthodoxy).

It is worth noting that desecularization concerns not only the rebirth of traditional religions. What is just as important is shaping new religious and spiritual traditions. A boom in

* Just recall Albert Einstein's quote: 'Humanity has all the grounds to place the ambassadors of moral values higher than the pioneers of scientific truths.'

** http://www.thenews.com.pk/Todays-News-2-139473-Number-of-foreign-Hajis-grows-by-2824-percent-in-92-years

* See note 150

new spiritual movements took place in the 1960s and 1970s when a pyschodelic* revolution, the development of a new spirituality in New Age communities, the rediscovery by beatniks and hippies of the 'wisdom of India,' the commenced interconfessional dialog, etc., all led to the active quest for a 'new urban spirituality.' In having overcome the period of original romanticism, this quest has now hit a pragmatic stage, where morning Yoga, meditation at work, and self-development evening courses have become a part of life for a significant number of urban residents in developed counties.

It is evident that the proliferation of new piousness in the world could develop along different scenarios and through different methods of promotion. In some cases, for example, within Islamification or the proliferation of Russian Orthodoxy, we can see the active support state and local major businesses that use religion for the establishing unified value-conscious standards (we also see in the case Russian Orthodoxy and Islam that opposing oneself to the 'Western' globalization project is a significant part of their current rhetoric, and this makes them rather unexpected allies). In another case, such as with the promotion of Catholicism and Buddhism, what we are witnessing is more a grassroots promotion meant to mobilize community initiatives in resolving social problems. A third case (especially religions and new-generation spiritual traditions) stresses personal self-perfection and personal effects. What is significant is that each of the notable religious and spiritual traditions offers not only person practices and the possibility of interacting with a community of like-minded people, but also their own project for world order, their own version of direction that should include the development of social evolution. The open question is to what extent will 'religious world projects' (Jewish-Christian, Islamic, Confucius-Buddhist, etc.) establish the path of value-conscious and ideological domination, and consequently, make their demands for the form and content of education in countries where these projects dominate.

Furthermore, the very perceptions of the values and goals of religious and spiritual movements underwent many changes over the past century (it is enough to mention Pope John Paul II's repenting in 2000 for mass crimes committed in the name of faith, including the crusades, persecution of the Jews, and justification of slavery). Over the course of the entire 20th century, 'religious parliaments,' world religion conferences, and other forums have been taking place that have called for dialog between religious traditions and for overcoming their disagreements. A number of attempts has been made (one of such recent attempts was the works of Karen Armstrong (ex. Armstrong, 2010) that were awarded the TED Prize)** to find uniform grounds for world religions that allow them to work together 'for the sake of the common cause.' Attempts are also being made to find a 'new healthy balance' between the scientific worldview and religious traditions, such as in the concept proposed by famous evolutionist S. J. Gould of 'non-overlapping magisteria' that presumes that science described the 'kingdom of empiricism, what the universe consists of and why it works the way it does,' while religion answers questions' 'extreme meanings and moral values.' What is notable is that these 'two conceptual spheres do not overlap between themselves and do not close the entire sphere of cognition (Gould, 1997). Thus, the place for religious and spiritual traditions in education could be to a significant extent revisited as the balance in the understanding of religion's place in society and the ethnical admissi-

** https://www.ted.
com/participate/
ted-prize/prize-
winning-wishes/
charter-for-com-
passion-karen-arm-
strong

bility of faith for students to change. How will this happen exactly is rather hard to say at this stage.

## 2.4.4 Factor of uncertainty: the future of states

The state is, and evidently will continue to be, a principal player in determining the design of national education systems. When creating the industrial system of education, states made (and developing countries continue to make) their chief investments in launching and maintaining institutions of basic and professional training. Therefore, the state administration model, one that is inevitably changing as new technologies are introduced and under pressure from new social and cultural factors, will certainly impact the future of education systems.

The main directions for the evolution of statehood:

First, there is a host of evidence that the public's demand to take part in education administration and to have control over state activities increases as people's economic well-being grows (Fung & Wright, 2003). Network technologies already offer a number of possibilities for monitoring the activities of state agencies and for proactive citizens to take part in forging solutions at all levels, from the municipal to the national, in industrially developed countries. Circulating 'open government' protocols (Lathrop & Ruma, 2010) increases governments' liability and allows for drawing up truly democratic solutions. In this sense, the world is seeing movement toward more openness, a transition to 'network' democracy models where specialized state processes are replaced by appropriated social processes (such development is completely natural, because the state is but an intermediary that re-allocates public resources among members of society). This process, however, does not mean that civil servants vanish completely, but rather that they make the transition to 'moderators of public discussions' where the 'state' retains the duty of ensuring equal rights for discussing and making decisions for all polylogue participants.

Second, the object of administration in the state changes. If earlier the state was responsible for a host of specific tasks, such as ensuring public safety, territorial defense, lawmaking, issuing currency, providing various services (medicine, education, social security, etc.), then now almost all these services can be obtained from private providers that (should there be a transparent and competitive market) grant them a higher quality of service. This list of services includes even such specific functions as physical defense and the right to violence associated with it (private armies and private police). It goes without saying that the Thatcher Cabinet's 'experiment in person' in Great Britain showed that there are limits to the privatization of state functions: a competitive environment and examination is needed at the very least.* We presume, however, that in the long term and coupled with the development of direct network democracy mechanisms, the state will transfer all the more functions to business and communities.

What is the role of states in such a world? All the processes described above function given the support of uniform 'protocols of interaction,' and in this sense there is a systemic function that is responsible for the commonness of a host of subjects that interact

* http://www.businessspectator.com.

together. This commonness was often identified in the past with ethnic affiliation, language, religion, and (most of all) territory; however, none of these characteristics will be able to precisely define the state where a multitude of ethnic groups (speaking different languages, professing different religions, living in many different territories, and spending a significant part of life in the 'common territory' of the Internet) could reside. What remains an object of administration is the identification of a state's citizens with their affiliation to this state. Hence, the future of states lies in the development of identity management.

As a result, in the coming 15 to 20 years we can expect the emergence of new (and the transformation of existing) players in the space of identity who declare their spot on the 'identity management market.' Major social networks such as Facebook are already bringing together hundreds of millions of people by becoming comparable to major states not only in scale, but also in controling mass opinions. We presume that an environment will manage to be created in the networks of the next generation where achieving inter-network status will begin to have a real impact on a person's life (not only through personal investment), and agreements within networks will begin to impact the circumstances of life (actual business projects, legislative initiatives, etc. will begin to take shape in them all the more often). The spaces of new networks structures will begin to acquire social significance through this. The extensive model of a 'society without a state' that is linked through an abundance of social networks is described in Zach Bornkheimer's article Techno-Anarchism*: in such a society, all relationships (including the right to violence) can be regulated using the reputation of individuals and groups in various communities. In the long-term future, we can also expect experiments with new state formats, such as 'virtual' states (that establish 'top-level' meanings and rules for the group existing in the network), and 'franchise' states (organized as a network of interconnected enclaves spread out across the world with uniform rules of life).

* http://scribd.com/
doc/78944315/
Techno-Anarchism

It is highly likely that these and other forms will emerge despite existing states, while their continuation will be for the purposes of replicating the culture and ethics of state leaders. Overall, states are extremely stable social institutions that have existed for thousands of years and that will not disappear when the first winds of change blow; however, their role on the global stage, resources available to them, and inherent processes will change drastically, and this is for certain. What is for certain is that as opposed to previous centuries when it was the states and their rulers who shaped history, in future nations and states, will be only one of a number of contrasting players shaping global and regional policy.

Nevertheless, the probability of this scenario in the coming decades will depend on whether new industries will mostly comply with rules introduced by national governement, or whether they will try to bend these rules to serve their ends. Information publicized by E. Snowden has revealed that nearly all largest ICT companies of the US have transferred (and some may event continue to transfer) the significant information about their users to the secret services. Technological sancations imposed by the US government towards 'outcast' countries force IT companies to decline customer support for users in those countries. Real business organizations that could have created future netocracies instead work to preservce interests of old governments — and not new elites. The war for the future continues, and the future organization of government will be one of its most dramatic battlefields.

**Table 5**
# THE IMPACT OF FACTORS OF UNCERTAINTY ON EDUCATION SYSTEMS

| SCENARIO FACTOR | KEY SCENARIO UNCERTAINTIES | INFLUENCE UPON THE EVOLUTION OF EDUCATIONAL SYSTEMS |
|---|---|---|
| RATE OF GLOBALIZATION | • Will globalization continue at the same pace as before? <br> • Can global economy go down, or be replaced by a set of macro-regions (each with their own economic & political standards)? <br> • Is there a chance that Internet global standards will be overruled by macro-regional or national standards (leading to Internet 'balkanization')? | • Speed of global standards proliferation in education <br> • Speed of educational innovations proliferation, incl. standardized global solutions (also in the case of 'nationalization' or 'balkanization' of the Internet / 'Splinternet' scenario) |
| NEW ROLE OF ASIA | • Will Asian economies be able to provide new meaning of globalization – given their ascent to the global leadership position? <br> • What will be the role of Asian cultures in the first half of 21 century — to what extent will they overcome the European cultural dominance and set their own standards? <br> • Will Asian schools of thought be able to provide new & important content for new models of education? (e.g. non-Aristotelian models of thinking) | • Asian educational innovations: new content & forms of education based on Asian national traditions (esp. India, China, Muslim countries) in cultural & scientific domains <br> • Alternative globalization models (incl. different value systems underlying such models), and their impact on the speed and depth of educational innovations proliferation <br> • New forms & models of thinking based on original Asian intellectual traditions |
| ROLE OF RELIGIONS AND SPIRITUALITY | • Will there be a revival of religions, a post-secular world with religious values dominate over economic & secular values? <br> • Will religions & ancient spiritual traditions be able to provide new & important content for new models of education? | • The speed of educational innovations proliferation <br> • New content requirements (religious movements as new education customers); possibility to borrow content from religious practices (incl. 'secularized' practices of self-regulation and development) |
| FUTURE OF STATES | • Will states get stronger or weaker compared to transnational business players and non-government network structures? <br> • Will states become more or less autocratic, especially in advanced countries? <br> • Will new states / governments emerge, will experiments in social design continue, and to what extent? | • New requirements for educational architecture depending on the model of national or international governance (incl. demand for education as a way to built new national identity) <br> • The rate of changes determined by the ability by non-government constituents to take over functions of the state (incl. basic and higher education provision) |

# 3. THE HISTORY OF NEW EDUCATION

This section recounts the 'stories' or 'narratives' of new education, ways of describing the 'map of the future' of the global education system. Upon having analyzed this map, we will have seen several of the brightest patterns that could be called trends, and they can be briefly generalized as follows: First, future education is becoming truly global, and not so much in the sense that all the more students are getting the chance to study in different countries, as much in the sense that the contours of the first global education systems are becoming evident, and for the meantime they are mostly concentrated in the United States. Second, education is becoming super-individualized (both because this is becoming affordable for students, and because this is sought after by the market, including employers). This, however, does not mean that people are stopping to study together, because learning is, first and foremost, a collective process, and collective forms of 'horizontal' learning will be all the more dominant in 'live' education. Collective learning will be carried out in two forms: first, any and all imaginable forms of game learning that will penetrate work and social life; second, the real collective practice that is linked closely to the creation and retention of knowledge in real time in communities of practice. All these new possibilities for organizing education systems could be realized in the coming years thanks to, first and foremost, information and communications technologies that are currently available or being created. Then, looming in the near future are technologies that have to do with the successes of neuro-computer science and cognitive psychology: NeuroWeb technologies that in the coming decades will be able to radically reconstruct the ways that we behold and perceive the world, but whose prototypes will begin to have an influence on education in the near future.

## 3.1 GLOBALIZATION

*We are making sure that the courses offered*
*at MITx and HarvardX are quintessential MIT*
*and Harvard courses.*
*They are not watered down. They are not MIT Lite or Harvard Lite*
*These are hard courses. These the exact same courses,*
*So the certificate will mean something*
**Anant Agarwal**, CEO of edX
(A MOOC MIT & Harvard joint platform)

### 3.1.1 Prerequisites: the 'normal' globalization of education

Globalization in education is not a new phenomenon. As the modern education system evolved, leading science and technology countries opened up an inward flow of students from across the world. This flow before the 20th century was concentrated more regionally: great Indian ashrams brought in students from Iran, Pakistan, and Tibet; Arabian madrasas drew in students from the entire Islamic world; German universities were the gravitational center in Europe. By the end of the 20th century when the world had become truly global, the Euro-Atlantic university system (first and foremost leading U.S. and British universities) also became truly international, while some countries (including Great Britain and Australia) placed their bets on the developing of 'education for export' as a significant economic industry.

Since this process dovetailed with the escalation of economic globalization, the battle for global talent that had already begun (and is intensifying all the more) had left its mark on this process. Access to the best human capital is recognized as the key competitive advantage, and therefore globally recognized markers of quality (ex. internationally recognized professional certificates) have set the guidelines for country education systems. This is especially noticeable in the world of science and academics, because science (at least the natural sciences and exact sciences) by nature is global. The number of programs in English is growing: for example, the number of such master's programs in the European Union has increased from 2007 to 2011 four-fold, from 1,028 to 4,644 (Brenn-White & Rest, 2012). The Bologna process is taking place within the European Union and the former Soviet republics. This process is adapting national education standards to a system of undergraduate/bachelor's (four years), graduate/master's (2 years), and Ph.D./doctorate (3 years). Instead of the accepted national systems of recognizing academic statuses (ex. the German layout of 'candidate' and 'doctor' of sciences), the Ph.D. is the most extensively used.

Transforming the education market into a global market has given rise to customer (students and employers) demand for the tools that ensure consistency with educational institutions and that assess their quality. As a result, a host of education ratings have emerged since 2003 for university programs (including Times, QS, ARWU, Global University Ranking, G-factor, etc.). In addition to creating user guidelines, these ratings serve another important purpose: transferring best practices between national education systems. The following are several important consequences from proliferating education ratings for universities

- Imposing academic recognition indicators for universities (number of publications and amount of times they have been cited, participation in leading research conferences, etc.) as a way to measure professor performance;

- (Result 1) changing in professor employment balance toward research and development work;

- (Result 2) transnational research collectives are formed in universities that contend to take part in global ratings (to increase their productivity)

- (As a result of this) developing international hiring standards, including the unification of a faculty 'ratings table' (geared initially toward research and then professor success) and spreading the American contract system in the world, including tenure.

The rapid expansion of uniform rules of the game thanks to ratings engendered two wonderful processes: First, a number of governments in quickly developing and developed countries use ratings as guidelines for developing their own education systems. China, South Korea, and Singapore (and India and the UAE to a lesser extent) have successfully implemented the 'ratings game' over the past decade. China added two of its universities to the top 100 in the QS World University Rankings and THE World University Rankings in five years through investing in academic capacity.* Second, a system of education franchises, where world leaders in university and business education create additional campuses and joint projects in developing countries, is taking shape, and at the same time these leaders capitalize on their high ranking by conveying education standards to new areas (Tamburri, 2013).

In turn, unifying the processes at the level of leading national university systems is beginning to impact both middle/low-level universities (that are either trying to get involved in the 'ratings race' or are trying to find their specific niche outside the ratings field), or the school systems, which is trying to adjust to the requirements of changing universities and to introduce their own international ratings and standards (ex. cross-country school success assessment ratings PISA, PIRLS, the TIMSS, 'international four-year degree' systems, etc.).

The process described can be labeled as 'normal' globalization that is unfurling at roughly the same rate and according to the same scenario as are countries that have become involved in the financial-economic globalization process by accepting international norms for imports and exports, and international financial accounting standards. The advent, however, of new education technologies is becoming a game changer capable of radically altering the rate and features of this process.

* http://www. topuniversities.com/ university-rankings/ world-universi- ty-rankings/2013

## 3.1.2 **Enter the MOOCs**

Distance education began to develop long before the Internet era. For example, the Soviet Union's preeminent results in mathematics and physics are based on a model of off-campus physics and mathematics schools that proved that it is possible to obtain a high-quality (in essence, elite) physics and mathematics education even on 'paper' technologies. This system under the old school would connect students (taking a program of increased difficulty in the natural science), university professors (developing the course content), and university students (for whom advising students was a part of their teaching practice and allowed them to better understand the subject) together into pen pals. Among other things, the distance training system served as a sort of funnel that would permit selecting talented young people from across the country for leading technology universities (those to have successfully completed a course could undergo preliminary testing and be accepted without applying). During the system's rise in the 1970s and 1980s, it brought in thousands and thousands of talented students. To be fair, we will note that the USSR did not invent this system. To be more exact, thanks to the opportunity to coordinate the operations of various universities as part of a large education system, the Soviet Union implemented the 'education-by-mail' format, which first emerged in the United States and Europe in the beginning of 19th century after the establishing of reliable postal communications.*

Massive open online courses (MOOC) in a certain sense reproduce this experience through a new technological base. The early success of programs that leading global universities have launched in the past several years (Table 6 below shows the largest projects**) allows to say that the defects in the 'first generation' of online programs are being surmounted (although far from all the expectations of the MOOC platforms for developing current higher education systems have been justified so far: see Box 'Udacity and San Jose University: better luck next time?').

Box 5

### *Udacity and San Jose University: Better Luck Next Time?*

MOOC platforms have created a lot of excitement among education system administrators in the United States, because the idea has emerged of cutting faculty costs at 'second-rate' American universities by using the MOOC courses of leading providers. San Jose University and the Udacity platform, with the help of California Governor Jerry Brown, launched the first such experiment in January 2013. The program offered three pilot courses in mathematics and statistics, each for 100 students, who had access to Udacity mentors. At the end of the semester, the students' course results were much lower than what students that took the program on campus had received (less than 25% of students received a passing grade). This failure led to the project being suspended in July 2013, and the future prospects for using MOOC platforms in California universities is still unclear.

* http://www. learndash.com/300-years-of-distance-learning-evolution-infographic/

** Given that the MOOC sector is growing rapidly, the situation within projects is changing quickly: new players are emerging, existing players are changing their format or their offers, obtaining additional financing, etc. Information in this section is provided as of April 2014 or earlier (according to the data available to us).

### Table 6
## LEADING MOOC PROVIDERS

| | EDX | COURSERA | UDACITY |
|---|---|---|---|
| PROFILE | A not-for-profit project launch by MIT and Harvard University. There are 34 partner universities from more than 10 countries, and 13 partner organizations (corporations and NGOs) | A startup founded in April 2012 by Stanford University employees. 108 partner universities from all over the world, including the world's leading universities (Duke, California Institute of Technology, and Princeton) | A startup founded by Stanford University employees, although without the university's formal participation |
| INVESTMENT | $60 million, $30 million each from MIT and Harvard University | More than $85 million at the end of 2013 | $300 thousand in startup financing, then $30 million was raised from venture investors. |
| NUMBER OF USERS (APRIL 2014) | 2.1 million people | 7.1 million people | 1.6 million people |
| COURSES (APRIL 2014) | 176 course, including physics, chemistry, engineering sciences, history, medicine, biology, etc. | 641 courses, including computer sciences, mathematics, business, social sciences, engineering, and education | 38 courses, first and foremost computer sciences, mathematics, physics, business, etc. |
| PERFORMANCE EVALUATION | Computer tests and homework | Computer tests, homework, and a series of assignments, such as peers evaluating each other's written work. Some instructors allow taking tests several times, with the highest grade being counted. | Computer tests, a series of assignments, programming assignments |
| CONTROL | Pearson test center employees grade some cumulative courses for a fee. To avoid cheating, students are given a series of tasks with difference randomly generated conditions | The student's formal acceptance of an honor code published on the project's site | Pearson test center employees grade cumulative courses for a fee of $89. |
| SPECIAL INTERACTION | Offline meetings for joint discussions with third-party universities and organizations using the edX platforms | Online forums and joint study groups, offline meetings organized by students in more than 1,500 cities around the world. | Online forums and joint study groups, offline meetings organized by students in more than 450 cities. |

|  | EDX | COURSERA | UDACITY |
|---|---|---|---|
| COURSE PROGRESS | Courses with a set beginning and end date. Course registration ends two weeks after the date it starts. Students can skip one week, but their grade drops if they do not do their assignments on time. | Most courses have set beginning and end dates. Courses can be registered for after they begin, but only before a certain date. | Students take courses at a pace that is convenient for them. |
| CERTIFICATION | Two types of certificates, one is given based on agreeing to an honor code, and the other is given once a third party grades final exams. The certificates have the name of the university offering the course, such as MITx, HarvardX, or BerkeleyX . | Some instructors sign course completion certificates on their own behalf (but not on the university's behalf), including for a fee. Beginning in 2013, several universities (ex. Antioch University) made it possible to count Coursera courses toward the main program, and a number of courses were officially recognized for credit at the American Council on Education. | Certificates that range according to a student's course success. The resumes of students to have successfully completed courses are sent out to employers, including Google, Bank of America, Twitter, and Facebook. |

Several facts that serve the stability and competitiveness of the MOOC model:

- High content demand: leading global universities have launched projects (Coursera is a consortium of more than 100 universities headed by Stanford University. EdX, a Harvard University and MIT project, includes roughly 50 leading universities and organizations) with courses that are given by the best international specialists in the appropriate subjects.

- Success of the learning process despite online limitations:

  - Careful attention is given to the possibilities of online pedagogy, including optimally splitting the lecture material into short (roughly 10 minutes in length) knowledge modules and a host of intermediate assignments that are done individually or in groups. It is worth separately mentioning the tools that are used by the special platform for learning Code Academy programing, where each step in studying the academic material is supported by the student's own actions (his own code line needs to be written), and such step-by-step interactive assimilation allows studying the material more profoundly than just listening to lectures.

  - The opportunities for student self-organization and joint learning online are not ignored, but rather actively used (although not enough). For example, specialized groups in social networks, where students discuss the course content and assigned problems with each other (it is worth pointing out here that the leading MOOC platforms offer students a special code of honor that prohibits exchanging answers to the individual questions assigned during the course.*

* http://online.wsj.
com/news/articles/
SB10001424052702
3037596045790934
00834738972

- Moreover, the actual MOOC online-learning process is becoming an enormous labo-ratory for providers to develop various types of online learning, to track learning patterns, to scan student-subject interest, etc. (which allows them to refine online-ed-ucation methods and separate themselves from the pack of those who do not do this). The chance is emerging, based on MOOC through processing large volumes of student-behavior data (big data models), to shape a fundamentally new evidence-based pedagogy built not upon individual pedagogic theories, but upon statistically proving the performance of any given academic formats, knowledge verification formats, etc.

- Free access to content. Knowledge is not limited by anything but the ability for poten-tial students to access the Internet. Courses are being monetized and will continue to be monetized according to current plans through supplemental services, such as paying for employer-recognized certification, job placement services for successful students, student consultations, etc.

- (Potential) access to opportunities that course-provider universities have, including the possibility of on-campus program selection for these universities and finding work in leading global companies that are partners of these universities. (Curiously enough, it is from talented secondary-school students, and not university students, from whom this option creates notable demand for MOOC education, including from developing countries that see an additional lift in these courses that gives a chance to students at these universities).

We will go into more detail on the last topic. When comparing the system of off-campus education in the USSR with MOOC education, we see that MOOC is an extremely effective tool for selecting the best personnel from all over the world. First, the fact of taking a course to the end and getting to the final test shows that student's are highly engaged in the subject (at present, 7-9% of registered student finish the courses). Second, test results allow for finding talents that possibly under different circumstances would not become visible for universities and their employee partners. As a result, the situation where a 15-year-old genius from Mongolia receives a personalized scholarship to study at MIT after having completed a course in macro-electronics is already becoming a reality.**

** http://www.nytimes.
com/2013/09/15/
magazine/
the-boy-genius-
of-ulan-bator.
html?pagewanted=
all&_r=0

What is significant is that MOOC platforms can provide potential employers with infor-mation that is extremely hard to obtain in offline education. In particularly, they can easily document a student's skills and qualities that are shown during the learning process (and not at the end), just as, for example, Coursera does: how methodically the student studies the material and completes intermediate assignments; how capable the student is of complying with intermediate and final deadlines; how effectively the student cooperates with others while completing an assignment. Personal learning patters (a sort of 'learning style') can show employers just how suitable a student is for any given position.

The current organization of MOOC, nonetheless, has a number of deficiencies, which points to the possible directions that this platform could even evolve in (movement in these directions has already begun):

- First, the courses being offered stand separately and are not integrated into an entire education program. Assembling individual courses into a program consistency will de-facto allow providing complete, long-distance programs of fundamental education and professional training (which is a significant additional asset for both students and employers). Preliminary information shows that this opportunity is part of the edX architecture, which declares itself as the 'university for a billion' project.*

- Second, the tools that develop content in existing MOOC platforms are poorly organized. When launching new online courses, the platforms pay a lot of attention to their structure (ex. dividing lectures into blocks) and to indirect quality control (ex. quality verification of the university where the professor works), but does not give enough attention to verifying the completeness and comprehensiveness of the course itself (through peer review tools, the blind buyer mechanism, etc.). Moreover, there are at least today no tools for rating professors and the courses they teach (including based on objective statistics, such as the number of students to have signed up for a course/taken a course). Students cannot assess the quality of provider other than through indirect signs (the professor and university's name), even if they have already taken the course before. Finally, no feedback keeps from encouraging professors to develop their course content, improve their teaching, etc. We concede that no ratings is meant to keep from scaring professors away from working with the MOOC platform; however, there is the risk that unsuccessful education experiences will scare away the motivated student audience, and therefore we believe that such mechanisms will be implemented in the foreseeable future.

- (Third, providers are launching courses that are geared toward independent students (at least for now). At the same time, education programs of second and third-rate universities could become one of the users, including from developing countries that fill the deficit of local skills with remote access to global skills. As far as provider universities are concerned, local universities could become their guides to a region, provide a flow of disciplined and engaged students, and create an additional source of monetization. We presume that such options are a logical step and that leading platforms will carry them out in the coming two to three years. The MIT development strategy already has the idea of a 'flipped university,'*** an educational format in which MIT** offers its partner universities its lectures and supporting materials, while local universities run the discussions, student projects, and laboratory work.

* http://www. topuniversities. com/student-info/ distance-learning/ moocs-future-high-er-education

** http://future.mit.edu/ preliminary-report

*** Similar to the flipped classroom in school education, where lecture and didactic material is studied online and independently, while at school students discuss the lectures and conduct joint create work.

- Fourth, the performance of MOOC learning is significantly increased through organizing mentoring, and there is the technological capability for this, which does not require spending the valuable time of leading professors. Connecting online and offline students from the university itself can organize mentoring, while mentoring for the latter could be an important practice that augments their understanding of the subject and skills in online teaching. If a course is repeated more than once, the professor can engaged online students to have successfully completed the course who can become 'second-rate mentors,' through which the mentor base could be significantly expanded. This plan is easily monetized, since mentor services can be paid for in addition, while the chance to monetize one's academic successes can create additional motivation for students.

- Fifth, new student motivation models must be drawn up that allow a large number of participants to take a course from beginning to end. Developing certification systems that allow for recognizing the results of independent online courses as part of a university education or advanced training programs are one of the variations.

Moreover, the following areas of MOOC learning development can be presumed:

- MOOC provider partnership programs with the corporate universities of leading global corporations (and various leading national corporations in developing countries), including MOOC integration in internal training programs and in metrics when promoting employees (such programs have already started to be carried out, for example, with the edX platform).

- Creating various MOOC education platforms that are vigorously using the opportunities of student self-organization and peer learning (the 'self-learning networks' topic is discussed in greater detail in section 3.3).

- Integrating supplemental learning formats in MOOC, such as education simulators, or creating MOOC around simulators.

- Using virtual game universes as supplemental MOOC education space (greater detail on this topic in section 3.4).

The original enthusiasm around MOOC platforms (including in relation to their capability to replace 'live' education) was very high, and now certain disenchantment is setting in within the educational environment (typical for this stage of technology penetration). We admit a host of limitations in the existing MOOC model, but we believe that most of these problems will be resolved in the coming three to five years (it is entirely likely that this will require one of two rounds of rethinking the MOOC business model),* and that the intention of leading MOOC platforms (ex. edX) to educate a billion students by the end of the 2010s

* http://www.
nytimes.
com/2013/12/11/
us/after-setbacks-
online-courses-are-
rethought.html

will be achieved (if only these platforms' operators do not shoot themselves in the foot by acting indecisively in creating and promoting new education models).

Developing online training systems to complete programs (with the opportunity to obtain a degree from the world's best universities) creates an interesting precedent that so far is unmatched. Within four to five years (by 2017-2018), supranational/transnational qualifications and skills models, which are starting to have virtually an instantaneous impact on national education systems around the world, will emerge and prove to be affordable. The barrier for students to enter the MOOC platform is very low, and this already is engendering real competition between MOOC courses and local provider courses. Since we are only at the start of the development of these forms, it is necessary to understand how they will restructure the education landscape.

The Coursera project, the most widespread among MOOCs, engaged roughly 7 million people in April 2014; however, these projects' ambitions are much greater: reaching roughly hundreds of millions of users (MIT professor and edX President Anant Agarval believes that this project will attract a billion foreign students over a decade).* When expanding the list of courses, the online platforms' capacity, and students' final opportunities, then there are no hurdles for this. As the round-the-clock life will become more and more a mass phenomenon, by the beginning of 2020 obtaining an online education will be a preferred option for more and more people. Students' preliminary training that allows them essentially to perceive course material is the only limitation (and this means that their proliferation will take place much faster in counties where quality schooling and primary university education is provided).

* http://www.forbes.com/lists/2012/impact/anant-agarwal.html

The language barrier could also be an additional limitation, as many students do not know English sufficiently enough, which for the moment creates additional advantages for local education providers outside the Anglo-Saxon world. This advantage, however, could be very quickly destroyed. First, leading MOOC providers are already beginning to provide translated courses (for example, Coursera is now translating its courses into 14 languages and has special programs for developing its own community of translators).** As the experience of the mass media education project TED shows, an engaged volunteer community around large resources can provide quality translations into a host of local languages. Second, and this is more significant, the likely emergence within the coming decade of semantic translators (which we discussed in section 2.2.2) could by the beginning of the 2020s essentially take down the linguistic barrier, and then having unique, modern, and quality delivered content is the only competitive advantage.

** https://www.coursera.org/about/programs

In this sense, assimilating the new (and still almost empty) market of complete online education has already begun, and it is very wise for the world's leading universities to head this process. Besides them drastically increasing their contact base and brand recognition, they are shaping a unique capability in online pedagogics that allows them to breakaway from other universities that will enter this sphere late.

As opposed to usual online education, new MOOC platforms are creating an entrance barrier that has to do with the complexity of technological solutions, quality of content, and unique statistics of education patterns. The last one is especially important, because it is the ability to find and foster the best pedagogical approaches in large masses of students that is the competitive advantage of leading MOOC projects. The volume of investment speaks to the extent that online education will leave others in the dust: for example, Coursera has already invested several tens of millions of dollars in R&D related to developing global education laboratories (such as those at Stanford University and the University of California-Berkley). This means that without access to human capital of comparable quality, creating similar online platforms with global ambition in other countries will cost several times more. Therefore, we presume that the 'university for a billion' in its essence is an engineering object comparable in complexity with a nuclear plant or Big Science devices in terms of the quantity of invested human hours (given the uniqueness of the technological and pedagogical capabilities). By virtue of this limitation, similar projects will be able to permit themselves only a restricted number of countries and investors.

It is presumable that in the next ten years (by 2022-2025), several—no more than five to ten—major alliances will be formed around the world's leading providers of online education. These alliances will take upon the main mass of online students. The principal share of students will be grouped together around the online projects of world leaders in offline education that provide basic content. Furthermore, several countries asserting their own agenda will try to shape their own platforms (likely with their national governments taking part). China, India, Russia, and one of the countries of the Arab world, at the least, will present their projects.*

* The first such platforms looking to capture the national MOOC markets were already launched in 2013, including the Russian project Universarium, the Arabian project Edraak, and more.

### 3.1.3 The future of education globalization: the goal of creating a global education architecture

The emergence of such mega providers, especially those laying claim to the entire global (cross-country) education market, will certainly give rise to two big questions:

1. **'Universities for a billion' challenging 'education imperialism':** This de-facto small number of players, at the same time engaging an enormous quantity of students, is beginning to convey (within courses, programs, and methods of intermediate and final assessment) standards, principles, and values that are related to a very narrow group of providers.** For a number of national universities, this is a potential risk having to do with losing their national agenda. There is already proof of that fact that online education will be used as a tool for applying political pressure: The U.S. State Department, besides economic and political sanctions to pressure rogue states (such as Cuba, Iran, and Sudan), prohibits the citizens of such countries from taking courses in American online universities.*** Moreover, there is yet another risk: 'university for a billion' projects de-facto lead to losing 'educational diversity,' when introducing new education practices turns out to be virtually impossible other than in the producer countries of new education (and this is a risk for a civilization that needs diversity in the forms and approaches for great stability and development).

** http://edf.stanford.edu/readings/globalization-edu-

*** http://www.wired.co.uk/news/archive/2014-01/29/coursera-restricted-by-us-government

2. A no less important question involves the problem of global 'personnel vacuums' emerging within the global labor market, namely mass job placement services based on the

results from taking MOOC-based programs that extract the best personnel from national economics in the interests of global players. As far as the governments of developing countries are concerned, such mechanisms can drastically increase the brain drain from local economies, while at the same time decreasing their competitiveness. Moreover, although the brain drain is by itself not new, its evidently being manifested through 'universities for a billion' gives rise to the question of who pays for basic education (that is a condition for being accepted to 'universities for a billion') and who takes the 'education revenue' (providing specialized education at the last stages of professional training, and then hiring and using the best personnel). (The likely answer to the liberal economic tradition is that distributing talents within the global market whatever the case will be optimal with the given restrictions; however, the situation, where mass secondary education in all industrially developed countries is a public good provided by national governments for local taxes, goes beyond the 'private market').

As a result, at the beginning of the 2020s, a non-systemic reaction can be expected from a number of national governments in developing countries (including Russia, China, and Islamic countries) to the retention of 'education sovereignty,' when national governments will try to regulate the content of MOOC, restrict global providers' access to local students and the chance to select local personnel. Developing such subjects is even more likely if globalization moves toward shaping competing large regional blocks between themselves (a topic that we discussed in section 2.4.1).

Expecting this possible reaction makes the beginning of a dialog over configuring the global education architecture in the coming years important. At least the two following models can be put in the foundation of this configuration:

- WEPO (World Education and Personnel Organization, modeled after the WTO): shaping a translational alliance that ensures equal opportunities for mixing talents, providing education services, and giving guarantees of compliance with uniform transnational standards.

- Education 'Kyoto Protocol' (modeled after the Kyoto Protocol to regulate greenhouse gas emissions): creating specific compensation rules for investing in talents between countries.

Beginning such a discussion will certainly be painful: this can be seen in the current situation with discussions over a new financial architecture as part of supranational structures such as the G20* or with resolving large-scale environmental problems such as the Great Plastic Island.** It is entirely possible that such a process will develop much more easily through dialog involving engaged participants of new education, not the representatives of national governments.

There is one more important topic that is related to the possible impact of large educational projects on the political landscape. As we discussed in section 2.4.4, the future of states hinges on the ability to manage collective identity. In this sense, mass education projects, to an even greater extent than social networks, are beginning to engender their

* http://www.
eastasiaforum.
org/2012/10/03/
is-the-g20-failing/

** http://www.unep.
org/regionalseas/
marinelitter/publica-
tions/docs/plastic_
ocean_report.pdf

own identity that is potentially just as significant as their national identity. In the distant future (within 20 to 30 years), we could very well see the first variations of transnational libertarian 'states,' with specialized education programs being the entry point to them. It is likely that when accumulating a critical mass of 'new citizens' in the more distant future (ex. in the second half of the 21st century), such transnational states will create 'another globe': carrying out their own territorial projects for new formats of social and political structure, including, but not only, through assimilating extraterritorial space (such as the projects being discussed now for floating states,* the territories of Antarctica and near Space).

* http://www. christianpost. com/news/ billionaire-pe- ter-thiel-fund- ing-libertarian-is- lands-to-build- new-soci- eties-54033/

## 3.2 INDIVIDUALIZATION

*Life isn't about finding yourself. Life is about creating yourself.*
**George Bernard Shaw**, playwright

### 3.2.1 Prerequisites: yearning for individualization

'Yearning for individualization' is initially inherent to education. Education at its base is a process of personal development that was originally built as a process of individual inter- action between a mentor and mentee, in which the learning process was shaped to the student's personal particularities and current goals. At the same time, developing mass education systems, especially in the industrial era, related to teaching a large number of people standard skills and knowledge, has forced its creators to come to a compromise.** Hence, the emergence of 'industrial' forms of education that have already become habitual (as if this was always the case) and that in essence operate in the logic of the 'average norm:' standard programs based on textbooks and solutions; national exams given as tests; school classes created according to the age principle of people the same age, etc. Individual educa- tion was also on the sidelines of this process, because it was very expensive and affordable only for the elite.

** Ken Robinson: Changing education paradigms http:// www.ted.com/ talks/ken_robinson_ changing_educa- tion_paradigms. html

Information technologies allow for bringing back the individual approach to the center of the education process, and by virtue of its affordability easily allows for making it wide- spread. In essence, this involves combining two masses of information: personal trait data (including peculiarities of disposition, personal learning style, etc.), personal history, and personal goals (set by the person himself or linked to him by the parent customers, employers, etc.). These two masses of information are combined with data on available opportunities provided by education programs and individual education decisions.

Uniform grounds are needed for such combinations, because individualizing learning involves the collection of a unique set of knowledge and skills, not obtaining a standard qualification. Competence models could serve as these grounds,*** in the sense that there is the capability to carry out a certain type of activity, fulfill a specific work assignment, or tackle a certain problem.

*** Tom Vander Ark: Future of Learning http:// www2.dreambox. com/l/14872/2013- 09-13/5jgqw

Proliferating competence models as the grounds for configuring an individual educa- tion trajectory creates the prerequisites for full-fledged lifelong learning models. First, the line between the education process and the application of obtained knowledge and skills is effaced in professional activities, because HR logic is aimed at management capabilities (obtaining them and applying them correctly). Furthermore, the professional activity itself is a space where capabilities are shaped or developed. In this sense, it is worth talking not so much about managing education trajectories, as much about managing education and career trajectories where education creates the prerequisites for a career, while a career establishes the prerequisites for additional education. The first full-fledged competence models that accompany education and career are already being developed in the IT sector. As was discussed in section 2.1.2, competence management models and the certification process in other sectors will be built in a similar fashion. The social network Linkedin, which offers members to endorse each other's capabilities, and Mozilla, which launched its Open Badges system in 2012 for independent certificate resources to endorse professional and education achievements, are the first models of such systems.*

* http://openbadges. org/about/

Second, professional education and career are only a certain aspect of a person showing their capabilities; only one of the opportunities for self-actualization. In this sense, the personal capacities profile can be built, refined, and applied over one's entire life and in all spheres: school, games, hobbies, volunteering, networking, sexual relations, etc. (Moreover, it is when all these spheres, from games to sex, will be natural and seamlessly integrated into the process of building a personal capacities profile that re-individualizing education will become sustainable).

## 3.2.2 Individualization as the order of employers

Proliferating individual education models will mean the radical reorganization of the existing education infrastructure, and to this regard it will also mean that the students themselves being engaged is not enough to move the education machinery toward individualization. Students, however, have a strong ally in this objective, namely business that is engaged in attracting new talents.

Business's main interest as an employer is to have the chance to see new talents or existing workers' actual achievements. It would be even better to see their abilities and capacities right away. In this sense, employers are interested in the advent of individualized education arriving as soon as possible and in tracking individual successes. A number of tools are already working on this objective:

▪ Personal work portfolio with recommendations (namely, outside evaluations) and a description of key abilities have long become the standard for self-introduction in several industries, such as design, photography, architecture, and ICT. A similar format is gradually beginning to replace the résumé in most industries where self-employment or project employment is common;

▪ Individual capacity profiles according to internal corporate capacity models are becoming the standard for managing career trajectories in most Fortune 500 companies. These models usually are coordinated with forms of professional certification within an industry (ex. programming or financial management) or a type of activity (ex. PMI certification in project management);

- A number of universities/business schools give employers access to electronic diplomas that reflect a student's main accomplishments, including digital copies of final exams, video recording of exams, and a portfolio of the student's main creative projects.

The main technical issue is that specific education institutions, employers, and sectors pass on this data. In other words, data on a personal education and career trajectory must be under the user's control and must accompany the user when switching from one education provider to another, from one project or job to another. The medical sector is going down roughly the same path (a little bit ahead) in that standards are taking shape for presenting personal medical information. These standards are independent of individual medical institutions and allow a person to switch between insurance companies or medical service providers without losing information on the state of their health or on treatment received. Based on the healthcare industry's experience, it can be said with confidence that such an objective is attainable. Therefore, we believe that within the coming five to six years (by 2017-18) the transition will be commenced in one or several OECD countries from the qualification model (proving professional skills through diplomas and academic course completion certificates) to full-fledged competence models, all with implementing proficiency diplomas that accompany people through their professional careers. The emergence of competence models will make obtaining an education more manageable for the student and will allow students to raise the issue of the contribution that each education element makes to their personal competence profile.

A mass transition, however, of global education systems to a competence-model-based education can take place only as a supranational architecture for administrating education takes shape (we talked about this architecture at the end of the previous chapter). Competence models recognized by international education and labor markets by nature must be transnational and require a strong technological platform at the level of leading global IT companies to support and develop them. For the moment we can observe the spread of such models in individual disciplines, first and foremost in information and communication technologies where online learning projects, personal training courses from leading vendors, and independent certification systems have completely unpacked the learning market by making traditional educational institutions but areas where learning programming in specific languages and final certification take place. In other spheres, especially where 'soft' skills are the chief subject of education, the advent of competence models will take place much more slowly. The opportunity to steadfastly manage investments in desirable and undesirable skills, one that we will discuss later on, will become an important condition for this transition.

## 3.2.3 Objectivizing human capital: personalized investments

In 2013, Upstart, a network offering the opportunity to invest directly in promising talents, was one of the most intriguing startups that caught the attention of leading U.S. venture investors.* The Upstart model, which is a version of a fundraising platform, allows for investing up to $200 thousand in a talented young man or woman for them to spend on their education or on a business project. The young talent is then obligated over five or 10 years to give the investor an annual, stipulated percentage of the revenue, but only from the amount that exceeds the subsistence rate (defined as $30 thousand in annual revenue). It is evident that the model is mutually advantageous, for a young talent is given opportunities that otherwise would not exist (ex. favorable terms for financial their education at a top-rated university), while the investor is virtually guaranteed income, since highly promising young people realize their ambitions much more often than highly promising projects, and because following a talent's potential is oftentimes simpler).

* https://www.upstart.com/how_it_works

Regardless of the Upstart's individual fate, it can be boldly claimed that providing the opportunity to invest in talent directly is a new and extremely important trend for education. This possibility to this day has been indirect, either through employer-offered projects or through investments in corporations that are partially intended for student professional training; however, each person can imagine themselves as their own project, approximately just as this has been done for a long time on the market of professional athletes, singers, and movie stars. Essentially, we are returning to 'legalized slavery,' only this time based on mutually beneficial and extremely market conditions.

Several conditions are necessary for the market for directly investing in talents to start to prosper, and there is no doubt that these conditions will be followed through upon in the coming years. The actual recognition of education as a service provided on the education market, consolidated by a provider's liability for its KPI, is the first of these conditions. Officially, this is recognition, but in essence it is not treated as such. If education turns into a service, then it can be presented with criteria and quality standards for how it is rendered, and this will engender the chance to lodge complaints for low-quality rendered services. As an indicator of this, we expect that 'education attorneys,' specializing in defending students in proceedings over the low quality of rendered education services, will emerge on the legal market within four to five years. On top of that, by the end of the 2010s, insurance organizations could offer their services, such as 'unawareness insurance' when the rendered education service, despite the promised outcome, does not allow a person to attain the required skills, which caused such person to not get a job or lose their job (investment insurance could be another simpler type of insurance in case a talent is unable to attain the expected level of income).

Second, it is necessary to develop the information support system in the education service sphere that allows for analyzing a variety of education and career trajectories, and for highlighting the most advantageous strategies (what education solutions and career moves had the greatest impact on personal income growth). To do this, it is necessary to have extensive information based on such trajectories (including on an individual's income evolution) and to create Big Data systems that are capable of statistically analyzing such information through large samplings. Most leading staffing agencies, including major job search websites (such as Monster.com) or professional networks (such as Linkedin) have such abilities. We expect that consulting on the optimal education and career trajectories (for talents and for investors) will become part of their packaged offers in the coming three to five years.

The perception of 'preventive result management' lies at the center of the direct investment model. Based off of preventive medicine, which is now becoming the main growth area in industrially developed countries (based on the ideas that it is easier to get to an illness through a healthy lifestyle than fight the pathology that led to the acute phase*), 'preventive education' creates the perception of desirable and undesirable routes of development. Some of these routes have already been highlighted empirically (for example, the career path of successful research in physics or neurophysiology is clear), but most of them still need to be determined, and in this sense big data models in education must stress not so much the study of the possibilities of online pedagogy (evidence-based pedagogy, which we wrote about in the previous chapter), as much the study of the optimal 'routes through life,' including social and financial success.

If the market for investing directly in talent is to grow, then we expect the emergence of man-llionaires by the beginning of the 2020s (owners of investment portfolios made up of talent with an aggregated value (according to expected income) of more than a billion dollars), roughly just as the first billionaires were made in the credit, bonds, derivatives, and direct venture investments markets. The emergence of man-llionaires once and for all legitimizes the market for investing directly in talent as far as mass investors are concerned.

Even more can be said in that unpackaging the potential of investing directly in talent in the distant future could flip the perception of the ways for organizing a pension system. The grave instability of the Bismarckian pension model is being widely discussed (providing payments to pensioners funded by income from the working public) by virtue of a change in the demographic base (if at the beginning of the 20th century when such system was introduced the coefficient of pensioners to workers was 1:10, then now it is drawing closer to 1:2 and less) (OECD, 2011). On the other hand, pension funds investing in financial instruments during the restructuring of an economy (see section 2.3.1) and the creation of a new financial architecture (see section 2.3.4) are also subject to risk. If a portion of the pension funds begin to shape their portfolios predominantly out of investments in talent, then they will de-facto create a modified model of the Bismarckian system, where specially selected, highly productive workers labor in the interests of 'favored' pensioners who have invested in the corresponding funds. There are the grounds to believe that such a model for operating pension funds could become one of the effective and prevailing strategies by the beginning of the 2030s.

* http://www.iom. edu/~/media/ Files/Activity%20 Files/Quality/ IntegrativeMed/ Preventive%20 Medicine%20Inte- grative%20Medi- cine%20and%20 the%20Health%20 of%20the%20 Public.pdf

### 3.2.4 Demand for manageability

The emergence of employers and investors demanding the individualization of learning will trigger the development of a management system through its own education (which will begin to be viewed as an investment in the formal sense of the word). This system's main objective is to make educational content correspond to the 'personal capitalization' goal as much as possible (which can be understand more broadly than just monetary capitalization: the accumulation of human and social capital is not less significant). As a result, education that 'assembles' and 'accompanies' a person throughout their entire life needs the right guidelines.

1. **The transparent organization of educational content systems.** First, the preceding discussion should have shown that an incredibly important transparency component is the description of the expected outcome of the educational product as a contribution to a competency profile: what qualities, capabilities, and knowledge does a specific course or program work on and where is it derived from? We expect that such standard metrics will emerge (something like nutritional facts on food packaging) as course markers within three to four years (giving education full-fledged service status will help this process).

In a certain sense, Knewton — a company that provides platform solutions for personalizing the education process — is tackling this objective.* Knewton's platform allows for linking independent educational products and their users by integrating a personalized learning trajectory and by determining next-step development objectives for students; however, since the metrics that assess the contribution to competence profiles still do not exist, Knewton is based on the existing knowledge metrics (ex. the GRE and GMAT). In this sense, the goal of creating new education metrics is still yet to be achieved, and how quickly and massive the process of individualizing education will be depends on this goal being achieved.

* www.knewton.com/ platform/

Second, education is an experience good, and the assessment of other users or market specialists is the only way for this type of products (which include films or wine) to know ahead of time whether a product is good or bad. As a result, educational products need to be rated, and ratings should not be limited to those of academic institutions (which say nothing about the quality of individual education modules or even the programs within these institutions). Peer rating systems in education have already begun to develop,** but for the moment they are only in adult education within the context of personal development.

** See http://help. coursera.org/ customer/portal/ articles/1163294- how-do-peer-assess- ments-work-

Such standardized descriptions and ratings could emerge, first and foremost, on platforms that aggregate and catalogue a large amount of educational online resources, or a sort of education libraries. We also expect that a full-fledged search engine for educational online services will emerge in the coming two to three years, most likely as a type of search within major search engine services such as Google, Baidu, and Yandex.

2. **Education trajectories as a commodity.** Since educational content libraries are intermediaries and are easily replaced by higher-level aggregators (such as the described search engines), their model is unsustainable, and they can exist only if they will offer additional value to the user. Offering the branded education trajectory, which allows for shaping a targeted competence profile (ex. a successful professional's aggregated profile in the industry or a specific profile of one of the industry leaders (heroes)), could be such a value. For example, below (Fig. 4) a variation for working with competence profiles is shown

in the a rose-petal chart (a set of axes that have a relevant or targeted expression of a student's specific competences): the student (or the recommendation system) identifies the rift between the current and targeted competence profile and determines what combination of education models allows overcoming this rift.*

Branded education trajectories can be assembled automatically through aggregated recommendation services (backed by the current and targeted student competence profile). In essence, this is a popular product that attracts education and career trajectory statistics. It goes without saying that this is a much more subtle approach than the existing industrial education system that offers content according to the one-size-fits-all principle but still ignores the large number of a student's individual particularities and demands.

The emergence of around-the-clock virtual teachers who are flexible in adapting the education trajectory as it is passed depending on the student's current results, goals, and psychophysiological state will be the next step in developing such recommendation and programming education services (we are expecting these solutions to be on the market around 2022). The emergence of 'The Diamond Primer,' a personalized complete textbook with artificial intelligence that accounts for all aspects of the student's life, current development challenges, and skills required for surmounting these challenges (modeled after the Primer described in Neal Stephenson's book The Diamond Age (Stephenson, 1995)) will be the culmination in the development of this type of products. It is most likely that these types of solutions will not emerge before 2030 (given the likely time frames discussed in section 2.2.2 for creating high-level artificial intelligence).

*This model was first compiled by our group at the educational 'meta-games' in 2008 (see Attachment 2) as a 'competence server' model, but we did not turn it into an alienable IT product.

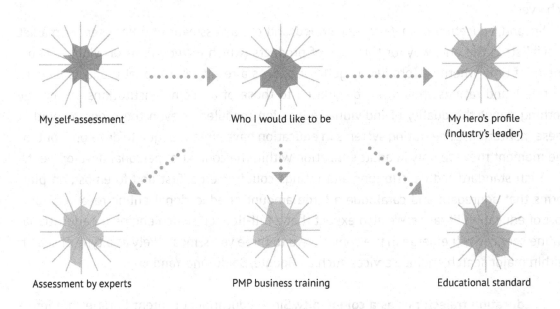

My self-assessment                     Who I would like to be                     My hero's profile
                                                                                  (industry's leader)

Assessment by experts                  PMP business training                      Educational standard

**Figure 4** The model for dealing with targeted competence profiles

The assembly of a custom individual trajectory, where a program (courses, projects, etc.) of educational products is selected in 'live' interaction between the mentor specialist and the student, is an alternative (and more expensive service at that) to automatic mass solutions. The mentor acts as the education navigator that lays out a route within a sea of education offers by relying on his instinct and perception of the student's needs. Such personal work will inevitably be supplemented by working with goal-setting and self-determination; with the student's capability to determine genuine life goals that meet more profound personal qualities and that are closer to his meaning of life.

### 3.2.5 Restoring the meaningfulness of self-development

1. **Demand for authenticity.** The preceding discussion in this section relied on economic logic; however, each of us is much more than an economic agent. Economics is a way for coordinating human beings for joint survival and to satisfy needs. At the same time, the need to unlock one's own potential, the need for self-actualization, and the opportunity to live a full life is the most significant, extreme, and existential need that goes beyond existing economics (Maslow, 1943). As a result, more and more people in industrially developed countries, especially from the new generations (Y & Z), prefer the chance to be more genuine, and to be more focused on the deep-seated needs of their persona, to social and economic success.* This phenomenon can be called the growing demand for authenticity (see section 2.3.3), which as part of modern economics is supported by the growing demand for 'following authenticity' as well in production and sales (Gilmore, Pine, 2007).

    Demand for authenticity means that a person is looking for the chance to move according to his own unique way in life by focusing on his own deep-seated interests and by aspiring as much as possible to unlock his creative potential. A person's independent demand for self-development and for supporting those who can direct such self-development (mentors, advisers, and gurus in the traditional sense of the word) is part of this direction.

    What is significant is that the 'demand for authenticity' directly coincides (and does not diverge from, as many think) with considerations of education's economic efficiency. The myth that the 'search for oneself' absolutely requires downshifting was created by the negative experience that generation X had in not being able to find the opportunities for self-realization in the economy of the 1980s, and therefore this generation was willing to sacrifice its career to be true to itself. If we look, nonetheless, at this from the other side of the coin, then if a person found a profession for himself that he is willing to fully dedicate and commit himself to, if he is willing to practice this profession even at the expense of his own resources, and if this is useful for society, then is it not in the interests of society to create an environment that would make such coincidences happen more often? Is it not better for society to have more doctors, teachers, and engineers, what is called 'from God,' rather than half professionals who chose their profession 'because their parents made the decision,' 'because it is fashionable,' etc.? In other words, it is economically expedient, politically beneficial, and simply humane to move toward a social system where the market or society will be able to find a domain for each of its members that they themselves will

* http://www.media-post.com/publications/article/170311/qa-gen-ys-youngest-demand-authenticity-via-tex.html

consider their calling (and also will have all the qualities for being successful at it), and to create an environment where they are able to practice this profession.

The individualized education model's principal structure in this case remains the same. The important thing that changes is that much more attention in this case must be paid to the 'subtle adjustments' that deal with diagnosing the psychological type, and the unique social and psychological situations of the student and his personal challenges. It is for this work that teachers in the original sense of the word are needed as advisers accompanying the student's development not only in one aspect (ex. in professional or in athletic achievements), but also throughout the student's life. Social-network-based recommendation services that allow people with similar qualities to find 'their own' teachers, and education support networks that allow such people to move within the education process and go through the challenges before them together, are becoming all the more necessary.

We presume that in the middle to long-term outlook, roughly 15 to 20 years, the demand for authenticity will become a significant social phenomenon, while 'live' education will migrate more and more to forms linked to developing authenticity by bringing back the original content and meaning to teaching.

2. **Life-long learning as a life path.** Education penetrating all aspects of human life and the shaping of the life-long education trajectory mean that the goals of education are also becoming commensurate with life. Pedagogy traditionally builds the structure of education around child crises and the stages of becoming an adult by clearly differentiating the goals and limitations of each of these ages (Erickson, 1959). It consistently helps to structure activities first around the emotional contact with the mother, and then around thematic manipulation and playing, and subsequently around academic activities (during which reflexes, reasoning, and goal-setting are shaped) and interpersonal communication and professional self-determination. Next, traditional education presumes improving skills and competences (mainly meant for social and career fulfillment), which is where the string of further accompanying development is broken, for an adult must tackle the challenges of becoming an adult, surmounting existential crises, children leaving the home, aging, and forthcoming death.

Weaving education as permanent functions of development into a person's life presumes returning the formation of separate types of activities into the mainstream that had fulfilled this development function, in particularly through returning the methodology and goals of psychotherapy. Planning investment in education for an entire lifetime and given not only external career goals, but also internal personal development goals, presumes including the corresponding psychotherapeutic tools in the education process. Today, the initial signs of this rapprochement are visible in the content of business workshops, in the emergence of meditation courses, and in biological feedback (see section 3.7.1) in both school and business education.

There was a time when both paths of development currently represented by education and psychotherapy were or could have been a single whole. For example, the Indian treatise Manu-smrti ('Laws of Manu,' the most influential collection of life laws of Vedic society written in the 5th century B.C.) puts forward four life stages: asharm training being the first; turning into the head of the family, work, and having children being the second stage; leaving one's affairs and passing them onto one's children, engaging spiritual affairs and charity being the third stage; and both meditating and preparing for death being the last stage. Each of these stages must be accompanied by passing through personal crises and individual work with an adviser (guru).

Accelerating changes in the world has possibly broken off a part of the formation of the 'internal,' psychological from the external, which has the goal of socialization and adaptation to the world. Personal development and the capacity for creativity in the new economy are becoming the foundation for a personal strategy, what Ken Robinson (Robinson, Aronica, 2009) calls 'your own element,' while O Sharmer (2009) calls it the 'inner place' or 'the source.' Therefore, the self-development process in life is long, what is essentially accompanying life itself, and will be the axis that education forms of the future will be threaded upon, whether it be transforming school, higher or supplemental education, or new forms of education that will emerge and that will emerge in the coming years. Education will absorb a host of psychotherapeutic qualities and will become the mechanism for surmounting age-related and existential crises.

## 3.3 COLLECTIVE EDUCATION PRACTICES

> *A good education system should have three purposes:*
> *it should provide all who want to learn with access*
> *to available resources at anytime in their lives;*
> *empower all who want to share what they know*
> *to find those who want to learn it from them; and finally,*
> *furnish all who want to present an issue to the public*
> *with the opportunity to make their challenge known*
> *Ivan Illich, Deschooling Society*

### 3.3.1 The public demand for teams

1. **Demand for cooperativeness.** You could get the impression from the previous section's discussion, just as from other discussions about the individualization of education, that future students are a sort of Leibniz monads, namely are detached subjects, each of which studies according to their own personal scenario and predominantly in an 'uninhabited' environments. People, however, are social beings, and the individual competences of each of us have value only in the context of being interlinked with each other (Boyd, Richardson, 2009). Namely, the capability to cooperate—to work in various groups, collectives, and organizations by fulfilling your part of a common goal and by supporting the group's work toward the common goal—is a key social competence whose role in the future will only increase.

Moreover, such capability to cooperate gives rise to synergetic qualities in organizations. These are capacities that a team wields rather than a separate individual. This brings employers and investors to the idea that it is not a separate talented individual, but a team capable of carrying out its duties or project goals that is the key component of the new economy.* It is the team that venture investors look at when making decisions to invest in

* http://www.rhrinternational.com/100127/pdf/V26N2-Leveraging-Senior-Teams.pdf

* http://upstart.
bizjournals.
com/resources/

a startup.* When hiring personnel, command-by-command hiring becomes extensive, especially in relation to R&D and administrative teams.** Furthermore, labor market patterns, including those related to the gradual displacement of humans from the sphere of routine intellectual labor (see section 2.3.3), indicate that the capability to co-create is becoming the key competence for the future worker, because this competence is the least exposed to the risk of automization*** Team co-creation competence is described as one of the key skills of the 21st century as part of the Partnership for 21st Century Skills program, which puts into practice modern approaches to learning using ICT solutions in U.S. schools and OECD-country schools.

** http://blog.
linkedin.
com/2013/09/24/
what-the-best-in-
business-look-for-
when-they-hire/

Teamwork is not only a new competence. It is also the most ancient competence whose role was diminished only in relatively new formats of industrial education (including school and university). As these formats increased rapidly in numbers, the original collective educational environment yielded the way to automation and competition (and we see the reflection of this, for example, in our assessment systems, which show by how many percentage points a given student passed other students). In the future, however, it will not be enough to be better than everyone: you will need to know how to be the best at something and together with others. In this sense, individualization not only should not suppress mutual aid, cooperation, and co-creation that have traditionally been in the education process and in life, but should rather develop them.

*** In particularl, see
the study by our
group, The Atlas
of New Profes-
sions http://www.
atlas100.ru/

2. **The deliberate demand for cooperation:** business and the state. It is entirely logical that two groups—business and government organizations—have the most far-reaching demand for education to training teams. The main demand is to provide such teams with the capability to work together congruously in the current environment and to ensure productive development for organizations.

The 'develop without destroying' challenge is one of the most serious challenges facing modern organizations. It has long been known that organizations pass through their life cycle as they develop, and as they grow, they become 'petrified,' losing the capability to change and thus become bureaucratized. This makes such organizations incapable of acting accordingly in response to the changing circumstances of the external environment. The history of business is full of hackneyed stories about how leaders of the technology market 'overslept' systemic innovations and became outsiders: Kodak, the creator of the first digital camera, risked not investing in promoting it and was displaced from the photography market by second-rate players; IBM, which in the early 1970s controlled 70% of the computer market, carelessly gave up the personal computer operating systems market to a small company called Microsoft. Organizations are restructuring their management systems from the principles of bureaucracy (standardizing processes) to the principles of learning in order to increase the ability to adapt within the logic of moving to hybrid network management as described in section 2.3.2. At the heart of 'learning organizations" operations is an environment that supports assimilating new practices, obtaining new information, and creating new products through experiments, free information exchange, systematic reflexes, and constantly retraining personnel.*1

*1 http://provost.
tufts.edu/celt/files/
Is-Yours-a-Learn-
ing-Organization-
by-Garvin-Edmond-
son-and-Gino.pdf

By following the goal to create 'learning organizations,' the world's leading corporations have begun restructuring training programs for their employees, especially middle and upper management and engineering personnel (ex. GE, BP, Boeing, etc.). Teamwork organization around real joint projects related to current corporate issues are being put at the heart of such programs (Katzenbach & Smith 2006). Moreover, in longer programs employees take on not one project, but a cycle of projects and have the chance to work in different countries and cultural contexts with different teams.

3. **Team education as a 'byproduct.'** There are organizations that have made the training of teams and employees that have made training teams and employees capable of working in a project team an inconspicuous part of their business models. These organizations are leading global consulting and auditing companies such as McKinsey, Boston Consulting Group, and Ernst & Young. When coming to work at such a company, the employee undergoes a rigorous selection cycle (which already guarantees his determined quality), and while on the job has the chance to work in various industries and countries, various contexts, teams, and administrators, and stressful conditions at that. In particularly, McKinsey, in following the 'up or out' principle, constantly gives its employees additional challenges that force them to either cultivate professional competences or to look for a more tranquil job, usually with their clients. Since working at McKinsey is a good school and recommendation, this company's former employees are willingly hired at other companies in administrative positions. In turn, Mcinsey vigorously supports the community spirit among its 'graduates' by using their contacts to obtain orders and new opportunities. In other words, we can claim that McKinsey and companies similar to it are in fact special educational institutions that provide the opportunity for young talent to increase their competences and their status, and all at the expense of clients who are willing to both pay for the day-to-day activities of these young professionals and to hire them once they have obtained a certain qualification. We will reiterate, however, that this model does not produce individual people, but rather it produces teams and networks that link specialists/teams together.

Startup accelerators, which are becoming the most popular model of venture financing, are yet another type of new educational institution that acts within the format of business goals. Selecting and accompanying startup projects from an idea to launch is the formal goal of accelerators (such as Y Combinator, TechStarts, SeedCamp, etc.). A significant portion of new businesses fail within the first months of a project before any notable results are obtained that allow the business to launch. This happens for two reasons: First, there are not enough resources (investors for understandable reasons do not eagerly finance projects at the early stages); second, and what is more important, the level of competences is not there. Startup accelerators accompany startups through the 'Death Valley' at the project launch by providing seed money and by helping them pick out that needed knowledge in several formats: through online/offline training courses, contacting industry experts, and working closely with mentors. Working with teams instead of individual businesspeople is a fundamental distinctiveness of accelerators, while the project's economic success is the main goal (since accelerators make money on buying a stake).

It is worth pointing out that building teamwork competences and fortifying learning processes through teamwork are both actively used in professional skills competitions as well. The Global Management Challenge (see the Box 6) focuses on management teams, the ImagineCup competition involves consolidating startup teams, and the EuroSkills competition stimulates inner-team education in trade specialties. It is worth noting separately the numerous robotechnics competitions, with this industry's specialists declaring that it is robotechnics competitions that are becoming platforms for shaping new teams of developers and robot manufacturers, since the goal of creating a robot by nature is interdisciplinary and requires the coordinated work of several types of specialists.

Box 6
*Global Management Challenge*
Small and medium-sized businesses' participation in various professional team competitions is one of the formats of new team training that is more suitable for such businesses. Global Management Challenge (GMC)–an international team competition held since 1980–is an example of such a competition. GMC is based on the computer simulation of business within a fast-growing industry: teams make management decisions, compete against each other, and try to get the best business results. Holding GMC competitions in participant countries allows teams to forge business competences and cooperation skills in stressful environments more profoundly, while the finalist teams often are hired for a new job.

Remark: Besides the main topic of our discussion – that the focus of attention in education, especially in professional education, is moving toward shaping team competences and team training – we see several important distinctions of new education models in the examples provided. First, education does not have to be an educational institution's main domain. On the contrary, an organization that uses education as an enabling domain to increase the likelihood of success can be an educational institution, no matter whether the organization in question is a business incubator, consulting company, research laboratory, group of interests, etc. Second, this organization can build a business model within its main domain where no one pays for education, but where there is stable demand for the organization's product that is obtained with the help of education. Namely education is clearly becoming a domain that creates added value. We concede that such models cannot currently be applied efficiently everywhere, for systemic school education is likely not to be organized as such; however, their very emergence and successful increase in numbers shows that education can have a host of 'non-systemic' players whose domain is not even yet recognized as educational, but who set new standards and new training models.

## 3.3.2 Communities as spaces of cooperative learning

1. **Revitalizing the role of communities as learning spaces.** As we discussed above (section 2.3.2), the economics organization model (and societies as a whole) are transitioning from hierarchically organized to horizontal network structures. Practice, the standard field with specific qualities, is the way to build an identity for such structures. Exchanging knowledge and experience in practice, or 'situated learning,' is the main designation for communities of practice (Lave & Wenger, 1991).

The communities-of-practice model is by no means new. It is likely that, along with learning within the family, this model is one of the most ancient forms of learning. Such groups have existed since the Neolithic Age (and possibly even earlier) as hunting and military alliances, groups of voodoo doctors, shamans, and priests, etc., and then later were formalized as medieval workshops. Their role in education was displaced to the periphery during the organization of the industrial education system. Now, however, the focused (or targeted) organization of such communities is a practice that is starting to gain more and more significance, in particularly as a knowledge control tool in learning organizations (Mestad et al. 2007). Although the difference between communities of practice and project groups is often stressed (McDermott, 1999), most projects can be organized in connection with communities of practice or serve as a tool for launching them. The Large Hadron Collider science mega project (see the Box 7 Large Hadron Collider as a New Education Project) could serve as an example of such integration that works to create a product and, at the same time, to both develop the competences of a large group of participants and build a sort of school.

The distinctiveness of communities of practice as spaces for joint learning is in their unique 'division of educational labor' organized with communities. A practical domain that can be organized as a project* or mission (each of which has a leader and team with a specific allocation of roles) is the nucleus of a community. The new participant studies predominantly in the domain by being part of the project working group in accordance with his competences and by gradually assimilating new (additional) positions.

A significant part of learning, however, takes place not within the project but in the space between projects (Figure 5):

- First, this takes place by exchanging experience from fulfilling specific projects (ex. a leader or participant of an analogous project or project that was assessed by members of the community as 'exemplary' can share experience or give recommendations for changing practice);

- Second, a norm or standard of practical is developed when accumulating the critical mass of projects and discussing them. Then specialists who determine or support such standards become the conveyers

Box 7

*The Large Hadron Collider (LHC)*

Built in 2008 at the research and development center of the Conseil Européenne pour la Recherche Nucléaire (CERN), the collider is one of the world's largest (and most expensive) scientific installations. More than 10 thousand scientists from more than 100 countries took part in creating it. The expectation is that the LHC will make a number of discoveries in the field of particle physics (the first of which was the Higgs boson in 2012). The LHC's educational effects concern several areas: (1) the preliminary research and design of collider component,, and the planning of collider experiments that through a common understanding bring together groups from several hundred universities (including those supported by a network of 140 computer centers in 35 countries); (2) teaching new technological approaches to several hundred suppliers (Autio et al. 2004); (3) simultaneously conducting research work and education programs in the field of science on the ATLAS component, which allowed for connecting (as part of 'missions') schools, universities, and research centers to studies (see http://www.atlas. ch/pdf/LA@CERN-Guide-of-Good-Practice.pdf)

* In practice, the notion of a project is so blurred that any collective activity with an established time frame and a comprehensible result, whether it be preparing soup or giving birth, may fully well be described as a 'project.'

of practice knowledge (in this sense, for example, educational institution ratings, in serving as the standard for schools and universities, act as the conveyers of practices within the education community);

- Third, the evolution of standards gives rise to demand for tailored learning and for certification to meet the standard. Namely a specialized (chosen) education process is engendered within the community.

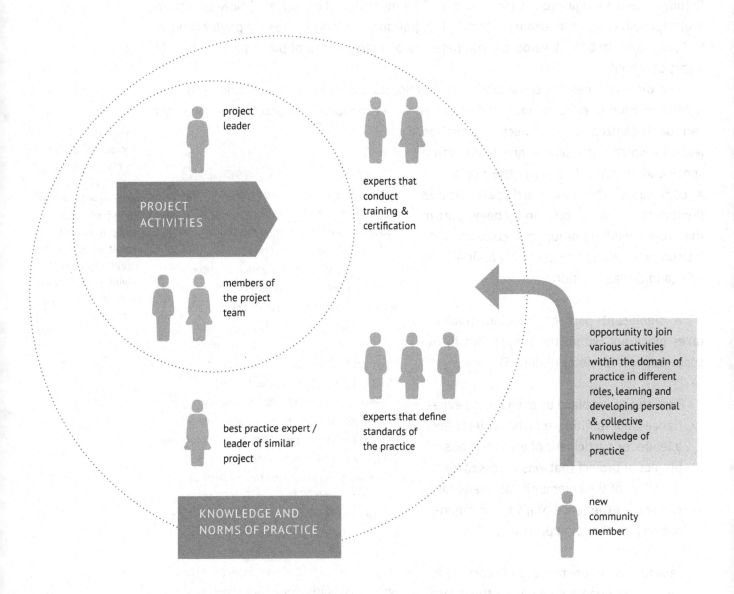

**Figure 5** The structure of the education process in communities of practice

In other words, a community of practice offers the opportunity for studying in the field, horizontal learning (experience exchange) and slightly vertical learning (learning standards and certification), as opposed to rigid vertical structures such as schools and universities. Communities in this sense act as spaces for mutual learning, as 'collective gurus,' where others can use each person's valuable experience for mutual growth (the topic of which we discussed above in section 2.2.6). It is in communities that are connected by a common practice that the principles of 'learning webs,' freely organized communities of education mutual exchange that Ivan Illich wrote about (Illich, 1971), can be realized (and are already being realized). These are spaces where one can present their difficulties, exchange experience with others, and indicate their willingness to help others resolve their problems.

2. **Learning in network communities.** Developing Web 2.0-based social technologies has given a big boost to the status of communities in the world by having allowed for forming a host of new communities around interests and practices. Communities at one time during industrial urbanization had a subordinate role since they were forced to group themselves around vertically organized structures. Now, with the emergence of the Internet, a thorough transition has taken place: communities no longer have to be limited to a territory. They have the chance to look for 'teammates' all over the world (what is also significant is that this allows individuals with unusual hobbies or capabilities to find people like themselves and join together). Web 2.0 tools (social and recommendation networks, exchange of results through forums and presentation websites) allow organizing the process of including new participants in a practice or a professional domain without direct contact. Moreover, social networks are becoming a mutual learning tool for participants with formal education. Mutual learning for MOOC participants is one of the typical and developing examples: MOOC creates communities online for working together on difficult course questions, and the participants help each other solve tasks and more. (The set of tools that enhance mutual learning through social media has been described as 'peergogy,'* and many of these tools are promoted by Connected Learning Alliance**). We presume that the MOOC design will gradually account more and more for the existence of these social groups by using them as an environment where course content is developed and refined (and, as we wrote above in section 3.1.2, 'experienced' students in such spaces can act as mentors for new students).

\* http://peeragogy.org/

\*\* http://clalliance.org/why-connected-learning/

3. **Mentor networks.** It is evident that the most significant learning effect inside communities is from the conditional horizontal transfer of information from more experienced to less experienced participants. In many cases, this can be a regular, not one-time, occurrence that registers the transition of an experience community participant to the position of adviser or mentor. It is mentors who are usually responsible for the systemic work of new community participants assimilating a practice (and the model of a startup accelerator described above that actively uses mentors in this sense is a type of community of practice, where experienced technology businessmen train beginning businessmen). In other words, mentors are guides to a practice, especially because they (based on their own experience in developing and surmounting challenges) see the student's needs to develop and are able to design a trajectory for the student as a set of challenges.

We believe that the model of mentor relations will increase more and more in popularity as economics and management systems switch from vertical to network organization. This will require creating mentor networks, spaces where mentors denote their competences and their willingness to provide mentor services. In turn, 'new practitioners' interested in mentoring offer themselves (and their undertakings) as an object for mentoring. There are a number of prototypes of such networks, including GetMentoring (business mentors), MentorNet (women advisers that accompany the schooling of secondary school girls interested in a scientific career), ICouldBe (an online network of mentors working with 'troubled' teenagers), etc. At the same time, the full-fledge realization of mentor networks is related to the competence profiles system and 'images of heroes' that we wrote about above (section 3.2.4), since this establishes 'a system of coordinates' for mentors and students to interact. It is entirely possible that the arising mentor networks themselves (which we expect to emerge by 2016-18) will also become a space where such profiles will be shaped.

### 3.3.3 New cooperative education tools

Since demand for network learning in communities is on the rise, and communities are beginning to actively develop as spaces for horizontal education, new ICT-based cooperative learning tools will be developed in the coming years. It goes without saying that there are already a host of solutions for creative collaboration and for exchanging experience in forums and Wikipedia. The most important new solutions for non-systemic 'horizontal' education will be related to objectivizing a community's educational effects for teams and individuals, and to developing tools to support these effects:

a. **Cooperative education opportunity exchanges.** Opportunity exchanges, spaces where an individual can find his team and a team can find a new member are probably the most important part of the future infrastructure of cooperative education. These exchanges (whose emergence is expected within two to three years) will be in some way similar to existing job search websites, but will also have several notable differences:

- First, existing job search websites are meant first and foremost for permanent employment, less often for project employment, and never for leisure and game employment. Rather, as we discussed before (section 2.3.3) and will discuss later (section 3.4), gaming is becoming one of the leading types of human activities in work, education, and leisure. 'Opportunity exchanges' have to consider this issue much more broadly by making it possible for a team to find a member suitable to the game task;

- Second, hiring for money is the main model of existing 'employment exchanges;' however, money is more a 'hygienic factor,' a work condition, but does not determine the main motivation to work. For example, the startup Genome (Marmer et al, 2011) conducted research that shows at least three other motivations for startup founders: gaining experience, personal reputation growth, and the ability to make an impact. As a result, exchanges must provide the chance to engage a team member for 'experience,' 'fame,' or 'ambition,' provided all three parameters must be expressed quantitatively;

▪ Third, and most important, is that 'opportunity exchanges' do not 'sell' users employment, but rather the opportunity for self-employment by taking part in new projects. These are meeting places for people and teams where a person can choose a project or game for himself according to his development goals, while team leaders can choose for themselves a new participant according to his competence profile, achievements, and growth potential. This process is in some way similar to putting together a baseball team based on analyzing players' statistics ('sabermetrics') or to select an NPC team in computer role-playing games (but only with the exception that all this takes place in real life).

b. **Issue exchanges** (communities as spaces to resolve them). Developing 'open innovation' models (which we wrote about in section 2.3.2) and crowdsourcing models give rise to a slew of open competitions to resolve research, inventive, and programming challenges (ex. the platforms TopCoder, Brightideas, etc.). The process for resolving real business and technical challenges is already starting to be integrating into MOOC on the basis that MOOC brings together processional audiences willing to resolve difficult issues.* Moreover, a shift takes place as part of the crowdsourcing paradigm from the vertical model, when companies or governments determine the range of issues for a community, to a vertical model of problem-sourcing, when the community itself determine the issues for itself using the same methods that it employs to resolve them (Davenport et al., 2013). Over the coming years, a significant number of communities of practice online will be able to acquire their own 'issue exchanges' where important challenges for teams are discussed and proposed.

* http://blogs.hbr.org/2013/07/a-new-use-for-moocs-real-world/

c. **Team-based competence passports.** If the team is the main participant in the education process and in real corporate projects, then collective competences are the management object in this type of education. Some of these competences are provided through team member competences, while others consist of what a team is able to do together (organizational competences). Organizations try to divide up their competences and work purposefully on improving them right away, but this field should also see the formalization of types of competences and the creation of tools for managing them (similar to what will take place in individual competence management — section 3.2.4). Moreover, individual and collective reputation management tools based on reputational capital can supplement collective competence management tools (see section 2.3.4).

d. **Creating the image of a community goal.** Cooperative education concerns not just current human and community interactions. Each community is a set of values and meanings, collective intentions and the common goals before them. This especially concerns cases where reference is made not so much to communities of craftsmen, as much to communities that come together for the sake of a certain reason or meaning. Having and supporting an image of a collective idea that the community members share is critically important for such communities. Modern literature on making predictions discusses how the practices of jointly constructing an image of the future (including foresight) serve as an 'organ for forecasting the state of the environment' for communities. This is roughly the same function that the emerging nervous system began to carry out for multi-cell organisms (Klein, Snowden & Pin, 2010). Shaping the collective competence of 'thinking about the future' and the supporting tools for the allocated construction of images of the future through wiki-foresights (ex. the Foresight Engine model used by the Institute for the Future)* is becoming a critically important component of all sustainable and self-developing communities of practice.

* http://www.iftf.
org/what-we-do/
foresight-tools/
collabora-
tive-forecast-
ing-games/
foresight-engine/

### 3.3.4 'Live' education: the time of horizontal structures

As network communities of practice and the support tools within their education processes develop, the role of structures that convey knowledge vertically—from 'older people' to 'younger people,' from the 'experienced' to the 'inexperienced,' from the 'teachers' to the 'students'—will decrease significantly. Of course, world-class individual gurus who will act as conveyers of unique knowledge through MOOC will not go anywhere; however, in most cases we are transitioning to the 'collective guru' (we wrote about this in section 2.2.6). Within the logic of collective gurus, each person can be the student or teacher, the bearer of valuable experience, and the person that can appreciate it. Conveying knowledge is becoming an auxiliary process of education, while uniting 'older people' with 'younger people' in the developing here-and-now process of joint practice is becoming the central process. As a result, structures where such a model is natural are taking on great significance as customers (and at the same time as providers!) of education. The two most massive types of these structures are communities and families.

1. **New 'student corporations.'** Corporations assimilated education as a development tool in the 20th century. In the first half of the 21st century, network structures will gradually replace corporations. As a result, education could see a new type of customer interested in cooperative formats of education and in 'cultivating teams.' Communities of practice can shape this demand within themselves by transitioning to more organized forms of learning (which is already taking place ubiquitously). What is more important is that they can shape it outwardly. As a result, forms of 'community universities' where practitioners collectively (or under the supervision of a council they have chosen) order training programs for themselves could become a frequent practice. The professional standard shaped by leading practitioners within a community is the nucleus of such programs, while supplemental programs meet the current interests and goals of a community's development (ex. Education Cooperative Project, a project for training businessmen in Oakland, is a model of such an educational institution. The Education Cooperative Project** is based on first having the group of businessmen invest money and shares from their own startups into a cooperative for conducting a joint program, and then once the cycle of programs has been completed, the community returns its learning investments through the success of their part of the startups).

** http://www.
coopedproject.org/

'Community universities' can emerge in online ecosystems as well around existing professional forums or MOOC. Thus, a portion of MOOC students are beginning to incorporate into communities to help each other in their learning both online and in groups that meet face to face. As the number of people obtaining education online increases, they will be co-organized similar to standard (or close to standard) education trajectories. By gaining influence, such groups of students will order education trajectories for training individual professionals and teams on both the online and offline education markets. Moreover, student communities can problem-source to tackle problems together* and to gradually make the transition to creating their own courses using the crowdsourcing logic. Finally, online communities can become a space as well for generating startup projects (even within the model of 'education cooperatives' described in the previous paragraph). Essentially, no one is keeping a platform from being put together – on the platform of professional IT online communities such as StackOverflow or Habrahabr – for generating and testing startup ideas, the best of wish will then immediately be able to be applied for financing from crowdfunding platforms such as Kickstarter.

* http://www.ssire-view.org/blog/entry/mooc_sourcing_for_social_good

In some sense, this process could be the beginning (based on an essentially new foundation and new motivations) of the rebirth of the model of medieval universities that originally were self-organizing corporations of students ordering their own education and, if need be, migrating from one teacher to another. For example, Bologna University from the time it was founded was a self-organizing community of students who elected a provost from among themselves and hired professors for a certain amount of time (who status-wise were dependent on the students and therefore gained influence from them exclusively through their own talents). Only later, as the university model became more frequent and rulers lent their support, power at universities began to transition to the faculty (and in many cases to the administration representing first and foremost the interests of the state). Discussing 'university spirit,' however, has now for three centuries been constantly bringing its reformers (whether it be Humboldt or Ortega-y-Gasset) to the idea that it is high student independence and autonomy that are most productive (in terms of the education's expected results), that the student should have the right to decide what content is useful for him and to go after his own interests. We will object here, however, because that it is not so much the individual by himself, as much the individual as a community of practitioner member geared toward standards of practice, collective goals and values. Developing non-systemic education and the growth of the technological opportunities for forging 'education networks' provides the real chance for 'community universities' to become a mass phenomenon within 20 to 25 years that compete with traditional universities (or that replace them).

2. **Demand for family re-integration and family teams.** Above (section 2.3.5) we wrote about reorganizing the modern family and about the search for a new identity, essentially about the search for a new cause and a joint image of the future. Families can conduct this search for identity independently or in communities, including in collectively created 'family universities.' The family is by nature a collective structure. The family presumes joint action and gives the potential for joint development. The modern family (which does not necessarily have to be a 'father-mother-children' nuclear family, but rather can be a commonwealth or commune) searching for its identity and for development opportunities will conceive a new order for cooperative education. Furthermore, all the tools that we talked about in the

previous section, especially the tools for shaping common goals, are entirely applicable to the family (or communities of families).

'Family teams' could become a new product of education systems that have forged their identity around their social mission. Stable reproduction of a set of competences within the family or family clan necessary for retaining or expanding family empire — business or professional dynasties, family corporations and other forms of family business — is an activity that far-thinking 'family politicians' have been conducted for a long time. Even though a society's dynamic development has a destructive impact on traditional forms of the family, family education can and will be sought after, especially when the education experience obtained in teams analyzes the notion of the advantages in using turnkey teams. Natural formed roles, traditions, sets of values coordinated since childhood, and predictive communications are just several of such advantages. Of course, family systems have their drawbacks as well that make modern nepotism an effective approach only in a very limited range of variations.

Indeed an efficiently operating individual education trajectories management tool can be mentioned only in a situation where all types of education and other influences are followed and accounted for; however, the field of education and communication in the family are almost completely independent spaces. The natural way to account for and use interactions in the family pursuant to individual development is to create general family education and life trajectories, in which all education and development influences in the family are accounted for and used within a uniform model. Carrying out such an approach points very clearly to the possibility and high likelihood of making family teams a reality, developing family competences, and the emergence of new approaches to family business and of team education forms meant to use as much as possible the interactions that separate families from working teams. It is through education, using the entire available arsenal of new humanitarian and technological solutions, that families will be able to restore their identity and become spaces for joint development.

## 3.4 GAME TOTALITY

*Play cannot be denied. You can deny, if you like,
nearly all abstractions: justice, beauty, truth
goodness, mind, God. You can deny seriousness,
but not play.*
**Johan Huizinga**, Homo ludens.

*Anyone who tries to make a distinction
between education and entertainment
doesn't know the first thing about either*
**Marshall McLuhan**, New Education

### 3.4.1 Returning games to education

It cannot be said that games at a certain point abandoned education for good, especially if reference is being made to children's education; however, gaming in the industrial system were allocated to leisure and sports. A large part of education, even if reference is being made to early school education, to this day is very serious. In recent years, it is an explosion of interest in playing that has forced the mentioning of gamification as one of the key trends of new education. The growth in student motivation, transparent education structure, efficient learning cycle management when mastering new skills, the low cost of mistakes when learning, etc. are singled out among the advantages of game approaches in education.* The question is whether this interest is a situational fashion or whether we are indeed seeing a change in playing's place in human life?

1. **New stage in children's games.**\*\* Games are a natural process for children, and a significant number of children's games have an educational load to bear. We can claim more: a child's psychological specifics are such that each object that a child interacts with for a long time becomes a learning instrument for such child, whether it is a toy, furniture, clothing or food. Hence, the emerging perception in the modern industry of children's toys and services is that all subjects of child customs must be designed as educational products.

Another important process that is taking place right now in the child industry has to do with the aspiring 'mediaization' of a product, when 90% of the product's value (be it a doll or clothing) is created by multi-character, long stories (such as My Little Pony or Winx) shaped in the transmedia logic (when a host of various media platforms, such as cartoons, comics, games, etc., are used for creating an additional image for characters and for telling their stories). Media characters shape children's perceptions of behavioral norms and values, establish behavior models and create their subculture. Moreover, basic psychological models used for developing such products are usually not discussed or comprehended at all. We presume that as the learning role of transmedia stories in child education, a system of various 'design models' will develop in the child industry, with the understanding of the educational effect of specific solutions (see the Box 8 Smeshariki regarding the design of unique education models within children's shows).

* http://paradigm-shift21.edublogs.org/2011/07/08/gaming-the-future-of-learning/

\*\* This fragment was built on our joint work with the Association of Children's Goods Industry to create a Russian road map for the children's goods and services industry

The demand for engaging their audiences is another important particularity of trans-media products and developmental environments based on them. Most of these products are meant for a specific gender and age group, but are interested in having the users 'live' with the product for many years. This forces searching for more complex types of products that can develop and change as the child grows. For example, Lego designs have different size and difficulty sets, from those with a small number of large pieces for the youngest children to complex sets with programming components. The future of the children's industry is in the creation of long-time use, interactive, and developmental (game) products that 'grow up' with the child and allow for tackling new tasks all the time. Some of these products will be placed in entertainment products such as cartoons, some in virtual worlds, some in augmented reality objects, and some in physical objects such as furniture, clothing, and shoes. Essentially, 'long games' are not a new phenomenon in pedagogy: it is on the principle of the 'long game' that R. Baden-Pauell built the scouts movement (Block, Proctor, 2009); however, as interactive environments develop and the possibilities to create transmedia products emerge, 'long games' could become truly a mass phenomenon that engaged a notable number of children in developed and developing countries). Anthropomorphic and zoomorphic learning robots that can look after a child's safety in games, accompany a child on trips around the city, offer a child socializing and intellectual games, all while changing its program of communication and the educational task as the child grows and becomes an adult, in the future could well be able to become the ideal type of 'long game' tool.

Games are efficient tools for shaping perceptions of values (because the metrics of the games themselves establish the axis of 'good' and 'bad,' of 'right' and 'wrong'), and this especially relates to 'long-cycle' games that accompany the child for a long time. The demand for this type of game products is on the rise: given the problem described in section 2.3.5 of value models eroding and traditional values deteriorating (to a large extent thanks to active participation in games that establish arbitrary value models), many social institutions will face the issue of how to shape the 'right' (as far as these institutions are concerned) value systems.

Box 8

*Smeshariki as an educational project*

The Russian cartoon Smeshariki (running in the United States and Canada as GoGoRiki), a series of 10-minute stories about funny, balloon-shaped little monsters, is an intriguing innovation in media products for children ages five to eight. Developing scenarios where there are no 'good' or 'bad' guys, and where all conflicts that occur between them are based on differences in perceptions of the world and are overcome through discussion and action, was one of the principles when creating this show. This approach shapes intrinsically different perceptions for children about the way the world works. To go from the perception of the world as 'an arena in the fight between good and evil' (the classic model from Aristotle to Hollywood) to the perception of a world where conflict stems from diversity and can be overcome through constructive communication. Moreover, the creators fundamentally refused to 'adapt it for children.' The show's characters use 'adult' language and tackle 'adult issues' (what children observe in real life, at the same time preserving the cartoon's conventionality of it all, which makes the show equally interesting for both adults and children. In other words, the show's creators clearly set pedagogical and development goals from the logic of 'future competences' as the main objective of the storylines and character design, and not just the objective of being comprehensible and attractive to the audience.

The Catholic Church is already actively using online games and offline quests to promote Christian values, while anti-globalist movements are spreading online games to shape environmental and anti-consumerist values. It is very likely that as transmedia 'long' games develop as one of the most important educational environments, the battle for control over meanings and value patterns integrated into these games will only intensify.

Another important function that games can ensure is to safely familiarize children with the adult world. In particularly, this concerns safety simulators: online or augmented reality games that can teach children to follow traffic rules, choose safe routes home, get out of dangerous social situations, or avoid criminals. Moreover, augmented reality allows creating 'special routes' for children that transform the urban space into a 'city for children' that, for example allows children to easily find workshops or education centers where they can use the game format to become familiar with adult professions and other activities.

Furthermore, games allow for engaging children into a complex field such as science or engineering creativity. There are already thematic science parks (were you can count on spending hours or even days) that are built around a specific game scenario (such as flying to Mars in an airplane, an archeological expedition, etc.). For example, the Canadian camp Science Quest, founded in 1988, offers several programs that create skills in programming, research, environmentalism, etc. through multi-day team game quests, in which the participants support the object's life functions and surmount unforeseen situations by using science and engineering developments that they create under instructor supervision. There is great demand for such programs, and many of them increase their duration and transition to a year-round format.

2. **School as a game space.** Developmental game environments are becoming a real competitor of school education. Since children outside of school are playing virtually all the time, it is becoming very difficult for the school to retain their motivation for learning without game elements. With this environment, the reaction of reasonable schools is to saturate their educational environment with game elements by making them less interesting but much more educational functional. 'Advanced' schools are already actively using game components in their educational work, sometimes for an individual class, sometimes for the entire school. Overall, however, reference is usually made to short games, because schools are restricted both in terms of their abilities to develop game movements and in terms of the available space for games. Therefore, game pedagogy in school is more a luxury or an experiment.

Although solutions for augmented reality are still in their early stage, it is clear that augmented reality will become ubiquitous in the near future. This will permit schools 'without losing quality' to refine their education processes using multi-user games specially developed for studying specific subjects (or groups of subjects), be it mathematics, chemistry, or a language, and that combine intellectual, social and physical activity. Gaming is becoming a process that organizes groups (often of different ages) around various types of assignments, while education takes place little by little while challenges are tackled. Playing could be a permanent process for young school children, while for adults it could be a part of their education process on par with 'serious' challenges. Teachers have the role of accompanying games (including as 'real-life' characters), making sure the rules are followed, and making 'subtle adjustments' that allow for tackling specific educational tasks. We believe that such 'long' games in school, which take up the majority of the game process, will be actively used in the coming five to seven years.

In the more distant future (ex. by 2025-35), schools could turn into a set of all different kinds of developmental games within the game universe, where the conventionality of roles and game mechanics will help students assimilate knowledge, subject and social skills. For example, students can dive into the world of the magic school of Hogwarts from Harry Potter, Baloo's Forest School from The Jungle Book, or Mumi School from Mumi-Trolls. Teachers' role in such a school is not only to be game teachers, but also to be 'master' characters that give students quest assignments through various tests. The child's goal (or group of children's goal) should be to get through the test, maybe even 'beat' the character teacher himself. Moreover, such 'fairy-tail' worlds could give relevant and up-to-date information: nothing is keeping from basing intergroup knowledge modules on important scientific knowledge (ex. through digital models, which we will talk about in section 3.5.2), while gaming could be adapted to developing scientific knowledge even without the help of intermediary adaptors (textbook authors and methodological textbook developers). The Classcraft environment, released in early 2014, could serve as one of the first example of such online environment for gamifying schools.*

* http://venturebeat.com/2014/05/31/class-craft-role-play-ing-classroom/

In this sense, schools could stop being a space for industrial learning, a place for meeting someone who has knowledge or a ready-made student primed for processing. Gaming is becoming the main education format. Academic activities, which shape skills, knowledge and abilities, and competences that are the goal of learning, are woven into the rules, scenario, and role of gaming. Provided that individual education trajectories are becoming the base methodology of education, and the goal of design and conducting such games is made extremely more difficult. This is because the game needs to have the conditions and goals of individual development for each participant, to shape the learning game processes that meet these goals, to establish control points and the means for establishing the level of related competences and capabilities, and to gather together all these elements into a collective game with an engrossing scenario. With a game environment that is balanced for a host of different players, the rules and capabilities, regardless of the students progress, are to remain within the zone of near development for each of them, namely to remain interesting and sufficiently difficult. It is virtually impossible to achieve this goal without the help of specialized game education movement designers; such systems still do not exist, although just their emergence would not achieve the goal completely. Besides them, augmented reality systems that are rather inexpensive and efficient will be required in order to become a part of the education standard. Systems similar to Google Glass glasses (or 'wearable' contact monitor lenses), will allow entirely getting rid of the learning process' dependence on a specific space because they permit creating an interactive space with set features in an arbitrarily chosen place. In addition, augmented reality systems will be able to resolve the contradiction between the necessity of individualizing education and the collectivity of gaming, since they will allow modifying the game scenario and conditions to fit each player.

3. **Recognizing game achievements as education results.** The educational role of games is recognized not only for child and school education. On the one hand, simulators for learning professional skills have existed since the computer era (and if we are to consider specialized simulators as educational games, they have existed for even longer). Training pilots, military commanders or company administrators for many years has included the game element. On the other hand, there are many games for adults that have the ability to develop all sorts of different skills, be it the capability to mobilize large teams, conduct tough negotiations, or manage the budget of a broad organization. These games, currently not perceived as education, have not just become legitimate; they have become a very important part of adult leisure by occupying their time, creative and intellectual capabilities.

Videogames are becoming a popular leisure activity for all age groups in place of 'non-interactive' entertainment (total videogame sales in the United States in 2011 surpassed DVD film and other platform sales, while 2012-13 videogames of the year Call of Duty and Grand Theft Auto 5 were the best-selling entertainment of all time). What is very significant in the penetration of virtual and game logic technologies is that the majority of the population in industrially developed countries is psychologically ready for a 'life in the game.' The generation of people aged 35-45 grew up on the first videogames of the 1980s, while videogames were already a part of studies and entertainment for today's students (16-25 years of age) (among the school projects, field trips, hanging out with friends and theaters that compete with them). The new generation (ages two to eight) does not even think about life without tablets, videogame systems, and Internet games. Above (section 2.3.3) we wrote about the proliferation of the kidadult model, where successful adults retain their interests in games. What is significant is that games are becoming a socially acceptable form of entertainment for pensioners as well (see the Box 9 Games for the Elderly).

Videogames, however, and especially MMORPG, are much more than entertainment. They allow for developing social skills, shaping strategic thinking, etc. For example, one of the most complex multi-user strategic games, EVE Online (with roughly half a million permanent players)*, is popular namely among professionals in strategic management and in security operations (for example, an American security specialist who died together with the American ambassador during the terrorist attack in Libya in fall 2012 was one of the EVE world's high-level players). Online games oftentimes are also serious investments: During the virtual battle of the very same EVE Online to have taken place in the middle of January 2014 and to have become the biggest battle in the history of the game universe, players 'burned' more than 300 thousand dollars worth of virtual property.**

Box 9

*Videogames for the Elderly*

The study 'Development of digital games for elderly users' showed that roughly one in every five Brits aged 51 to 65 regularly plays computer games, while two-thirds of them play at least once a week. The Finnish research center VTT reports that one in two (52%) Finnish pensioners (65 and older) plays computer games, while one in five (22%) plays computer games every day. According to Dutch researchers, more than a fourth of American retirees play videogames (Ijsselsteijn et al. 2007)

* http://www.eurogamer.net/articles/2012-09-12-us-official-killed-in-syria-was-a-senior-eve-online-player

** http://www.polygon.com/2014/1/30/5360208/Eve-Onlines-Bloodbath

The following is one of the questions that is already emerging on the labor market: if games are in fact becoming legitimate, mass activities with an educational function to them, if players are spending hundreds of hours perfecting skills that are needed in everyday life (as well as spending serious time and money on playing games), then why are they not shown in a person's résumé? We believe that this cultural stereotype will soon be surmounted (only individual Silicon Valley companies are acting as the pioneers so far), and the game level in MMORGP will have no less significance when being hired than your university grade-point average.

Moreover, if virtual game worlds allow both shaping and exhibiting competences, then they are the ideal environments not only for learning but also for verifying skills. We expect that within three to five years games will be actively used in education through academic projects and final exams, while certain game achievements will be counted as elements of education (this is currently happening usually in an elementary format).

Game environments could become an important supplement to the MOOC model. MOOC is now mainly targeted toward codified knowledge (be it courses in neurobiology or electrical circuits), while the possibilities for shaping skills in them are limited. Using specialized game environment (ex. management simulators us as the GMC model described above in section 3.3.1 or the SimCity urban management simulator, of standard game worlds (such as Sims Universe) and specialized 'virtual laboratories' (see section 3.5.2) in the future will help integrate a process for shaping skills in MOOC. It is MOOC that can begin actively using game environments for taking discipline-specific exams as well.

The listed formats continue the trend in gamification that has been taking place in education for several decades already; however, we believe that gamification will be much broader: it already engages the 'serious' activities of corporations and social institutions, while in the coming decades it will encompass our entire everyday life.

### 3.4.2 Game pragmatics: resolving 'serious' tasks in game form

Game designs are one of the most potent tools for orchestrating team performance, spurring on creativity, and being able to think outside the box. Now, gaming is making its way into serious business, becoming a way to package business or scientific research. In particularly, administrative work, new product development, etc., are all undergoing gamification (Deterding et al. 2011).

1. **Simulators and virtual worlds for advancing professional skills.** Game mechanics have long been a tool for professional training programs. Educational military games can serve as an example: chess or xiangqi are well known for having been used to train general officers and military commanders. Simulators have been used for many years to develop professional skills in transport (pilots and train conductors), industry and energy (power plant operators or hazardous industrial facilities), medicine, and managerial activities. Now, two important additions are being made to this training model. First, highly realistic, special virtual worlds are being added to simulators to train specific skills. For example, the Federal

Deposit Insurance Corporation (FDIC) commissioned BreakAway Games, the leader in the 'serious games' market, to create a virtual world where financial auditors are able to improve their risk assessment skills by interviewing personnel during a game-simulated audit. Integrating educational game solutions with augmented reality is the second important trend (de Freitas, Liarokapis, 2011). Here, for example, safety training can become a game where the employee earns points for proper behavior and loses points for improper behavior. The same logic works, case in point, in teaching medical workers difficult professional skills using real-world objects such as remote surgeon training using augmented reality.*

Virtual worlds can serve more than learning purposes for already hired employees. The development of new industrial sectors in the coming years (section 2.3.1 and 2.3.3) will require large-scale retraining in new competences. Game worlds could fill this role by allowing adapting 'extra people' to new tasks, either by giving them competences in self-employment, by themselves or in teams. (Moreover, just being in virtual worlds allows partially tackling the problem of 'extra people,' when education acts as a 'space for overexposure' (see item 3 below).

2. **Gamifying the workplace.** Game movements are suitable not only for educational purposes but also for motivating participants to do difficult, unusual or, on the contrary, routine tasks as part of one's main work. Traditionally, an image of a field requiring will, concentration, and reliance on external motivation has been consolidated in the term 'work:' receiving subsistence to exist and achieving a status. Work usually has the traits of a routine, uniformity, limited accessible options and scenarios, 'boredom' in a broad sense; however, it is work that the term 'benefit'—both personal and social—is often related to. Game activity, on the contrary, has the traits of creativity, joy, relaxation, spontaneity, and is done through natural, game motivation. Gaming is often associated with social or personal benefit, responsibility, and someone being socialized in society. Working is gradually and for various reasons gaining the traits of gaming. Elements of gaming are being integrated into several monotone types of operator activities to support the needed level of attention. Competitions and tournaments are gradually becoming a universal part of working, while the motivation in these competitions and tournaments is gravitating to becoming intangible for good. In 2012, the company Gartner predicted that 70% of 2,000 major global companies would take advantage of game mechanics, namely have at least one game application for users and employees.** There are also several trends taking place in the process of engaging game mechanics in serious tasks.

First, games are becoming a form of crowdsourcing that allows organizing the mass generation of new ideas. Here, game organizers offer a sort of deal: they obtain valuable solutions in exchange for pleasure from the game. Foldit, an online puzzle game about protein folding that was released in 2008, could serve as one of the good examples in this field. This game is part of a research project conducted at the University of Washington, and the player's objective is to fold a structure of selected proteins as best as possible. The best user solutions are analyzed by scientists who can use these solutions to help them find a solution to real scientific puzzles related to developing vaccines and to biological innovations. In 2011, players were able to transcribe the crystal structure of the M-PMV virus,

* http://www.forbes.
com/sites/john-
nosta/2013/06/27/
google-glass-teach-
me-medicine-how-
glass-is-helping-
change-medical-ed-
ucation/

** http://www.gartner.
com/newsroom/
id/1844115

which causes AIDS in monkeys, in just 15 days (the outcome of a crystal-graphic analysis later confirmed their findings). Prior to this, leading scientists were unable to find the solution to this problem for 15 entire years.[*]

* http://fold.it/portal/node/990356

Urgent EVOKE, a game created for the World Bank and held in 2010, could serve as another example. The game took place in 2010, with the players faced with various social crises (for example, the threat of hunger in Tokyo) that they needed to surmount either alone or in teams. Although conveying the World Bank's vision about global prospects and threats, the selection of talented social activists in developing countries and the teaching of new skills for dealing with social challenges were declared as the main goals of the game, and participants from all over the world could generate hundreds of distinct approaches to resolving crises (Waddington, 2012). These approaches could full well become the foundation for future World Bank projects and policies.

In the future, it is extremely likely that game conventionality could replace not only the form, but also the content. Here, the structure of a work assignment has to be specially shifted into a game metaphor by one or several games for one or several users. Solutions such as 'I conduct a customer's calculations while playing a space strategy' or 'I conduct marketing research while battling zombies' could be the result. The presumption can be made that such game environments will likely be adapted to challenge classes that will allow them to shape competences in rendering real problems in game mechanics: calculating tasks, producing creative solutions, collecting user data, etc.

Furthermore, we presume that workplaces will begin to acquire all the more traits of game environments — especially in cases where the issue concerns tasks that require routine or increase attention — not only in specially sessions, but also in one's regular work. For example, the company Cisco is using game solutions to increase the work performance of its salespeople and call centers (Penenberg, 2013). Using first-person shooters for carrying out actual military operations (ex. for controlling military drones, including for 'consensus' control, when a host of players instead of one chooses how to control the drone's real movement) is one of the bizarre but from unlikely possibilities. Such possibilities are out there for civil use as well — for example, for fulfilling operator or dispatcher assignments — and we are also confident that they will begin to be used long before the 2010s are over. The situation described in the novel Ender's Game could serve as an analogous of such solutions. Here, the main character is a genius military commander child who, in taking part in simulated battles with his computer, in fact is managing a conflict between a real terrestrial fleet against aliens.

3. **Gaming as a social adaptation tool.** Organizing a system of social order and the practice of punishing for breaking the law are one of the biggest problems facing modern industrially developed. U.S. prisons have roughly 2 million people, and they are mainly working-age men. A significant number of these people are repeat offenders, since after being released they have a social stigma and rely on their prison contacts. Russia, which is second (after the United States) among major countries in the number people in prison, has a share of repeat offenders in prison that is even higher. The problem is that the archaic system of imprisonment does not re-educate convicts, but rather isolates them from the rest of society, and as a result, dissimilates them.[**]

** http://www.unodc.org/unodc/en/justice-and-prison-reform/prison-reform-and-alternatives-to-imprisonment.html

Education, especially new forms of it, could become an effective new way to arrange the penitentiary system. Educational and penitentiary institutions can give prisoners (first voluntarily, then through new motivation systems such as getting a positive, adaptive personal profile that allows adapting to society after being released) the chance to not just take education courses, but also get the chance to take part in education programs that are specially targeted toward transforming personal profile features that led to deviant behavior into socially acceptable features. American court verdicts that hand down 'educational punishment' (such as having to take anger management classes or male nurse courses that lead to working in clinics for those who are guilty of having made someone suffer) are frequent in 'penitentiary education.' The possibility of creating realistic virtual worlds will emerge by the end of the 2010s as the technological base of virtual simulators develops: 'Virtual prisons' meant for experiencing situations again and again, and the illegal actions committed from the point of view of the victim, members of the victim's family, guardian of the law, and third-party citizens. When sufficiently realistic and when being immersed in the game experience, this gives the criminal the chance to acknowledge his crime and its repercussions as much as possible (such a model is in some way similar to the Indian model of karmic punishment, where committing a crime leads to probably regeneration of a similar crime in the victim's body).

'Virtual prisons' are new 'special overexposure' where criminals are temporarily isolated from society, while at the same time they work out their dysfunctional behavior and assimilate socially acceptable behaviors of action. Furthermore, nothing is preventing from integrating the learning of additional, useful skills into a virtual prison's game mechanics. The same goes for real tasks, as is described in the previous item, in particularly ones that are calculated or routine. As it so happens, prisoners in Chinese prisons are already carrying out routine steps in game worlds at the request and in the interests of prison administrations (ex. earning money by 'mining gold' in World of Warcraft).* Then, of course, in this sense the 'virtual GULAG' could be at times not much better than the real GULAG; however, if a system is transparent and organized in the interests of prisoners themselves, then this system could very well be suitable as an alternative to current forms of punishment.

Moreover, if there is the chance to create human systems of overexposure and re-education (including such systems that are built on the principles of self-control, shaping perception, learning socially useful behavior, etc.), then the line between 'intentionally dissimilated' criminals and 'inadvertently dissimilated' citizens (ex. dismissed from their job for being disabled) could be erased). We concede that virtual worlds will be widely used for 'special overexposure' and professional advancement beginning in the 2020s as a cheap alternative to retraining systems at employment centers.

Applying the virtual prison model could go beyond correcting dissimilating behavior. In essence, what is being referred to here is overcoming certain inefficient behavior (or even lifestyle) through acknowledging it, living it universally, and overcoming the reasons for it. Gaming for these objectives has been used at the least since the mid-20th century in the context of psychodrama, namely the practice when a therapy group participant can repeatedly experience a traumatizing event, provided that this is not only from the person's own position, but also from the positions of other people involved in the story. We presume that

* http://www.
theguardian.
com/world/2011/
may/25/china-pris-
oners-inter-
net-gaming-scam

virtual prison technology will be suitable for psychotherapeutic purpose and will be able to aid working through traumatic experiences and stopping dysfunctional behavior for most conditionally normal people. 'Psychodrama worlds' where people will play out and experience each other's life stories together could become a working alternative to group therapy by the beginning or middle of the 2020s. Psychodrama worlds can be applied not only (and not so much) in the format of clinical psychotherapy, but also a part of the education trajectory of normal people (in our understanding, this format, which is meant to teach a person new ways to act and to develop personal qualities, is also a form of education).

### 3.4.3 Game totality

The gamification of education is, in essence, already an established fact: gaming may not yet have penetrated school, university, and professional education for good, but there is no serious opposition to this process. Following this process, the gradual gamification of 'serious' spheres, such as research and development involving the creative resource of game communities, is taking place right before our eyes. We presume that gaming will return their status in society, similar to what they had in antiquity and in medieval times within the coming generation; gaming that penetrates the political, the military, the economic, and the cultural. The onset of the era of total gaming is taking place before our eyes, and below we provide several signs and expected events from the advent of this area.

1. **Gaming as a way to control creative ability.** We have repeatedly discussed the subject that the capacity for goal-oriented (individual or collective) creativity is becoming the principal advantage for people in a world where routine physical and intellectual work is being passed onto robots and artificial intelligence. Furthermore, the modern system of education and organization of working environments is more counteracting rather than aiding the development of creative abilities (Robinson, 2011). The transition to game models in education and the organization of labor is a way to create spaces where the capacity for goal-oriented creativity is aroused, retained, and developed (Penenberg, 2013). We already mentioned the possibilities for creating virtual environments with a game component for work, including Ender's Games, which will restructure routine and complex assignments into puzzles and quests. The decision to gamify working processes is a clandestine 'revolution from within' because it requires companies to critically analyze which organizational processes are routine and do not motivate very well, whether they in fact are necessary, and whether they can be automated or transformed into 'working games.' This decision means that an organization makes the transition from the industrial model of 'working according to standards for a wage' to the post-industrial model of 'creative work for interest,' namely aspiring to create a space of high productivity for creative personalities.

The spread of game models in the economy is beginning to shape a new behavior model where a person's mistake is not fatal. In most cultures, especially in traditional, non-European cultures, a social mistake (for example, a failed project, bankruptcy, etc.) often creates a stigma: a person to have made a mistake looses their status or overall becomes a social outcast. And although all cultures admit that making a mistake has educational value to it and provides experience ('learn from one's mistakes,' 'failure teaches success,' etc.), actual social punishment causes people to act more carefully to keep from making more mistakes. The experience of venture ecosystems, and Silicon Valley in particularly, shows that making mistakes, recognizing them, and getting a second chance are together an important condition for the innovative economy to be effective. Google and other high-technology companies* have their corporate culture built on these principles, which can be labeled as a 'culture of mistakes.' It is in a game environment (where a player can make a mistake as long as he stays in the game, and this mistake is not fatal, but rather teaches a lesson that allows shaping and perfecting skills) that this culture of mistakes takes shape. The culture of mistakes is necessary to preserve workers' high creative potential, because creativity must allow for the chance to make mistakes and try again. This is also why game environments will become the preferred way for organizing the workplace in developed countries.

* http://hbr.org/2006/06/the-wisdom-of-deliberate-mistakes/ar/1

Returning to the statement that the seriousness and routine of schools is destroying children's creative capabilities, one could look to an area that Mitchel Resnick's group at MIT Media Lab is developing, called life-long kindergarten. Resnick and his colleagues' idea is that the kindergarten** atmosphere — with developmental games and opportunities to actively experiment — should remain in schools, universities, at the workplace, and in the urban environment as a whole. Ritualized games in the form of interest groups are becoming more and more sought after in society, be it competition between fan clubs, biker shows, or the re-enactment of famous historic battles. At the same time, there is also demand for spaces that allow for unspecific, unorganized playing, such as what happens when children play in stores or at restaurants (where kids have many opportunities to play collectively or by themselves, while those watching over them make sure only that the children do not hurt each other). We believe that clubs, which we call 'adultgartens' (places where adults go to 'remove' their social roles and obligations, return to being children, and play a game that interests them or do something creative without the risk of being condemned by others), will emerge and begin to develop in the coming decade. Such adultgartens can be both educational and therapeutic, and they can become a part of 'serious' organizations that need a boost of creativity, be it innovative companies or startup incubators (the first such experiments, still with limited functionality, were conducted at the campuses of Google, Pixar, and others). Limited types of adultgartens are already appearing in the urban spaces of many big cities as new forms of public art, when a game, poetry, theatrical improvisation or a handcrafted article is made not only (and not so much) by professionals, but by anyone and at their pleasure. It could be said in this sense that an adultgarten is a form of the reprivatization and deprofessionalization of art, of the restoration of the true 'folkness' of art, the way that art existed in village communes, and now can exist in an urban environment and with modern technologies.

** http://llk.media.mit.edu/

2. **Playing as a form of gentle social control.** We already discussed virtual prisons as a way for gently correcting socially unacceptable behavior; however, gamification has much broader possibilities. In essence, any social behavior can be restructured as a game that will begin to motivate people to behave 'correctly' and to decrease the likelihood of their

behaving 'incorrectly,' not to mention to act in the interests of people themselves. Jane McGonigal discusses these possibilities in detail in his book Reality Broken (McGonigal, 2011), claiming that transforming part of our everyday reality into practical games could work in favor of our longevity, increase our psychological stability, strengthen our connections with other people, and make us happier; and not only through games themselves, but also beyond them. In this sense, according to McGonigal, game developers are becoming 'hackers of happiness' that are allowing us to regain happiness within game environments that has been lost in industrial civilization.

For example, games can stimulate our interest in sports, as do social competitions based on Nike+ or Bitbit acceleration gauges, which let us compare our daily running or walking achievements with our social-network friends. The SuperBetter application offers a daily game that increases our physical, psychological, and social stability. The geographic locator application Foursquare lets us compete for the number of visits to specific places (restaurants, offices, museums, etc.) with other visitors, or to earn points for visiting places that are new and unusual to us. It is clear that such gamification is only the beginning of a large-scale process (especially, as we discussed in section 2.2.3, as augmented reality technologies become widely used). Using gaming to stimulate a healthy lifestyle — if this includes not only tracking movement activity or a sleep schedule, but also diet and encouraging a desirable lifestyle through earning game points, winning badges, etc. — could fundamentally revolutionize medicine and fitness. An urban space saturated with augmented reality game solutions allows improving social moral by, for example, encouraging help the elderly or disabled, stimulating socially safe behavior, etc. Games that encourage business cooperation or social activity are also possible. Social games in pregnancy are also imaginable, with some of them being able to increase the birth rate, while others (something like 'Grow a Tamagotchi in You') help learn how to correctly raise your future child. Bonus points accumulated in games with reality are becoming reputational capital (see section 2.3.4) that gives a person access to new opportunities for development, gaining experience, and getting pleasure. A pretty good illustration of such a future, where virtually one's entire life turns out to be gamified, can be seen in the short-length Sight.*

* http://vimeo. com/46304267

As gamification encompasses more and more parts of human life (not only school or work, but also health or social interaction), it can be said that any gamified practice begins to transform into education, because the game has within itself the perception of the desirable and undesirable (namely assessment and self-assessment), and the mechanisms for shaping skills and self-improvement. All spheres of life can be represented as 'long games,' in which a person grows from standard academic levels to higher levels of expertise. In this sense, the personal education and career trajectories described above (section 3.2.4) are most conveniently realized in game models.

3. **The transition to a game society.** Duality between gaming and non-gaming, between the serious and the condition, is still preserved in the society that we described above; however, the reorganizing of industry and economics taking place in the world could lead us to a fundamentally different reality. As we described above (section 2.3.1 and 2.3.2), new means of production (3D printing and new materials, biotechnologies, robotechnics, smart

grids, and autonomous energy sources) assume the high localization and automation of production. Production as such and the related services sector could one and for all transform into a small part of human activities, while the main population will be involved in things that are in no way related to production, and in this sense there will be a definitive post-industrial transition whose beginning is described in Daniel Bell's famous book (Bell, 1973). For the moment, however, it can only be presumed what meanings this new society will put at the forefront. The image that some futurologists propose is that of a 'digital Athens' * that will be built not on exploiting human labor, but rather on using machines that will replace humans in any type of routine labor. Most likely of all, when automation and autonomous intellectual systems free up a person's personal time and creative energy, those new spheres that will absorb the majority of people (including attention management and broadening experiences) will be much more people-centric.

Games are the most organic form for such reality:

- First, games let anyone become any character, be it a real or made-up character, which gives a lot of opportunity for being entertained and realizing one's potential;

- Second, the most interesting games are those with a lot of people, where people can help each other get experience in direct interaction. Games can create collective experiences (ex. historic or imagined events) or concern personal issues (as in the psychodrama worlds described above). A joint game in this world could be a collective cause (ex. as in club formats) or hired work (ex. similar to animators or ceremony hosts);

- Third, part of the experience can be obtained in the passive, rather than active, model; then outstanding players' behavior becomes the object of audience attention. Even now are the best gamers in quests and shooters putting up their game progress on YouTube and getting slews of views, while virtual racers are getting contracts in real racing shows. For many players, their own life could become a show à la Big Brother or Russia's Dom-2 that can be shown to the world; participating in such interactive shows could become the main profession for a significant portion of the population.

In other words, in the distant future of our prediction (the 2030s), gaming could turn from an auxiliary activity into a main activity and begin to occupy a significant amount of time for residents of developed countries. This will no longer be the game formatting of 'serious' activities, which will likely be gradually integrated into gaming as one of the courses of action. The gaming society could become complete by dissolving individual social roles within it (even such stable roles that the institutions of the family establish (ex. husband-wife, child-adult, etc.)) and the borders of social institutions. Of course, roles and rules are not disappearing, but becoming demonstrable, clears, and acknowledged, which means that they are becoming more manageable for people themselves. It goes without saying that the transition to such a 'game' society cannot happen in a single step. It is very likely that there will be (it could be said that there already has been) a break between 'man

* Similarly to ancient Greek Athens, where free citizens could be involved in the arts and politics, while women and slaves who made up the main portion of the population did all the work.

playing' and 'man working,' and that the essence of this break is to know how to refuse excess serious attention to oneself and one's roles, to accept the conventionality of a host of social games, and to allow oneself to take part in these games with full commitment. There will be those who accept the new way things are, those who oppose it, and those who even do not understand what is going on. It could be that the way things were in the 1960s, when the 'flower child' movement tried to 'take apart' the conventionality of the norms and rules in the Euro-Atlantic culture, but only this time the scale of the shift could be much greater. In other words, along with the 'psychological break' in assimilating the new tools of the NeuroWeb (which we will talk about in section 3.6.3), accepting the rules of the 'total game society' will become one of the cognitive barrier factors in the transition to new models for organizing the lives of human beings.

Games are one of the fundamental activities of living beings that are older than humanity itself. People have mastered games (or games have mastered people) since the beginning of human culture, and in ancient civilizations game behavior penetrated all spheres of life: war, politics, arts, commerce, and male and female relations. Industrial society put games in their own unique pens—in entertainment and sports—by separating them from 'serious' engagements, such as science, economics, and lawmaking. Games have 'forgotten their nature,' and people now leaving the sphere of routine labor for the creative sphere allows us to recall that 'all of life is a game' is not just a metaphor, but also the way things really are.

## 3.5.1 THE NEW SCIENCE MODEL

*Thought is not the only and original reality;*
*on the contrary, thought and intellect are one of the reactions,*
*to which life obligates us and which finds its own source*
*and its own meaning in the radical, primordial and intolerable*
*necessity to live*
*Pure and isolated reasoning has to learn*
*to be life-long reasoning*
**José Ortega y Gasset**, Mission of the University

*The army form a square! Mules and scientists in the middle!*
Napoleon Bonaparte's order before the Battle of Alexandria (1801)

### 3.5.1 The Evolution of Science: Where Are We Now?

It would be bizarre to expect that science would remain on the sidelines of change during the dramatic transformations that virtually all areas of human life will experience under the influence of new technologies. Since education (especially higher) is closely linked to organizing cognitive models, we will try to understand what factors will move the evolution of science in the coming 20 years.

Science in its current form is a phenomenon of exclusively the industrial stage of society's development. Science during the pre-industrial era was linked to general philosophical and religious cognition of the world (first and foremost through speculative conclusions, self-observations, or the search for discoveries), and in most cultures was based on the interpretation of religious texts. The idea of systematically organizing the research of nature in order to assimilate it and subject it to man is a purely European project that Francis Bacon in its essence shaped in his treatise New Organon by proclaiming 'knowledge is power'. European scientists' experiments on nature, beginning in the 17th century, in fact did begin to produce a number of new technologies that served for technical superiority in war and in manufacturing (and the success of European colonialism is evidence of this). As a result, science by the 19th century transitioned from the status of a 'gentlemen's hobby' to a regular activity that was carried out with the support and control of governments (science in Kaiser's Germany in this regard was exemplary). It goes without saying that science served to raise the state's prestige and could create new types of useful materials or medicines; however, ensuring military superiority was its main purpose. Science has finally begun to occupy its current niche—areas where it creates economic innovations and allows national companies to compete effectively—in the second half of the 20th century when economic competition replaced military competition, only after two World Wars that were truly 'triumphs of science,' a war of mechanisms and the means to produce them, and ending in the explosion of the extremely powerful atomic bomb. It is this pragmatic role that determines the structure and model for the organization of science in industrially developed countries today. Modern universities were built as factories meant to produce new knowledge whose quality is assessed by communities of professionals and users (state institutions and private companies). Scientific competition is closely related to economic competition: bidding to conduct important research in a specific field directly correlates with a country's capacity to retain technological practices in the corresponding sphere, and to use them to develop existing business models and build new ones.

As a result, science is being made pragmatic, and Charles Sanders Peirce described the logic of this process (Peirce 1931): when choosing a hypothesis and experiments, researchers must look for the most cognitive bang for the buck; however, it is impossible to keep up permanent and growing bang for the buck. Just as in any other sphere, science sees inevitable diminishing returns from its resource (if the aggregate of tools of scientific cognition, including theoretical perceptions, research methods, experimental devices, etc., are considered to be this resource). This causes a number of repercussions:

- The cost in traditional disciplines of research that create new knowledge is gradually increasing. Hence, the need for scientific cooperation increases as a way for sharing expenses, especially in the natural sciences (ex. the already mentioned Large Hadron Collider, the first thermo-nuclear reactor ITER, the International Space Station, the pan-European Human Brain Project, and more);

- The inevitable diminishing return of traditional paradigms (namely the chance to engender new knowledge and applied solutions based on it) is also necessitating that new models for describing reality are searched for. This search is easiest to do in an empty space 'between' disciplines. Hence, the explosive growth of inter-disciplinary research that in the process engenders new disciplines. Having a very profound mastery of relevant material within one's discipline is the sole competitive advantage for researchers that remain within traditional disciplines.

- The amount of knowledge, measured in the number of published articles, registered patents, etc., that institutions have produced is the mediated performance indicator of research institutions. This causes exponential growth in formally structured knowledge.* Furthermore, far from all this knowledge is obtained accurately: knowledge is subject to the problem of 'half-decay' as new facts are accumulated (Arbesman, 2012). The 'half-decay' problem exacerbates the explosive growth in the amount of second-rate and third-rate journals, in which the bar for research quality is falling quickly.**

- The risk of cutting the quality of research and the spread of plagiarism has become a separate side effect of the demands for showing results, which thus has necessitated creating additional systems to 'protect from idiots.' At the same time, the competitive nature of modern science, which raises the issue of recognizing scientific merits and distributing intellectual property at the end of studies, has gone nowhere. Since this problem is not new, it does not block scientific cooperation, but does increase intermediary expenses.

- Finally, the increasing break between the scientific system and society is one of the most significant problems. Scientific knowledge (and the technologies based on it) has become too specialized and detailed for the majority of society to be able to understand it. Therefore, tracking scientific achievements ceases to be the standard for an educated person. As a result, scientists are forced either to demonstrate the applied significance of their research (which works out in far from all areas) or to be satisfied with their low status and funding.

This brings us to rather gloomy conclusions: if the presupposition that the 'diminishing return on the cognitive model is correct, then there is the threat that science as an industrial system for obtaining knowledge about the world could soon reach its limit of growth. This limit stems not so much from science's incapability of making further progress, as much from society's not being willing to provide the resources for science to progress (Nobel laureate in physics Steven Weinberg pointed to this real problem in his article 'The Crisis of Big Science' (Weinberg, 2010)).

(Incidentally, this position could change for a certain amount of time, because new technologies in the field of bio- and nano-technologies, robotechnics and ICT, and cognitive technologies that allow creating new types of armaments and for shaping a new war model. In addition, the 'compactness' of new technologies gives many more opportunities for attacking small terrorist groups. As a result, it is highly like that in the 2020s there will be an arms race, where not only major states will be able to participate, but so will independent

* Which is often mixed up with the 'quantity of information in the world'

** http://theconversation.com/open-access-and-the-looming-crisis-in-science-14950

radical groups, and this will heighten the interest from leading countries and corporations in science. In preventive logic, DARPA is already assimilating these areas of research.)

Second — and in the long term this problem is much more acute — when exact and inter-disciplinary research increases, so does the division between researchers, a sort of new Tower of Babel when even in adjacent fields of one discipline do specialists not know about each other's research and not understand specific problems and terminology (Stanislaw Lem predicted this threat back in 1963 (Lem, 2013) by calling it a 'break in the science front'). As a result, science is starting to collapse under the weight of its own knowledge that is trans-forming quickly into ignorance.

Third, the demand in this situation increases for knowledge that could immediately prove its value, namely be created right away as knowledge in practice. In other words, the 'pure' scientific search that was the ideal of scientific schools until the mid-20th century (Soviet Physicist Lev Landau's famous statement: "Science is a way to satisfy one's own curiosity at the government's expense") is now being replaced by the resolution of strictly pragmatic tasks, within which researchers can integrate their 'scientific curiosity (such as, for example, an astrophysics model of gravitational waves could be developed when creating new methods to search for oil and gas deposits*).

* Real example that was told by one of the former Vice-Presidents of the National Science Foundation.

Moreover, the following 'non-systemic' researchers start to gain an advantage:

- Specialized management and engineering consulting companies (ex. The McKinsey Global Institute, which regularly publishes influential reports on the development of economic and technological practices);

- Independent developers of new hard and soft technologies that oftentimes transform their developments into startups (the Koios platform for resolving complex social problems created on the basis of the ideas of Douglas Engelbart and Thomas Malone on collective intellect (namely the development creator does not write a scientific article, but rather turns the scientific idea into a practical solution) could serve as an example of such type of development;

- And new generation 'amateur scientists' (for example, members of the bio-hackers society who run serious independent research on gene modification).

Independent researchers have a number of strategic advantages over 'systemic' scientists in that administrators of science do not hold them to strict requirements, and they can be more flexible in setting their goals and in managing the research process (since they attract targeted funding for practical developments). They can offer and test more daring ideas (since they are not restricted by the need to publish their developments in specialized journals). Limited funding forces them to be more ingenious and pragmatic in achieving their goals. We presume that 'non-systemic' science will become all the more of a noticeable part of the sphere of cognition and knowledge control, just as it will also become more and more a part of the education sphere.

Science, including science at universities, is feeling the pressure of the listed factors above, although this pressure is sufficiently indirect. Through increasing demands for high citation rates in publications, criteria for progress in one's scientific career are becoming stricter and procedures for obtaining funding for research are becoming more difficult. More and more researchers, universities, and countries are discovering that they are taking part in the Red Queen race from Alice in Wonderland: they are forced to run just to stay in place, while they need to run twice as fast to progress. And there is the risk that more and more runners will drop out of this race.

### 3.5.2 Fighting for effectiveness: the transition to digital

Since the crisis described is a systemic process, it can cause long debates about whether this process in fact exists or not (roughly as with the debates over global warming, except that the scientific community here will be mainly on the skeptical side). As a result, specific problems will show up within the community's scientific practice, for which specific answers meant to 'increase science's output' will be proposed. As in the case with education, increasing performance and reorganizing processes will have mainly to do with applying information and communications technologies in research work.

1. 'Decreasing output' from existing cognitive paradigms, especially when reference is being made to modeling complex systems, is the first and most important challenge for developing science. Creating a new language for describing complex systems is one of the chief goals that science started to tackle beginning in the second half of the 20th century, and the contours of these possible future solutions are already beginning to take shape:

- **Transitioning from analytical to algorithmic models.** According to the pattern established by classic physics, mathematical law (usually expressed in differential equations) for a long time remained the idea of a model; however, sets of equations are very inaccurate in describing complex systems (ex. a cell, body organ, ecosystem or human community). At the same time, systems of agents that interact according to simple rules are well described (ex. a simple set of rules that is proposed in Craig Reynolds' boid model (Reynolds, 1987) is exact in describing the modeling of the complex movement of flocks of birds and schools of fish). As a result, many industries of science have made the de-facto transition to a new language for describing complex objects, when we do not try to remove the laws of communication of measured parameters but rather describe the algorithms of how complex system components work. Moreover, a computer retains the structural model;

- **Virtual worlds are becoming new laboratories.** Digital models long ago became one of the chief research components in quantitative physics, chemistry, biology or economics. In recent years, 're-usable' simulations that are gradually being refined to conduct various qualitative experiments have been actively developed (ex. in qualitative biology this is the cell model of Stanford University and Craig Venter, as well as the models of the brain, heart, liver, immune system, and more). It is evident that virtual laboratories decrease the total expenses (and speed) in conducting research by replacing experiments in vivo/in vitro (for which special equipment, agents, and often live creatures are needed) for experiments in silico (for which only structural models are needed).

'Re-usable' models can become more accurate as experimental data are collected, because one of the most serious problems of existing simulation models is their low quality of input data. The research and development process has to create a large amount of data, new algorithms to process them, and models to package them. Organizing research transforms into a 'dialog' between data collection systems and analytical systems where a scientist carries out the role of dialog 'moderator.' This will mean the next step in the development of science, the 'fourth paradigm' that is expressed in the transition to highly intensive data work (Hey, Tansley, Tolle, 2009).* The latest scientific installations of 'big science' are already starting to create a flow of data to be processed: for example, the already mentioned Large Hadron Collider in 2012 created 22 petabytes of data, while the SKA radio telescope that is supposed to be completed in 2024 will create more than 1 exabyte of data per day (this is more than all the Internet traffic for an entire day at present).**

What is most important is that patterns based on data flows can produce systems themselves of artificial intellect that conduct the processing of mass data. The Cambridge-based company Nutonian's Eureqa System is an example of this type of solution.*** This system is capable of producing scientific laws based on Big Data analysis: for example, in 2009 tests, the system was able to 'rediscover' the second law of Newton mechanics in a matter of hours.*[1] In this sense, a change takes place in the role of the researcher who transitions from finding patterns within experimental data to designing experiments and to controlling the search.

Scientists making the transition to processing qualitative data will mean increasing the intensity of their intellectual labor, roughly the same as the transition that is taking place in other industries from manual labor to mechanical, and from mechanical to robotechnics. Therefore, the pragmatics of managing science will force researchers (and research sponsors) to move down this path.

2. An additional decrease in expenses for conducting research is also possible through network allocation, which more efficiently combines existing research resources. This process has already begun, and several modern formats can be mentioned, including the following:

- The already mentioned 'virtual' laboratories. These are general use digital models whose access can be organized for any interested research group, at least as part of the national science system or large research consortiums (for example two digital models of brain activity are being built on the same logic, namely the European Human Brain Project and the American BRAIN Initiative);

* As the next step after experimental science (first paradigm, from the 16th to the end of the end of the 18th centuries), theoretical (second paradigm, from the end of the 18th to the middle of the 20th centuries) and qualitative science (third paradigm, from the middle of the 20th to the beginning of the 21st century).

** http://www.researchtrends.com/issue-30-september-2012/international-council-for-science-icsu-and-the-challenges-of-big-data-in-science/

*** http://www.nutonian.com/

*[1] http://www.wired.com/2009/04/newtonai/

* See. https://www.
gov.uk/government/
uploads/system/
uploads/attachment_
data/file/249715/
bis-13-861-big-sci-
ence-and-innovation.
pdf

** https://www.
zooniverse.org/about

*** http://hubble.
galaxyzoo.org/story

*1 https://scicast.org/#!/
about

- Remote laboratories (a significant number of radio telescopes in the United States is already operating remotely).* Within the framework of a number of big science objects (ex. LHC), it is possible to collect 'requests' for research from remote research collectives. Finally, remote laboratories allow allocating risks when conducting dangerous research.

- Involving users, including non-professional scientists, is becoming a very important new tool in cognition as a new stage in citizen science. The agenda now calls for using 'collective intellect' to resolve complex scientific problems. The Zooniverse**, which has been in development since 2007, is meant for searching for new and important scientific solutions (the website Galaxy Zoo, which allowed for creating the broadest classification of known galaxies and to discover a number of new space objects, was the first stage of this project)*** At the beginning of 2013, Harvard University researchers used users' creativity for a calculative biology problem (Lakhani et al., 2013). The SciCast platform, launched at late 2013, allows making crowd-sourced scientific forecasts regarding important research problems (provided that the problems themselves are dissected by artificial intelligence that scans relevant scientific literature for the emergence of new ideas and concepts.*1 In all likelihood, many research projects await us in the coming years that are based on 'collective intelligence.'

In the future, the model of allocated scientific resources could create an open experiments market (that the appropriate exchange and recommendation system would support) ,based on which experimental resources are proposed both in regards to big science objects and research teams, standard laboratory equipment, and engaged amateur scientists.

3. **Reorganizing the science publications system.** A notable number of scientific works is related to the researcher participation in communications within the scientific community (conferences and scientific journals). The proliferation of digital technologies is beginning to alter the standards of scientific communication by allowing increasing the transparency in the scientific process and scientists' responsibility for their outcome. Research and development materials of countries where serious scientific research is conducted are virtually entirely converted into digital archives and indexed (although only page by page at the moment), and control over plagiarism is provided based on published archives. We presume (largely by sharing Richard Lynch's point of view (Lynch, 2009) that the following standards of knowledge organization will become widespread by 2020.

- Reorganizing the form of scientific articles by transitioning to complete hypertext structures (given that the vast majority of articles are already being circulated and read digitally, today's pre-Internet citation standards in scientific journals do not withstand any criticism);

- As a result, publishing results could be organized through threads where you can track a line of arguments and hold discussions in real time (and not only and the end of the yearly cycle for editors and reviewers);

- Integrating raw research data (measurements, calculations, visualizations, video observations, etc.) and using structural models in scientific publications (including being able to reverify an outcome or to further promote something based on such outcome);

- Proliferating structural models as independent objects of scientific achievement presentations, and developing the means to index them (as the format of 'virtual laboratories' develops, we also expect the emergence of a search engine for scientific structural models, similar to the existing search engines for articles and databases).

As a result, there will be a change in the perception of what a scientific contribution is. The latter can be done not only as a publication, but also through an idea voiced in a group discussion, as a data set, or as a contribution to common digital models. This allows assessing research performance not only on the basis of the number of publications or citation rating (but also, for example, on the basis of the number of accesses to a digital model or of post ratings in online discussions).

In the near future, the opportunities for tracking individual (and group) contributions to creating scientific results (including to discoveries) will be significantly broadened through the complete indexation of intermediate developments and scientific contacts between researchers/collectives and the accumulation of stories of interaction (hence, the chance is emerging to 'half-automatically' assemble recognition of a contribution or of intellectual property rights). Moreover, proliferating end-to-end digital environments that accompany the entire research process allows establishing best practices and introducing common quality standards for the discipline (incorporated into the digital environment). Both processes have already essentially taken place in the field of applied science and technological developments, and in the near future could become common practice for any scientific sphere.

### 3.5.3 Surmounting the 'curse of the Tower of Babel?'

Digitalization in the described logic partially deals with science's existing problems as far as increasing its performance is concerned, but at the same time risks exacerbating the 'curse of the Tower of Babel,' because when transition to 'automated' scientific work, the volume of results will only increase.

The collapse of common perceptions (both society's and researchers' themselves) about the scientific world map is the main problem of this 'curse.' In essence, the whole is being replaced by a host of fragments that is only marginally connected together. Even now are researchers from adjacent fields able to conduct research on the same subject, but not have any idea about each other's results. This problem is especially palpable in research of complex systems, such as population biology, psychology, and science about society, or in such broad fields that require uniform grounds, such as the physical sciences.

Among other things, the division of scientific communication is being made difficult by the existing policy of journal publishers who restrict access to materials, their indexation, and the integration of new formats for presenting results. Of course, journals have a number of advantages, including a long-standing reputation and policy, groups of editors and reviewers, and a constant audience consisting of the professional community. Moreover, their figures are integrated into the metrics of managing science (and researchers are forced to look to publications if they want to advance their career). What is clear, however, is that journals in the long term do not have any strategic advantages over open platforms such as arXiv, where researchers can publish their results. This is because it can be made much easier on open platforms for the scientific community to discuss materials, review them and rate them, and have cross citation.

The main challenge for science is to ensure systemic theoretical generalizations of results that retain the integrity of the 'science front.' Wikipedia, where the user community is able to retain quality and relevant cases or describe approaches for most topics, is the first example of such generalizations (collections). To be fair, we will say that the Knol project, released in 2007 by Google—the creation of an lone standing Wiki by professional researchers specially selected for writing articles—failed and was shutdown in 2012 most likely because of not having a critical mass of the community needed for operating wiki-mechanisms). It can be said that the formula for promising scientific communication in the coming years is arXiv + Wiki-collections.

Further advancement in structuring science will depend on whether (and if yes, then when) a technical solution will be found for segmenting the Internet. Our base prediction (see section 2.2.2) relies on the presumption that several variations of such technologies will be created before the end of the 2010s, and that these solutions will allow overcoming the many years of stagnation in the field of the construction of artificial intelligence.

If the expected breakthrough in semantic technologies will be made, then it is to the organization of scientific knowledge that new developments will first and foremost be applied. The situation could develop in line with the following scenario:

- First, there will be the possibility to build 'science maps,' in which semantic technologies identify the meanings of each publication or development, cluster them according to their foundations, and then build bridges between individual developments by 'sewing' them together into a uniform meaning field. The first such developments have already been created: for example, Eric Berlow and Sean Gourley showed how an agenda of hot topics in technological and cultural development can be taken from the presentations of TED conference speakers based on semantic clusterization;*

* https://www.ted.com/talks/eric_berlow_and_sean_gourley_mapping_ideas_worth_spreading

- Second, since this very process of building on meaning links is very similar to creating 'ready-made products' for wiki-articles, artificial intelligence could become the creator (or co-creator at the initial steps) of wiki-collections that generalize perceptions of individual disciplines;

- Third, the working process of scientific collectives (as a rule, allocated and during the entire stage, from establishing the problem to presenting the final results) can be accompanied by such semantic systems that determine the promise of developments and their place in big 'knowledge maps' that set the requirements for the current research step, organize the intermediate performance results, consolidate them with the contexts of other collectives' performance, analyze the weak spots, development holes, etc. (at this stage, which we expect to be within the next 10 years, the role of artificial intelligence in collective work will be so noticeable that some collectives will indicate it as a co-author*);

- Fourth, if there is an end-to-end system for indexing preceding scientific (experimental and theoretical) results and digitizing intermediate results of research, and collections generalizing them, then existing publication practice is fairly rapidly becoming out of date and inefficient. A significant amount of scientific articles and monographs are dedicated to plunging into the context (links and citations), while they themselves fulfill the role of collecting results, namely acting as intermediaries between the live work of a researcher/scientific group and the scientific community. When completely digitizing the process and results of scientific works, and when having semantic systems accompany this work, then a scientific article as a form of communication is superfluous. It is not 'committing to text' that becomes the knowledge criterion, but rather the 'committing to digital' (most likely are complex digital models, namely information processing algorithms). This is virtually the 'end of the Guttenberg era.'

We will establish the situation that we are in.

In the 4th century B.C., Aristotle by himself wrote a corpus of texts encompassing virtually the entire aggregate of knowledge of the ancient Greeks, from zoology and physics to the theory of theater, poetry, politics, state administration, logic, and ethics. Several dozen authors wrote the 18th century French encyclopedia, which as envisioned by its author Denis Diderot was supposed to present all the existing knowledge about the world. There are several million researchers in the world being published in international and national scientific journals. There are approximately 20 million Wikipedia editors (with roughly 300 thousand of them writing actively). Moreover, none of the authors (and none of the people alive today) can image the completeness of the organization of human knowledge or the correlation of various disciplines between themselves.

The 'scientific world map' in the way that schools and universities have been presenting it since the early 20th century — a uniformity of perceptions about how the world is organized, developed upon materialistic and secular prerequisites — is starting to fall apart; however, there is no way back to mythological and magical thought (although there will periodically be attempts to increase the presence of the religious component of education in schools, to teach creationism instead of the modern theory of evolution, etc.); the artificial technological environment that people created is too complex, and fragmented mythological and magical thought cannot withhold it. The place for a 'new Aristotle is still vacant, and it is most likely of all for the indicated reasons that semantic artificial intelligence will take this place (although there is another possibility that we will discuss in section 3.7.3 that people at the next stage of development will be able to occupy this place: neurocollectives based on communities developed according to special rules and linked through neurotechnologies).

* One of the Hong-Kong-based investment funds, Deep Knowledge Ventures, has already nominated AI as a member of its Board of Directors in May 2014 (http://deepknowledgeventures.com/)

Whatever the case, we can point to the post-Greevsky stage of science's development as the hypothetical 'fifth paradigm:' when dealing with data in the world of high-intensity data is bound by semantic technologies, and adjusting 'machines that deal with meanings' capable of creating various data processing models in the context of using them in economics and culture is the main area of work.

This stage, which will onset (given social inertia) within 25 to 30 years, sees a significant portion of practices and rules, to which we have become accustomed relating to 'good science' but which simply were substantiated by past choices made by scientific organizers and administrators (what is called the QWERTY effect*), lose meaning. The line between theoretical and applied science is effaced definitively, and the very essence of 'fundamental' science completely changes as well. Constructing productive working ontologies for assembling data processing models becomes the role of 'fundamental' scientists (together with the systems of semantic artificial intelligence that support them); but these data and models are used immediately by conditional 'applied' scientists, engineers, technological businessmen, and managers for creating new technologies and products based on such technologies or for making administrative decisions.

'Live models' built around communities of practice and continuously being updated by semantic artificial intelligence based on collected data about the world and human practices are becoming the standard for working with knowledge. We will also note that as 'live' models proliferate, the textbook culture virtually dies, because the textbook establishes molds of past knowledge and always lags behind live practice. Conveying knowledge-in-practice (and the grounds necessary for assimilating this knowledge) must rely on communities of practice, on the condition that the integrity of these individual fields of knowledge in their common frame of science is withheld by the position of the 'new Aristotle.' Therefore, practice itself, a sort of 'training in battle' will be the main method for conveying knowledge for adults; game universe-based simulators that integrate digital models of reality within themselves (in application with new models of school education, which we talked in section 3.4.1) will fulfill this role for those assimilating the 'base,' namely conditional (!) 'school children' and 'students.'

The particularity of this new world is that digital 'live' models allow for creating all the more exact reflections of reality and all the most perfected technologies, but the mechanics of the models themselves is passed onto the apparatus level and is all the less comprehensible for researchers themselves. The technological environment is 'coming to life' (in the sense that in terms of complexity it is becoming comparable with live creatures and ecosystems) and is becoming a partner in cognition for us.

Futurologist and Astrophysicist Alexandr Panov, in making an argument very close to the one made in the introduction to this section (section 3.5.1), claims that science as a progressive phenomenon in the near future will forfeit its leadership and 'some other leader whom we still do not know anything about should come take its place.'** We believe that the live practice itself of civilization's development in various domains of human activities is becoming this 'leader' (a sort of 'progressorship'),*** for which rejuvenated science will be not so much a 'life teacher,' as much a source of solutions for social and personal development.

* http://www.econ.ucsb.edu/~tedb/Courses/Ec100C/DavidQwerty.pdf

** http://2012.gf2045.ru/read/120/

*** A term from the novels of Arkady and Boris Strugatsky that means 'agents of change' who consciously help take society to a higher level in developing technologies and social practices.

# 3.6 ENCLOSING TECHNOLOGY: NEUROWEB*

*We are evolving to meta-intelligence group-minds*
**Peter Diamandis**, Businessman
Founder, Singularity University

## 3.6.1 **The cognitive revolution: the future starts now**

In a certain sense, all existing learning technology—be it oral lectures, textbooks, or multimedia online courses—are intermediaries between the person with the knowledge or skill and the person who wants to assimilate it. The dream of many science fiction writers is skills that you can obtain immediately, just as in the famous movie The Matrix, where the main character instantaneously studies Kung-Fu by downloading it into his nervous system, or in Larry Niven's story The Fourth Profession, where taking alien memory pills allow the characters to student translation skills and even 'miracle-making.'** We presume that roughly the same science-fiction storylines will become a reality before our very eyes within the coming 15 to 20 years through mastering and proliferating potentially cognitive technologies currently being developed (and that we already described in section 2.2.4). It is entirely natural that these technologies, if they are to be made a reality, will force us to reconsider the model for education to a much greater extent than what has been listed above; however, in order for our discussion to make practical sense, it is worth reviewing only the technologies that are in fact accessible for the general public or that will become accessible in the coming years, as well as their possibilities as part of models of education.

1. **Neurointerfaces**. The idea that nervous system signals can be recorded directly from the nervous system dates back to scientific physiological works of the mid-20th century, when their first neuron models emerged, although even in the 19th century physiologists used extra-stimulation of the brain and nervous tissue to determine their functions. Beginning in the 1970s, a number of powerful instruments would emerge for studying the brain non-invasively, such as magnetic resonance imaging, magnetoencephalography, and eletroencephalography, which in the past several years have been supplemented with a powerful optogenetics tools that permits 'turning on' individual neurons. Brain research and the successes of neurosurgery allowed for addressing the potential of neurointerfaces, namely devices that directly link the nervous system with technical devices. And although the idea of applying neurointerfaces caught the imagination of science fiction writers right away, it was only in the second half of the 2000s that they began to be actually applied. It is important that technologies that to this day are limited in their application (mainly clinical and military) can become truly large-scale technologies. Users' understandable fear of invasive solutions (inserting chips directly into the brain), caused mostly by culture, was one of the hurdles for proliferating these technologies. In recent years, neurotechnology's potential*** has been realized by leading players in the IT and medical industries, while we justifiably can expect to see large-scale neurosolutions, some of which we will describe below, in the foreseeable future.

*This section was prepared based on the work of the Russian NeuroWeb group (to be presented as the Report on the Future of the NeuroWeb in 2016)

** This story was written in the early 1970s, when the preservation of memories on unique RNA molecules was the main hypothesis regarding the composition of memory. Fortunately or unfortunately, this hypothesis later turned out to be wrong (Rose, 1993).

*** As well as their predecessors in the field of biometrics and personalized health monitors

There are several applications of neurointerfaces that will impact the development of this area in the coming years:

a. Medical applications. The medical sphere is one where applying neurointerfaces is very sought after and where users are forced to overcome their fear. Some neuroimplants, such as cochlear implants, have already become widely used, while others, such as cyber-artificial prostheses controlled by brain signals, were used for the first time in 2010. It can be expected that initial success in creating neuroprotheses for lost limbs and sensory organs will take root, including as prosthesis production and operating become less expensive.

Moreover, non-invasive solutions that serve to rehabilitate the disabled are gaining acceptance. In particularly, in Paul Bach-y-Rita's famous series of works, patients with damage to the vestibular apparatus had a prosthesis created for them that transferred the sense of balance to a stimulator placed on the tongue. The patients would gradually relearn how to use their sense of balance and even rehabilitated their ability to keep their balance without the stimulator through the neuroplasticity effect (Doidge, 2007). In the same way, using exoskeletons controlled by interfaces (ex. eLEGS by the company EKso-Bionics) can allow patients with spinal damage to move, and possibly, in some cases to restore their mobility.

b. Military and industrial application. Neurointerfaces are intriguing militarily for controlling complex battle equipment, including remote control battle robots. DARPA had been financing developments in the field of neurointerfaces since the 1970s, and now this work is producing a lot of practical results. In particularly, prototypes of effective exoskeletons for use in battle have already been developed (ex. XOS2 by the company Raytheon), and as well as systems for controlling military drone.* Moreover, DARPA is supporting work on such projects as remote control anthropomorphic robots through neurointerface (it was declared that the first models of such robots would be released by the end of the 2010s)** and silent communication interfaces between soldiers on the battlefield using Silent Talk neurointerfaces.*** As opposed to large-scale commercial use, military use fully allows the use of invasive interfaces.

Neurointerfaces can be used not only on the battlefield, but also in industry. For example, control of industrial robots operating in hazardous environments can be organized more efficiently using the same technologies as applied in battle robots. Moreover, neurointerface control allows building productive operator groups to control complex industrial facilities. Neurointerfaces can also be used as a support tool for distributed groups conducting complex industrial developments.

c. The entertainment industry. The first large-scale neurointerfaces emerged in the computer industry at the end of the 2000s as input-output devices for attaining new boundaries of the game experience. A number of companies (including Emotiv, NeuroSky, and Neural Impulse Actuator) offer devices that are meant for controlling

* http://news. nationalpost. com/2013/06/05/ thought-con- trolled-helicop- ter-shows-poten- tial-of-brain-pow- ered-devices/

** http://www.wired. com/danger- room/2012/02/ darpa-sci-fi/

*** http://www.nytimes. com/2011/09/18/ magazine/the-cy- borg-in-us-all. html?pagewant- ed=all&_r=0

game characters: by presenting the corresponding patterns of movement, you can make your character run, stop, turn around, jump, shoot, and more. Others offer neurogames, where the player makes an object move through relaxation or exertion (the most famous of such games is MindBall, which is a battle between two players, with the winner being whoever is able to relax the most). It is presumed that as such game devices become less expensive, they will become widely popular in the coming five years, along with more accustomed input-output devices (we also concede that the emergence of game solutions based on neurointerfaces in the coming years will engender the 'neurosport' phenomenon, with neurogame tournaments that with time will become very popular entertainment).

2. **The body as an interface** (biomonitors, BF, and more). In addition to neurointerfaces themselves, employing body patterns and parameters as input-output devices is one of the extremely promising fields. It is clear that existing interfaces (monitors, keyboards, computer mice, etc.) are temporary solutions (what is more, they cause a lot of additional problems, such as obesity from a sedentary lifestyle, deteriorated vision because of working with a monitor, etc.). Technological development will move toward 'naturalizing' interfaces. The game industry is proposing the first such solutions, in particularly solutions such as Wii and Kinect, which allow turning player movement into game action perceived by the computer.

Wearables are one of the most promising markets for computer equipment in the coming decade. This market's volume in 2012 had already drawn near to a billion dollars, and it is expected that it will increase roughly 20-fold by 2016 (from the current 14 million to 300 million devices).* Wearables allow for recording any bodily indicators, processing them and returning them to the user. This allows making unperceived bodily processes perceivable and controllable. In particular, wearable accelerometers, often combined with heart-rate monitors, that allow for determining the level of the user's physical activity (Adidas, Nike, Fitbit, and others make such devices) have already become widely use. Other devices (ex. Tap Tap) allow transferring tactical information. The third type of devices monitors your health and allows providing timely help. For example, Sano Intelligence is a device that allows for continuously monitoring glucose levels, the kidneys, and metabolism levels for diabetes patients.** Healbe, a Russian device, was considered one of the promising wearable devices that allow tracking how many calories you have consumed and burned in real time, which permits arranging one's diet and physical activity in a completely new way.***

The ability in real time to give feedback (at the least provide information about the body's condition, but oftentimes as will give instructions (including non-verbal) about the recommended state) is the advantage of wearable devices. For example, wearable devices are able to monitor stress levels and give a signal when a person has low stress, high stress, and what will help the person lower their stress level. Namely, an educational scenario can be built into wearable biomonitoring devices with biological feedback (BF) that teaches the users the 'right' behavior. This allows for creating various educational products meant, for example, to teach the user so-called resource states: the state of being highly concentrated, relaxed, mobilized, etc. We review the possibilities for using cognitive technologies in education below.

The large-scale proliferation of wearable devices is also important because it is respon-

* http://www.businessinsider.com/wearables-create-new-mobile-markets-2013-9

** http://go.gigaom.com/rs/gigaom/images/wearable-computing-the-next-big-thing-in-tech.pdf

*** https://www.indiegogo.com/projects/healbe-gobe-the-only-way-to-automatically-measure-calorie-intake

sible for a large volume of content in communications networks that is related to new sensor channels: if content originally was text, graphics, and sound, then thanks to 'wearable' devices content is now tactile, motor-operated, and even connected to the sense of balance, sense of space, or various emotions. These new types of content will have their own packaging and information transfer protocols that will begin playing all the more of an important role as neurocommunications expand.

## 3.6.2 Cognitive technologies: the potential for education

1. **Treating age-related dysfunctions and fitness for the brain.** Proliferating technologies that operate directly with our body and mind will directly depend on society's willingness to accept them; however, it is cognitive technologies that can provide a solution for one of the most serious problems of the coming century. Above we discussed the trend of the increase in the average life expectancy to 100 years and more, which really raises the question of the productiveness of the elderly (at least of their activity and being engaged in life). Decreasing intellectual productivity with age, and age-related diseases of the nervous system such as Alzheimer's and Parkinson's, are becoming all the more prevalent in industrially developed countries. According to the Alzheimer's Association, annual losses from Alzheimer's disease are roughly 1% of global GDP.[*] A number of studies show that the brain is one of the organs whose functioning depends on the intensity of its use (use it or lose it), and therefore regular cognitive activity, especially in old age, helps prevent age-related dementia (ex. (Wilson et al., 2013)). One of the options for creating such activity is to organize 'brain fitness' special education programs.[**]

The 'brain fitness' industry is made up of program applications and technological solutions for developing various cognitive capabilities, including memory, mental arithmetic, pattern recognition, etc.[***] This industry is becoming a new, fast growing market in developed countries, and its size by 2015 could reach 5 billion dollars.[*1] Not only (and for the moment not so much) people at risk for dementia are demanding 'brain fitness,' but so are people in the active phase of life, for whom this fitness is become as much of a mandatory part of their lives as fitness for their bodies. Special games and tests for developing attention, memory, the ability to concentrate, quickly relax, and to 'turn on one's creativity' are increasing all the more in the App Store, Google Play, and Windows Store. Lumosity, which offers education programs through daily training for memory, attention, information processing speed, etc., with the training content adapted to individual weak spots, is one of the most successful providers. More than 40 million users have signed up for Lumosity programs, while its smartphone application has been downloaded more than 10 million times.[*2] We presume that this market will actively grow in the coming years, and that program solutions such as Lumosity, Mind Sparke, and BrainHQ will gain in popularity among all age groups.

Moreover, several companies in the past two years have announced the release of portable and inexpensive devices for monitoring and controlling human health that are positioned as both neurointerfaces and as devices that are a base for brain fitness: for

[*] http://www.alz.co.uk/media/100921

[**] http://todaysgeriatricmedicine.com/archive/020110p22.shtml

[***] A prototype of this industry can be found as Sunday crossword puzzle applications and Sudoku collections

[*1] http://sharpbrains.com/blog/2012/05/02/brain-spa-trend-travel-for-mental-fitness/

[*2] http://techcrunch.com/2013/04/03/founder-stories-lumositys-mike-scanlon-on-exercising-the-brain/

example, Melon*, Emotiv Insight**, and others. Commercial biological feedback devices have been on the market for many years, although it was only last year that medical quality could be 'packaged into a convenient product for less than a cell phone. Light and sound stimulation devices, such as line of mind machines from the company Mindplace that are specially developed to work with the iPad and iPhone, are also products from 2012. The trend of developing these products stems not so much from the emergence of technological possibilities, as much from the ideology and values of modernity all the more including not only the physical in the concept of health, but also the cognitive.

2. **Learning resource states and working with attention.** The connection between mental states or optimal psychiatric work routines and activity efficiency has never been a secret, but for a long time corporate personnel management practices and education programs ignored this sphere. The situation, however, is beginning to change, and fairly quickly. In particularly, the proliferation of meditation practices in the corporate world and the discussion of spirituality as a factor of labor productivity*** are the law of change.*1 In particularly, Google founded the Search Inside Yourself institute of leader programs, which teaches meditation to engineers, and this course is one of the most sought after at the company because it allows company employees to deal with stress more efficiently and be more productive.*2

Cognitive technologies provide new and very effective ways for learning resources states. In particularly, the company Wild Divine has developments that use the BF tool to quickly and independently study meditation practices.*3 The company's products are a combination of video courses that famous meditation instructors teach, and simple videogames, where winning is done by entering the targeted states of relaxations, pacification, concentration, and mobilization. In addition to learning 'traditional' states well known since the times of ancient meditation practices, some business schools are starting to practice teaching executives special states for making decisions, such as the 'state of clarity' (Kopeikina, 2005) using BF devices. The capability to identify and control one's own states by shaping states for creativity, decision-making, vacation, etc., is gradually becoming the inherent competences of a high-level manager, and therefore the demand for the appropriate education programs is on the rise. Videogames that teach self-control using BF could be popular not only among adults, but also among children. For example, the game RAGE Control was very successful in teaching children with emotional disorders the skill of anger control.*4

In addition to managing resource psychophysiological states, cognitive technologies can be used for teaching attention management. The oversaturated information environment is a serious challenge for the human mind, since there are many media products that hack the neurophysiological mechanisms of attention management by superfluously employing search and orientation reflexes (Doidge, 2007). As a result, many adults start to suffer disorders related to 'flooding' on the Internet, while children are diagnosed with ADHD (Attention Deficit and Hyperactive Disorder). The capability to control one's attention, as an ability that increases competition in society, is steadily becoming all the more valuable, and the proliferation of literature and workshops on ways to concentrate attention and manage perception, for example, are evidence of this. BFB tools have been clinically proven as effective in treating ADHD*5. Some of these developments have been used in commercial

* http://greatist.com/health/melon-mind-fitness-tracker-preview-part-one

** http://www.kickstarter.com/projects/tanttle/emotiv-insight-optimize-your-brain-fitness-and-per

*** For an expanded list of scientific work, see http://www.eegspectrum.com/applications/adhdadd/

*1 http://www.wisdom-2summit.com/

*2 http://www.wired.com/business/2013/06/meditation-mindfulness-silicon-valley/

*3 http://www.wilddivine.com/iom-feedback-hardware/iom-active-feedback-hardware/

*4 http://www.eurekalert.org/pub_releases/2012-10/bch-vg102412.php

*5 For an expanded list of scientific work, see http://www.eegspectrum.com/applications/adhdadd/

applications, such as the company Play Attention, which uses neurobiological feedback to teach children attention management, including as part of specialized school education modules.* We believe that within the coming 10 years, especially considering the emergence of a large group of 'children brought up by tablets' (see section 2.3.5), demand for similar education programs will grow significantly, and they will become a part of standard training programs in schools, universities, and business schools.

Furthermore, a number of cognitive technologies are meant to expand the range of attention by transferring signals from the unconscious to the conscious. The DARPA CT2WS project, where army binoculars are incorporated with an EEG interface capable of noticing a soldier's unconscious reaction to events in his field of vision that allows to more than double the subject's capacity to identify potential dangers (during field tests, soldiers with CT2WS binoculars noticed 91% of dangerous objects, in comparison with 47% of dangers that soldiers with regular binoculars noticed).** It is evident that the field for applying such solutions goes far beyond military purposes. For example, 'comprehending the incomprehensible' is very important in operator work (ex. managing complex industrial facilities) when public transportation enters metropolises, when difficult negotiations are held, and even as a basic skill for every person who wants to take care of their health and well-being. Therefore, we believe that 'attention management schools' that combine traditional tools such as meditation courses and new tools such as augmented reality devices with modules of neurobiological feedback can by the early 2020s become a sought-after format.

3. **Objectivizing the parameters of the academic process.** The ability to objectively assess the education process and its results is one of the most important aspects in applying cognitive technologies as far as education foresight is concerned. In particularly, in other section (2.2.6 and 3.6.3) we wrote that a student's psychophysiological parameters, which show the concentration and mobility level (neurointerfaces essentially do not need to be used for this, since biomonitoring bracelets that track the pulse and level of the skin galvanizing reaction deal with it), can be used for assessing the quality of the education process, its 'flowability.' This allows, for example, for determining to what extent a class gets students interested, and to adapt the content on the fly so that students are kept engaged. With simultaneous education given group work on a project, various solutions can be proposed that show the objective engagement of each participant in the work and how energized the group is as a whole. With asynchronized learning systems, including simulators and MOOC platforms, biometric data can become one of the parameters of education statistics that are used to adjust education courses to be in line with where the student is at (speed of conveying material, difficulty of text assignments, etc. Sometimes the recommendation is to postpone the education session until another time if the student is tired and cannot comprehend the material).

Another very popular ability that cognitive technologies will be able to provide in the future is to objectively control whether the student has assimilated any given material or skill. If the student has been working with a neurointerface for a long time, then you can create an individual brain map and use it to track whether there is brain arousal in areas that are responsible for any given types of knowledge and skills. Namely, you can record

* http://www.playattention.com/

** http://www.forbes.com/sites/katiedrummond/2012/09/18/darpa-threat-recognition/

how learning changes the brain's structure. It is evident that as soon as it becomes possible to make objective measurements, it will be possible to manage the process. In the future, we can expect the development of individualized high-speed learning programs made directly for the morphology of a subject's nervous system. We are still rather far from creating such tools, but the launch of two global brain morphology projects (the BRAIN Initiative in the United States, the Human Brain Project in Europe, and the DARPA programs, which were described in the previous section, such as Silent Talk) make it possible to expect that the first products that register the objective assimilation of knowledge could be released in the coming 10 to 15 years.

4. **The psychopharmacology and the second psychodelic\* revolution.** At present, psychopharmacology is more a tool for clinical psychologists who get people out of serious psychological disorders or compensate the effects of systemic neurophysiological problems, such as ADHD or dementia. Psychopharmacology's resource, however, is grossly undervalued by the education system, and legal (or specially developed) psychoactive substances could become one of the important educational tools meant to fortify human health's capabilities and abilities: memory, attention, concentration, creativity, and other cognitive functions.

Some of these substances with a background in nature have already long been part of our accustomed ration, and we cannot reflect completely on their role in increasing our work performance; the most well known of them is tea and coffee. For many people, a morning cup of coffee is an indispensible part of self-regulation, while tobacco and alcohol serve this purpose for others. A whole line of substances, some of which have obvious negative effects, have become inaccessible for most people, while its active functional substances have become part of medicinal drugs. At the same time, pharmaceuticals are not standing still offering the market all the more safe and effective medicines for normalizing weakened cognitive functions that often also strengthen a healthy person's cognitive functions. Many of these substances are part of the class of so-called 'nootropics:' Medicines that have a specific activating impact on integrated brain functions and that stimulate learning, improve (restore) memory and mental activity, make the brain more durable against aggressive influences and hypoxia, and strengthen the connection between the cortex and the subcortex. Nootropics do not have the expressed psychostimulating or sedative effective. In many developed countries, in particularly in Great Britain, students are already actively using nootropics to improve their academic results.\*\* Therefore, the academic community is starting to discuss the legality of using nootropics, and some authors believe that using them is the same as cheating on an exam or plagiarism.\*\*\*

It is left for us to only note, on the same exact grounds that using coffee in offices gives some workers an 'unfair' boost and increases their competitiveness compared to the rest, while using aspirin gives people with a cold an 'unfair' opportunity to recover their ability to work more quickly. Moreover, All of medical pharmacology 'unfairly' increases a person's chances to survive. Should we turn our back on new technological possibilities? The answer is clear: the history of human civilization from the very beginning is the breaking of established practice by people who have risked using new possibilities, including those created by man himself.

\* The original term proposed by psychiatrist Humphry Osmond in a written correspondence with Aldous Huxley soundly like psychedelic ('spiritual clarification'). One of the leaders in the 'psychedelic revolution,' T Leary, proposed the variation 'psychodelic,' which he thought sounded better. This name was much less popular in the United States and Europe, although it caught on in Russia. We prefer using a term that indicates, first and foremost, the therapeutic and transformational application of psychoactive substances.

\*\* http://www.theguardian.com/education/2009/oct/01/students-smart-drugs-boost-grades

\*\*\* http://www.neulaw.org/blog/1034-class-blog/3969-nootropics-use-in-educational-settings-and-implications-for-neurolaw.html

Since the early 1990s, research activity in the development of new nootropic and other psychoactive drugs has greatly increased. It can be presumed that the explosive development of biotechnologies will allow creating entire lines of harmless drugs in the coming decade that significantly strengthen man's cognitive functions, including given individual genetic particularities. In combination with classic and hardware resources for self-regulation (including biological feedback, light and sound stimulating hardware, transcranial magnetic stimulation hardware, etc.), these drugs will allow creating completely new way to learn by increasing the complexity and depth of education.

It is worth pointing out one more enticing capability. Developing DIY technologies (which we wrote about in section 2.3.3) will give rise to households having not only 3D printers for creating everyday items, such as clothing, devices, furniture, etc., but also biological molecular synthesizers capable of creating 'task-specific' individualized chemical drugs based on chemical 'sketches.' There are already around ten prototypes of such devices, and several more simple mass-produced models (for example, the CHIP chemical printer by Shimadzu); * one of the fathers of this field, Lee Cronin, claims that this 'chemputer' will allow doing for pharmaceuticals what Apple and iTunes did for the music industry: liberate developers from the oppression of 'industry monsters.' **

Of course, developing biotechnology draws us close to the ability to provide man with individually designed, safe, and effective tools that will model how the nervous system works, will be able to improve cognitive capabilities, accelerate rehabilitation after different types of stress and increase efficiency in carrying out not only tasks related to memory and attention stress, but also to creativity. Part of these substances will have features that are the same as modern stimulators or nootropics, while the other part will have purely recreational features (such as the substances described in the famous works of Alexander and Ann Shulgin (Shulgin & Shulgin, 1991);*** another part will be meant to study internal mental spaces. In other words, soon after the emergence of mainstream use pharm-printers, we can expect a new era of self-research using psychoactive substances synthesized for home use; what can be called the second psychedelic revolution. Since the times of the original psychedelic revolution at the end of the 1960s, which was a grassroots revolution and which caused the conservative part of society to react glaringly, the world has had time to prepare. Therefore, the second psychedelic revolution using the achievements of psychology, pharmacology, and pedagogy will be recognized, calm, and manageable, and its effects will be able to have a positive impact on social evolution and people's personal growth.

### 3.6.3 The emergence of NeuroWeb: the 'psycho-explosion,' psychosis, and the 'end of pedagogy'*1

The possibilities described in the previous section are based on 'near-future technologies' that already exist or that will emerge in the near future. We believe that these technologies will prepare human culture for 'future shock' related to the advent of a radically new environment of communication: the NeuroWeb. As we said in section 2.2.4, the NeuroWeb is a

---

* http://www.ssi.shimadzu.com/products/product.cfm?product=chip

** http://phys.org/news/2012-04-3d-diy-drugstores.html

*** The books PIHKAL and TIHKAL by Alexander and Ann Shulgin document the research of several thousand hallucinogenic drugs from a group of phenethylamine and tryptamine

*1 This section is a brief presentation of the results obtained by the Russian NeuroWeb group. The group's detailed material is provided at www.globalneuroweb.org

'technological inevitability,' the most important stage on the path to the 'Internet of everything.' As far as our civilization is concerned, however, the emergence of the NeuroWeb will mean a change in the rules of the game that will be even more radical than the advent of the Internet.

1. **The NeuroWeb is a new communicative environment.** We believe that the communication environment based on the direct interaction protocols of nervous systems (such as the 'thought transfer' protocol HTTP-2 described in section 2.2.4) will emerge in the coming 10 to 15 years. The first neurocollective projects that are still in demand (and first, of course, we will see assemblies of 'local' networks, and only then of global networks) will have a purely utilitarian meaning:

- First, these are communication environments for soldiers in battle, the first option for which is the already mentioned DARPA Silent Talk project. It is evident that these environments will include not only human soldiers, but also military robots (flying, running or crawling drones, such as military quadcopters or robots such as Big Dog and Cheetah that are currently being developed by Boston Dynamics for DARPA).* In other words, military groups armed with neurocommunications will be able to act as a single whole, where each member will know exactly where the other is, share pressing information with them without using words (including sharing their feelings, such as the feeling of anxiety) and controlling air or ground battle robots just like parts of their body.**

- Second, these are environments for controlling complex industrial facilities, such as automized factories, large ships, or space stations, where a small team of operators coordinates together to control various devices, including neathropomorphic devices. Such neorocollectives can be used for complex control tower operations such as to control air transportation traffic in an urban space with a sharp increase in the number of unmanned flying devices.

- Third, these are environments for creating new engineering developments, from airplanes to communicators, similar to the digital environments that already house industrial design and engineering in specific teams, but with expanded capabilities to work together at the early stages of development (when the generative design takes place).

In all instances, groups of neurocollectives, when they work on a clear goal, use digital communications environments and 'live models' of knowledge supported by artificial intelligence (similar to what was described in section 3.5.3); there are usually neanthropomorphic robot helpers that act as parts of the 'collective body.' The point of using neurocommunications protocols for these collectives is to accelerate decision coordination and making; this is so that neurocollectives can work as a whole. Exocortex technology — artificial parts of the psyche supported by machines and synchronized by natural psyche (ex. additional external memory, an 'expanding' sensory and effector system, auxiliary mental functions

* http://www.boston-dynamics.com/robot_bigdog.html

** Some of the possible solutions for these future battle groups can be seen in the recently released Call of Duty: Black Ops II, which takes place in 2025. The game was made using professional military experts, and one of the goals in making the game, according to its creators, was to model the methods for conducting future military special operations using new technologies. http://content.usatoday.com/communities/gamehunters/post/2012/05/interview-black-ops-ii-consultant-peter-singer

such as conducting complex calculations, etc.)—will play an important role in the emergence of such collectives. In essence, neurocollectives are nothing other than several human psyches linked by an exocortex into a uniform collective subject.

It stands to reason that applying civil protocols of neurocommunications (HTTP-2) will quickly go beyond applied industrial and scientific purposes, such as how the emergence of HTTP allowed the Internet to quickly go beyond scientific and professional communities. The NeuroWeb environment—a new Internet—will be built on inexpensive, large-scale neurointerfaces that by the early 2020s will become one of the standards for input-output devices. Of course, the entertainment industry will be the pioneer of proliferating new technologies, first and foremost the game industry and (similar to the penetration of the Internet), of course, the pornography industry. The emphasis here will be put on the abilities of total submergence in the experience (transferring not just video and audio, but also bodily sensations and even emotions), and on the ability to experience unusual (closer to psychedelic) sensations through stimulations of deeper zones of the brain. Furthermore, neurocollective technologies will be sought after as such in multi-user online games, where they will be used as a base for productive game teams to quickly be assembled.

It is evident that pioneers, who will offer services within the NeuroWeb for learning, communication, creativity, and group management, will begin to assimilate the NeuroWeb. The main difference from today's Internet will be that the NeuroWeb will be built on the communication of unique nervous systems without, in essence, it being mandatory to use a natural language, but rather using special unique languages that combine nervous system 'maps.' Therefore, communication will take place faster and more accurately, and it will be possible to 'express the inexpressible'; to pass on states to each other; to exchange not only verbal experiences and feelings, but also psychoemotional ones; to create complex and highly realistic sensations for each other, etc. It is most likely that the development of exocortex technologies, which are becoming a sort of 'external map' of our psyche, its intermediary in communications (at the same time it is highly likely that in the future, and learning will consist of joint and mutual learning of man himself and his exocortex), will become the foundation for all these processes. We believe that the emergence of such solutions is realistic within 15 to 20 years, namely by 2030-35.

There are now two main barriers on the path to building the NeuroWeb, and technological solutions, in all likelihood, will be found in the coming decade for both of them.

- First, this is the precision of the existing interface revolution. If an interface is invasive (such as an electrode in the brain cortex), then it is possible to determine down to the neuron where arousal is taking place, and through this compile a unique map of brain activity; arousal can be not only registered, but also created. Only the rare user, however, will agree to perform trepanation of the skull and insert electrodes into his brain. Only non-invasive neurointerfaces are acceptable for the majority of users, and their 'permissive capability' is extremely small: they can 'record' only signals regarding the arousal of large areas of the brain (ex. that are responsible for large movements but not for individual verbal patterns). Creating an interface through such devices as neural dust (microinvasive chips that are implanted by injection and that can provide a 'brain map' in high detail* is a variation that could be seen as the most acceptable. With time, as biocomputer interfaces develop, NeuroWeb access devices will become as natural as possible (roughly like 'neuro-bio-connectors' as with the fauna on the planet Pandora in the James Cameron's film Avatar).

* http://arxiv.org/
abs/1307.2196

- Second, since each brain is unique, there must be complete maps of individual nervous systems for each user when accessing the NeuroWeb. This requires calculation models that are much more powerful than existing silicon computers; however, the actively developing the quantum computer, in all likelihood, allows surmounting this problem.

If these problems will be resolved, then it is likely that a mass NeuroWeb will emerge that will begin to quickly spread 'over and above' the Internet and include all the more participants. People within the NeuroWeb will have colossal advantages over those outside of it in terms of understanding the ability to act and coordinate with others, just as it was with those who had access to telecommunications networks in previous generations, such as with the telegraph, telephone or Internet. We can only fathom indistinctly about what will happen when the NeuroWeb will become a part of our communicative reality (and a part of our bodies). Therefore, all further reasoning should be classified as science fiction; however, we will still run the risk of making several presuppositions, because as we said before, the emergence of the NeuroWeb promises to rewrite many norms of human practice, including norms of education.**

** We will stipulate
immediately that
this section is rather
futurologistic and we
call on viewing it as
more of a possible
'distant horizon' for
the development of
modern technologies
where neurological,
biological, and infor-
mational technolo-
gies come together.

2. **NeuroWeb threats, the psycho-divide and 'new luddites'.** Radical technologies are often perceived as a threat and sometimes as an apocalyptic threat (take the well-known quote about how railroad passengers would inevitable suffocate from the high speed). The NeuroWeb's threats have been described in many science fiction novels, played out in films and in computer games since the early 1970s, with one of the NeuroWeb participants ('neurohacker') gaining full control over the nervous system and body of another partici-pant, genuinely 'stealing one's identity,' being the most evident such threat. It is possible to imagine the threat of such 'neurohackers' implanting false memories, mental dysfunctions, programmable nightmares, and even an order to kill.

It goes without saying that the NeuroWeb could be a very dangerous space; however, life itself is dangerous. Technological security systems and rules are being created that can decrease possible risks in order to make life less dangerous. A car can serve as a means to kill or to commit suicide, so people first go to driving school, take an exam, and obtain their driver's license before hitting the road themselves. As for the NeuroWeb, it is most likely that the same principle will apply: school, exam, and obtaining access rights.

It is almost inevitable that when the NeuroWeb arrives, society will be split between those who are willing to take part in the new communicative environment and assume its advantages and possible 'side effects,' and those who will resist it. This is provided that there will be at least two obstacles to taking part: first, this is the fundamental capability to assimilate new communicative protocols; second, this is the willingness to do so (with all the possibilities and risks that stem from this). The NeuroWeb will divide the world into those who assimilate cognitive technology, and those who do not want to or cannot do this, similar to how the Internet divided society among those who have access to the web and those left on the wayside, what is called the 'digital divide.' We are calling the coming and highly likely divide the 'psycho-divide,' the threat of society dividing along the criterion of access, the ability to use, or the knowledge and capability to take advantage of a new generation of cognitive technologies, including communications technologies (NeuroWeb protocols), new individual ICT tools (neurointerfaces, intellectual agents, augmented reality based systems, etc.), and communications formats (education in NeuroWeb groups and life-long education).

As opposed to the 'digital divide,' the psycho-divide reflects a situation where not only the economic factor, but also first and foremost the psychological factor, are the important factor that determines on what side of the divide any given person will end up. The digital divide was a divide in access to ICT tools and activities that carried them out, and only to a small extent, through a divide in thinking (although we de-facto see a completely different user success rate in using digital space tools, and this success rate has to do with users' willingness to accept and apply new rules of the game). The NeuroWeb and the social practices related to it to a significantly greater extent transform a person's psychological tools, in particularly his thinking. The emergence in the foreseeable future (10-15 years) of new generation neurointerfaces, capable of interpreting a person's intentions and thoughts into various human and technical languages, completely changes the rules of the game by creating an environment for a much more profound disconnection of user groups according to types of thinking and languages used than even today's conflict of civilizations.

It is very likely that a part of society will begin to openly perceive the NeuroWeb as a threat at the early stages of the NeuroWeb's development. Moreover, this is happening even in regards to technologies that are the early predecessors of the NeuroWeb: there were several attacks in 2013 on people wearing Google Glass or with cyberprostheses.* Social conservatives resisting the development of cognitive technologies will become the forerunner of yet another stage in neo-luddism. This resistance could begin even before the widespread proliferation of neurotechnologies, anthropomorphic robots and total labor automation gain the status of a real challenge to civilization. A host of cognitive tech-nologies serves as the main point in the development of 21st century innovations. Even biotechnologies do not prove to be a very big interference in human nature, traditions and culture, and this includes new eugenics, which the Chinese government made a decision on in summer 2013. The merger of man and machine, the change in human psyche, the emer-gence of thinking and sensing machines, the transfer of linguistic functions to the techno-logical environment, and the modification of intellect and psyche are all a greater challenge to traditional consciousness than a sex change, making a bodily modification, and drastically lengthening life through biotechnologies. Technologies, in developing faster and faster, are ever increasing the divide between those who are on the front line of technological devel-opment and those who are bringing up the rear in this process. The divide will be much greater by the mid-2020s than today, while today it is already much more expressed than during the beginning of the digital divide. We believe, however, that the 'NeuroWeb elite' will be able to act in different time scales and in a different logic (although not separate from

* See http://io9.
com/5926587/
what-may-be-
the-worlds-first-
cybernetic-hate-
crime-unfolds-in-
french-mcdonalds

the rest of the world), which a priori will make resisting the NeuroWeb pointless (roughly in the same way as how now no one tries to counteract the Internet and digitalization despite the vast possible side effects).

What is very important to say is that the emergence of large stable neurcollectives is in no way a fantasy of 'psychonaut' fanatics, but rather a necessary step in civilization's development. The main problem with modern systems of social control is that in operating as a system to coordinate individual interests, they give preference to solutions that have quick output and work in the interests of specific people or small groups. Such control structures that operate in the majority's interests (regions, peoples, nations, and humanity as a whole) need to be created. This is, in essence, the condition for our civilization to survive, and a necessary step toward our civilization building a genuinely sustainable socio-economic system that does not allow for large-scale destructive conflicts (wars, genocides, etc.); a society that is in a productive dynamic equilibrium with nature, and at the same time preserves the internal capability to develop. If we want to achieve this goal, we must stimulate the development of groups that personify the 'soul of Humanity' and that are capable of acting productively and in concurrently over long periods of time. Creating the technical environment for such groups to emerge is the NeuroWeb's primary objective.

3. **The 'end of pedagogy' and the Psychozoic era.** In taking the risk of going too far (and we are intending this Report to be first and foremost a practical document and not an example of radical, transhumanistic futurology), we will briefly describe where the situation could go, if our technological forecasts turn out to be right.

First, fundamentally new forms of communication emerge in the NeuroWeb environment. Virtually since the beginning our existence, for likely several hundred thousand years has humanity lived in a culture of natural language that serves as a way to package the meanings of current activities and to preserve culture (namely the memory of previous generations). Over the past six thousand years, written language, the language of signs and symbols emerging over, above, and based on natural language, has been added to oral language, the language of oral signals. Education is a product of language just as, incidentally, all human culture is. This culture is configured to talking, reading, and writing texts; however, in the NeuroWeb (and maybe before it, in the Internet) we see the likely collapse of linguistic culture and the emergence in its place of post-linguistic communication. With the Internet, this is infographics, the developing field of a new package of meanings (not just in texts, but in complex visual and textual structures). With the NeuroWeb, this could even be the direct communication of meaning and feeling that sees natural language as a superfluous and inaccurate intermediary, and in its place there will be artificial language that is supported by artificial intellect only and exclusively in the communication of a specific group or even two subjects.

Post-linguistic communication makes super-fast learning and super-fast communication possible. In some cases this could be the super-fast download of knowledge and skills from 'external' carriers directly into the nervous system (as in the already mentioned scenes from The Matrix). In other cases, this could be several people learning together who are connected by the NeuroWeb to the neurocollective, where exchange and joint learning take place through super-fast and/or super-condensed communication that includes not only the verbal stratum, but also a stratum of directly exchanged feelings and experiences. It is evident that such education processes (if they are technically able to be implemented, and all the prerequisites are currently there to do so) will mean other roles for 'teachers' and 'students,' other meanings of the 'academic process,' 'result' and 'assessment.' In other words, as neurocollectives emerge, 'pedagogy as we know it' will lose its meaning, and 'experience engineers' will take the place of 'knowledge conveyors.' This new pedagogy, however, will emerge from network pedagogy that is taking shape right before our eyes thanks to the tools that we had talked about in the previous sections.

And finally, where will the emergence of the NeuroWeb take us? The NeuroWeb development trend clearly shows that communications between users will be much more dense than today. Neurocommunication protocols, neurointerfaces, and artificial intelligence are semantic translators, the use of psychofarms and adjusted ways in which our consciousness and thinking can lead to people's intellects being very closely interconnected (and with supporting technosystems) and at a many levels of consciousness. The main effect from this will be in 'bringing intellects together' and in changing the notion of 'identity.' Developing exocortex technologies that seamlessly supplement natural parts of the psyche with artificial components, and the emergence of external organs as additional sensors or robots controllable through an interface are all already blur the perceptions of the lines of one's own 'me.' When neurocommunications protocols unite several people, the lines between individuals also begin to be erased and the new reality of the 'neurocollective' emerges.

Let us imagine that the neurocollectives described above are structures that have features that are strange even by today's standards. They have individualized consciousnesses that are united into a uniform collective mental subject, and part of this subject is certainly artificial (artificial intelligence that supports communicative protocols). Such subject has many bodies, some of which are biological, while others are cybernetic (and are often even neanthropomorphic). There are processes within this subject that operate with its collective consciousness and its collective unconsciousness. This is the way that the conditional military unit or design group in 2030 will look; however, today's working groups would probably look no less exotic to our ancestors several hundred years ago.

Furthermore, the 'collective unconsciousnesses' preserved in the exocortex of such collective can have jointly created 'mental artifacts:' for example, states of high effectiveness that a group felt, or special sensations (such as the sense of time, the sense of crowd, etc.) that a group was able to develop in itself using biological feedback tools. This will allow for using neurocollectives not only for utilitarian commercial or battle objectives, but also for joint therapy, games, or studying unusual states of consciousness. It is very likely that new 'neuro-sectarians' will emerge among these neurocollectives that constantly support their own participants in the changed states of consciousness, in a type of 'collective desperation,' and 'collective therapeutists' that work with them and that will be able to bring these collectives to the area of productive communication.

Gradually developing technologies of collective neurocommunication will bring us to the emergence of special neurocollectives, which we call 'forests of consciousnesses,' because it will consist of a host of independent yet densely interconnected consciousnesses whose cognitive abilities will significantly surpass the capabilities of a single user and will be comparable in capacity with strong artificial intelligence. What will be the chief particularity of these 'forests of consciousnesses' will be that they will be the preferred form of existence for its individual participants, a type of 'tribe' or 'commune' built on a new technological base and with much greater connectivity between participants. A host of serious, general-systemic studies and program works, including the well-known Cybernetic Manifest by Valentine Turnchin and Cliff Joslyn (Turchin, Joslyn, 1989), in the past 30 years have predicted the emergence of such mental structures.

It may initially seem that the emergence of these 'forest of conciousnesses' scenarios are threatening (in literature similar phenomena in analogous with insects are sometimes called 'swarming intellect' or 'the ant hill consciousness'), but there is nothing scary about them. It is not difficult to understand that 'forests of counciousnesses' are possible only for people who achieve the greatest personal self-realization possible, because only such people will not have the contradictory motivation that creates possible 'opaqueness' (conditionally do something else besides the things that they feel a calling to do). In other words, the 'forest of conciousnesses' is the natural transition from individual consciousnesses to the collective without losing individual diversity, and the culmination of one's self-realization.

What is most likely of all is that experiments to create 'forests of consciousnesses,' in not being put together for a specific task but in being sustainably and continuously existing neurocollectives, will begin right after the NeuroWeb emerges (around 2030-35) and will gradually become all the more massive; within 10-15 years (roughly by 2045) they will succeed in creating the first truly collective meta-consciousness. And if this takes place (and in all likelihood this is the only evolutionary transition and will give humanity the chance to survive in the 21 century), then having such collectives emerge will mark 'the beginning of the end' not only for traditional education but also for many customary institutions and cultural norms. What is most likely of all is that, beyond this transition, there will also be 'new pedagogy' meant for self-learning and mutual learning in neurocollectives (it is evident that the very notion of learning in this case will become secondary, while joint development will become primary).

Today, in 2014, the emergence of 'forests of conciousnesseses' in just 20 years looks to be an improbable event; however, the practice of the information revolution shows that many improbable events take place earlier than planned. The NeuroWeb is both a threat and an opportunity. In this chapter we make what are currently too many futurological presumptions in discussing technologies, with the emergence of some of them in the coming years not being a given. Since this is an applied Report, we believe that it is necessary to keep an eye on this scenario (especially because creating leading technologies for it is within the priorities of countries that are the leaders in technologies), but the near and mid-term future possibilities, available now, need to be focused on. At the same time, the logic of evolutionary development shows that — sooner or later and through any given technological solutions — we and future generations will continue to move toward the 'Internet of everything.' The only question is whether we will go toward this progress blindly or with open eyes, and what principles will we put at the base of this movement, because the NeuroWeb environment is the environment of constant education where we teach each other for the sake of the common good; a principle that the systems of new education already coming into place are shaping.

## 3.7 THE IMAGE OF THE FUTURE: 'THE STUDENT'S PATH,' THE EDUCATIONAL TECHOENVIRONMENT, FINANCIAL TOOLS, AND NEW POSITIONS IN EDUCATION-2030

*Education is a process of living and not a preparation for future living*
**John Dewey**, My Pedagogic Creed

*Education is the understanding of life as an integral process*
**Jiddu Krishnamurti**, Education and the Significance of Life

In the sections above, we tried to show from different angles how future education could look. This is an education that is becoming more technological, international, highly individualized, being conducted in communities and within games. The education system is turning into an education sphere that surrounds a person for his entire life. Below we will try to describe how this environment could look from the point of view of the student himself, how it does look as far as the education providers are concerned, where it gets its resources from, and what new types of specialists are supporting its existence. (The only thing is that although the shift in the cognitive model will play a significant role, especially in reorganizing university education, we are still factoring out this topic given its specifics).

### 3.7.1 The place of education in human life cycles

We started this Report by indicating our understanding of education as an end-to-end process that accompanies a person from his first years of life to the very end of life (section 1.3). The education solutions that we described above mean that the place of education in people's everyday lives is changing, both in terms of the place in the entire human life cycle and in terms of regular life cycles (daily, monthly, annual) (similar ideas were proposed in the European Memorandum of Continuous Education).*

When imaging the place of education now, then it is first and foremost the 'run-up before the start,' getting prepared for independent adult life. Subsequently, a person continues to refine their qualifications through advancement courses, but their intensity is comparatively low; after retiring, education comes to a halt. As a consequence, education in its current form deals with two main objectives: socializing (helping assimilate the rules for interacting in society, the 'protocols of communication,' and general perceptions of how the world works)

* http://www.bolo-gna-berlin2003.de/pdf/Memorandu-mEng.pdf

and professionalizing (career training in the field of choice). Future education accompanies a person through his entire life and addresses not only his social success, but also his inner growth (see Figure 2). As far as intensity is concerned, then education today begins with preschool, then the intellectual and psychological load gradually increases, hitting its peak during university education. Then, a sharp drop-off occurs (since a big part of professional education is already no longer formally considered to be education), while people in their last years of life present almost no interest to the education system. With future education, learning and development take place through a person's life. It starts immediately after being born, and often before birth (see 'school in the womb,' section 2.3.5), and then accompanies a person to their last days (Figure 6). This does not mean that education is asserting its claim to a substantial amount of time and energy: as we said, the educational environment of 'non-educational' activities is recognized (such as project work or playing in multi-user environments). Therefore, a person inevitably spends a lot of time within education. There is also a certain culmination, when education is as intense as possible. At this time, a person makes the transition from the life of a child to independent adult life, and this transition can be labeled as an 'initiation ceremony' or 'maturity exam' (as we said in section 2.3.5, this will be a 'floating' period and will depend on the level of psychological preparation).* It could be that the time when a person will finish their professional career and transition to the 'third part' of life is the second 'culmination': since life expectancy and the quality of life in old age are increasing, then elderly people's lives will be a separate stage in self-realization that requires educational training).

*It is entirely likely that there will be several such peaks in some cases, because it is clear that there are gradations in adulthood depending on the person's maturity and willingness to take responsibility.

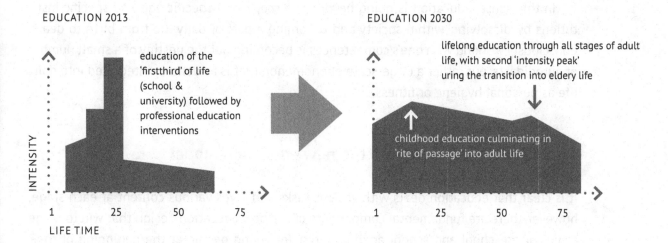

EDUCATION 2013

education of the 'firstthird' of life (school & university) followed by professional education interventions

INTENSITY

1    25    50    75

LIFE TIME

EDUCATION 2030

lifelong education through all stages of adult life, with second 'intensity peak' uring the transition into eldery life

childhood education culminating in 'rite of passage' into adult life

1    25    50    75

**Figure 6** Education in the human life cycle: from sprinting to marathons

As far as short cycles are concerned (ex. monthly or annual cycles), there is a specific time within these cycles that is put aside for taking education programs, mainly within specialized educational institutions (kindergarten, school, colledge, or university). School children and students dedicate the majority of the year to education programs (and the rest of the year to playing/leisure activities, and sometimes practice), while adults often-times dedicate several days/weeks of the year to education, combining them with work. The education cycle in future education is becoming continuous: both children and adults can spend part of their time year-round on personalized online education, including education that is integrated with work or playing (instead of having to specially head off to class at a separate academic institution). Online education will be combined with offline education, which will be more intensive and focused on tackling issues together and on collective creativity.

Finally, education for children (now preschool and school) and beginning professionals (now university) can expect the most significant changes in the daily cycle of life. First, the share of traditional education formats (studying lectures and taking tests) will gradually decrease, while the share of learning-in-practice will gradually increase (through commu-nities as of practice, as changes are to the dominant models of cognition and knowledge acquisition, as discussed in section 3.5.3). Second, although formally students can dedicate less time to academics and more time to playing, leisure activities or hanging out with friends, what they do will be assessed as far as the impact on their personal achievements portfolio and competence profile is concerned. Meanwhile, the majority of everyday activi-ties are clearly becoming educational in how to develop a person for formalizing knowledge. Third, the role of learning through gadgets, videogame consoles, and mobile devices will grow in this education process. For example the 'wearable' bracelet that we gave examples of in section 3.6.1) is becoming a personal fitness coach that monitors physical activity and gives recommendations for recovering during the entire day.

In this sense, education is going beyond the scope of a specific age and specific insti-tutions by 'dissolving' within society and becoming a part of daily life from birth to death. Consciously working with one's competences is becoming not the destiny of a small number of autodidacts, but rather a large-scale phenomenon that is as densely integrated into daily life as personal hygiene or fitness.

## 3.7.2 'The student's path' in the new education model

It is clear that education deals with various tasks and gives various content at each stage; however, there are fundamental components of the new education design that will look the same for preschool and school-aged children, for young people at the beginning of their careers, for adults developing through self-growth, and for elderly people changing their career path (Figure 7).

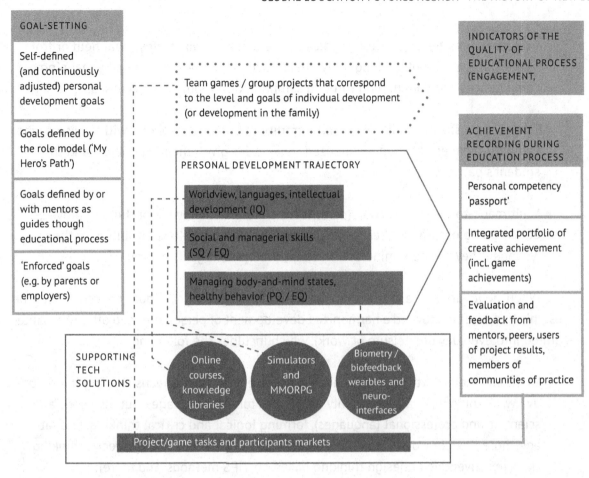

**Figure 7** Learner's path in 2030 education (demand side)

The individual growth trajectory (section 3.2.4), which during the late school and professional career stage is a education and career trajectory but which accompanies a person his entire life, is at the center of this universal design. The education trajectory determines at each stage what the education goals are (in the 'close development zone'). Goal-setting is essentially the first stage, the student entering the education sphere (although goal-setting is not done all at once, but rather goals are revised and updated based on changes in the student's life or achieved goals). As we said in section 3.2.4, development goals can be shaped using several methods based on the student's motivation and maturity:

- The most socially and personally mature students with their sights set on self-learning (autodidacts) are capable of independently determining their development goals and establishing their own trajectory based on these goals (we believe that there will be more and more such students willing to actively manage their own development as the 'life-long learning' model becomes more popular);

- Drawing up one's own personal development trajectory based on 'heroic' models is another variation (possibly, most popular in the near future). These models come from the competence profiles of typical leaders in a certain professional field or from profiles of specific outstanding individuals (such profiles are drawn up by mapping out competences and data mining through sampling development trajectories;

- Finally, some students will follow more traditional paths by working with advisors who will help them establish individualized trajectories given their experience and the student's particularities;

- Adult made-to-order education (parents for children, employers for their employees, etc.) is going nowhere either, to the extent that 'elders' take responsibility for the 'younger,' they can determine their future development goals as well.

When goals are set, a comprehensive training program (individual trajectory) can be established, targeted toward a harmonized development of personality, and oftentimes integrated into everyday life (leisure or work), which includes the following:

- An intellectual growth track: for children and teenagers, this means shaping their worldview, learning languages (not only native and foreign languages, but also specialized scientific and professional languages), forming logical and critical thinking. At a later age, more flexible work is done on subject knowledge and teaching special thinking skills (ex. inventive or design thinking based on TIPS methods, and more);

- A social and administrative skills shaping track. These are general skills for interacting with other students and the outside world, and specific social and administrative competences, including co-creativity skills, leadership skills, and more);

- A psychophysiological track. This concerns not only physical education and sports (given the logic that universities and schools today provide this), but also the ability to control one's body and health in various situations (the ability to concentrate, relax, overcome stressful situations, etc.) (see section 3.7.1 below regarding the revitalization of attention to controlling one's psychophysiological state in education).

What is significant is that these tracks will not draw up in a 'parallel' logic as is, we will say, a set of successive courses, where a student learns about physics at one and does physical activities at the other. Education of the future has to become integral, with intellectual, social, and psychophysiological development woven into one single 'thread'. In particularly, since studying blocks of knowledge material should mainly be organized as independent work with libraries (section 2.2.6), the student is given first and foremost knowledge-in-practice: knowledge that he must assimilate to resolve practical tasks and overcome challenges. For example, a teenage student could study physics in a special simulator where he and other students are in a Martian laboratory, and their team must battle external threats. To survive, they have to understand a block of material on physics and solve a number of tasks based on this material. Another scenario is where an adult working in production or at a charity accumulates knowledge, social competences, and self-control skills (ex. the ability to control oneself in stressful situations). At the same time, the project he is working on was specially picked so that he would have the environment to develop new, desirable competences.

The technological environment is a student's active partner in supporting the various components of the student's education trajectory:

- For dealing with knowledge, there are online courses such as MOOC (section 3.1.2) and knowledge libraries, including encyclopedic generalizations on specific disciplines (section 3.5.3) that are adapted by artificial intelligence for the student's level;

- For dealing with social and administrative skills, there are various simulators for teamwork (section 3.3.1) and game multi-user educational environments such as MMORPG (section 3.4.1);

- For psychophysiological development, there are, in addition to traditional means, various simulators of psychophysiological state based on biological feedback and neurointerfaces (section 3.7.2);

- Moreover, there are technological solutions that register from end to end the student's achievements throughout the education process.

The education process could take place alone, but joint learning with other students — in communities, families (section 3.3.4), and in real organizations — will take up a significant part of it. As a consequence, a person's individual goals for education must be synchronized with the opportunities that are out there in the joint learning spaces in order to have cooperative education work for individual goals and vice-versa. Collective education can be organized as joint work on real projects in business, the social sphere, art, or as a joint game. As we were saying in section 3.3.3, the education opportunities exchange — where new education opportunities are offered to promote team objectives — is one of the important tools that connects collective education spaces (ex. role playing) and the individual student (ex. who is ready to act as a player).

Moreover, the set of tools used for learning will depend on the stage that material is assimilated. Most likely at the stage when a student must assimilate introductory (basic) knowledge or skills, it will be sufficient for him to use automatic learning tools: for example, a set of online course or simulators that can be taken alone or in a group of similar beginners. At the next stage, he can start working (or playing) under the supervision of an older adviser (ex. take part as a volunteer in a research or applied project). Finally, at some point the student assimilates the subject enough to become a full-fledged member of the community of practice. From this stage forward his learning is built mainly on exchanging experience in joint work with other practitioners. Essentially, this plan in many areas is already a reality, but it has not taken root institutionally. Meanwhile, when the tools for managing individual education and career trajectories are widely used, the terms for a student's transition from one status to another, just as in the medieval shop-floor system of 'student-apprentice-master' statuses, must be formalized and consolidated by the communities of practice themselves. We will note that as opposed to the medieval situation, when the transition depended on the decision of a local guild leaders protecting their status (and therefore oftentimes did not give students the opportunity to progress to the status of master), modern-day 'competence levels' can work toward 'de-elitization,' if the terms for obtaining student statuses are built on objectively proven achievements and are rid as much as possible of national/local standards (ex. anyone having obtained a set of knowledge in a neurosurgical simulator and having passed knowledge tests will be able to obtain the qualification of neurosurgeon and the chance to work in operating rooms at most hospitals in the world. The set of such statuses and terms for obtaining them (including remotely, through online simulators) will gradually be shaped by supranational communities of practice themselves, just is done now in one-on-one combat, ERP system programming, 'careful production,' and more.

Finally, learning leads to certain results or achievements that the student can record in various forms:

■ First, this is one's own increase in competences that takes place during special education sessions, playing games or solving real tasks: a personal competences passport that is updated through one's entire life (in addition to a competences passport that reflects special abilities, there can also be a meta-competences passport related to one's learning style,* quality of communicative skills, etc.);

■ Second, these are artifacts created during the learning process (both in reality and in virtual worlds): a personal portfolio that also is supplemented throughout one's life;

■ Third, these are reputation indicators that are collected as a cross assessment that a student gets from his classmates (members of the game team or participants in his own academic or real project) and advisers who accompany the student in the education process, people using the project results, members of communities of practice, 'master characters' in 'live' games, and third-party observers. All these assessments work, first and foremost, to shape an accurate competence profile (since competence is evaluated using the assessment), and second of all toward reputational capital.

\* Moreover, the process itself of documenting skills—such as demonstrating them in academic or work environments—can be at the same time the process for documenting meta-skills (namely not only what a student learns is registered, but so is how the student learns this).

The personal competence passport, personal profile, and personal reputational capital are on the student's side, when the student enters the 'education opportunities exchange' looking for new projects, new games, new friendly meetings, or new career positions.

Assessing personal achievements maybe is the pragmatic side of education, but the very quality of the education process that the student himself can assess is no less important (see section 2.2.6). As Mihaly Csikszentmihalyi (Csikszentmihalyi, 1996) writes, there is a special continuous state, in which one can 'be completely engaged in an activity for the sake of the activity itself... Each action, movement, and thought follows from the past one, as if playing jazz. All your essence is engaged, and you apply your abilities to the limit.' Existence in a continuous state is not less (and maybe more) important than the results obtained at the end. One of the secrets of existing in the flow is the fine balance between the complexity of a task and a subject's skill that keeps tasks in the zone where 'it is already interesting, but still not too complex' (and best of all, this balance is being achieved in videogames). The ability to manage a student's quality is happening through scanning his psychophysiological state and behavior patterns (section 3.7.2). As a result, intellectual education systems (such as 'virtual teachers' or 'The Diamond Primer'—section 3.2.4) can be adapted and make the educational experience as engaging as possible, all the while making it possible to make a skill as well trained as possible or to get to the sagacity of knowledge.

The cycle described (Figure 7)—the movement from goal-setting through the education trajectory (individual or team) to a set of achievements with the support of technological solutions—accompanies the student his whole life. Of course, a child learns predominantly in game and developmental environments, while an adult learns through real work, social, or artistic projects. Subject content depends on the interests and goals of personal development that the student sets out (at the beginning with the help of his parents and advisers, and then all the more independently). Childhood achievements, and especially reputation, likely have less weight than those during adulthood; nonetheless, the essential plan that both schools and universities can use, as well as (all the more often) independent education providers, remains more or less the same.

### 3.7.3 The technological platform for supporting new education

The education model we are discussing can be successful only in one case, namely if there will be a cloud of interconnected technological solutions that allow for carrying out the functions of an industrial education system that is more successful and less costly. Each student in the new education sphere, regardless of age and status, will be surrounded by infrastructure on the 'supply side' that ensures work for educational institutions and independent providers. We will examine the possible elements of this future technological infrastructure (Figure 8).

The nucleus of this infrastructure (solutions that are necessary for new education processes) consists of four elements that are already partially discussed in section 3.2 and in the previous block:

- The education trajectory control interface is the chief element: a system, in which the student (and his 'live' or automatic advisors) can set out goals and either create or change the planned set of education programs (lectures, game lessons, etc.) and track his progress in these programs;

- Big libraries or (semantic) search engines concerning independent providers, in which you can select individual courses (such as MOOC), entire course programs, or education simulators (allowing to perfect abilities or working to develop personal qualities) are the second component. A rating and recommendation system should be put together as part of libraries/search engines. This system should allow selecting the courses and simulators that are the most effective and relevant to the student's demands.

- Implemented assessment and certification systems are the third component. These systems allow for obtaining an external, confirmable assessment of knowledge and skills. Test systems and competitions are already an existing part of such evaluation systems, including those organized online; however, as we discussed in section 2.2.6, this system also must include student behavior assessments in various processes that have an educational component (including real projects, games, interaction in social networks, etc.).

- Achievement confirmation tools are the fourth component. These tools partially exist already. For example, many social networks allow presenting one's own electronic portfolio. Other such tools have yet to be implement, such as the system that was discussed in section 3.2.4 for registering a current competence portfolio that allows noting all situations (work, game, or social), in which the person employed any given competences (and received the corresponding assessments of having these competences).

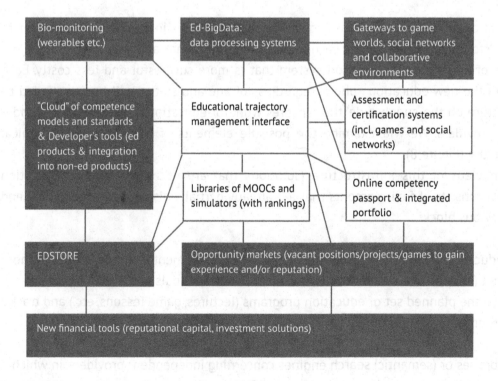

**Figure 8** Learner's tech environment in 2030 education (supply side)

Biomonitoring systems will be the additional component of education infrastructure. These systems describe a student's biological, medical, and psychological profile, as well as control biomonitoring and neurointerface parameters (see section 3.7.2). These tools allow giving the student feedback on his current psychophysiological health, the optimal learning schedules depending on the state and on more ways to transition to more productive states. Furthermore, they can be used to adapt the education process to the student's current state or to stop it, if the student is not able to work. Biomonitoring data can serve as an additional information channel, to which certified educational applications will have access (through preliminary user confirmation).

Moving on, we talked about how, in addition to educational products created for exclusively educational purposes, there is an entire range of applied and leisure products (ex. project management systems or game environments) that can integrate education components. There is no need to create a special game world for learning, if it is still possible to study in existing worlds. Therefore, special gateways will be created to connect the education process with playing, communicating, or working. The purpose of these gateways is to integrate education into non-education services: integrate a task within a game or project into the education trajectory (as part of an opportunity exchange, see below), confirm that a student came to the corresponding virtual world or an education project, and that his actions must be reflected in his achievements profile. These gateways must at the very least include the gates (a) to game worlds (MMORPG or augmented reality games), (b) to social networks (as spaces for communicating and presenting oneself) and (c) to collaborative environments for creative work on a project.

Moreover, in order for a student to be able to correctly establish his participation in games and projects, he needs a tool to the education opportunities within non-education activities: the education opportunities exchange, already discussed in the previous section and in section 3.3.3.

Some of the educational solutions in libraries and search engines of educational content will remain free, just as they are now; however, as the independent education market grows, there will be all the more providers looking to monetize their MOOCs and/or education simulators. As a result, one or more exchanges will be created for such providers, a type of EdStore (modeled after the AppStore or Google PlayMarket). These exchanges will most likely be organized based on either educational content search engines or education trajectory management.

New education funding mechanisms, which we discussed in section 3.2.3 and which will be discussed in the following block, will be required for working with paid education services (and for taking part in the education opportunities exchange). Among these mechanisms will be various investment and insurance solutions, as well as a reputational capital management system.

To have the new education system work efficiently, there have to be specialized environments for developing courses and simulators, as well as for integrating education components into non-education solutions, modeled after work environments for engineers and technicians (such as AutoCAD, SolidWorks, CATIA, etc.), multipliers, architects of ERP systems, etc. These environments consist of several components. First, a cloud of competence models and education/professional standards based on them that are composed (and saved digitally) in communities of practice (some of which are directly connected to education) are necessary guidelines for developers. Second, there must be the tools to develop education trajectories and education programs (such as sets of educational solutions: courses, simulators, text assignments, etc., during which the student gains a certain competence). Third, there must be tools that allow for integrating education components into game environments (ex. when a game character's achievements simultaneously change a player's competence profile) and other digital solutions. In essence, education developers' tools must become the superstructure that allows for transforming virtually any 'non-educational' digital environments into educational digital environments.

Finally, for the new education system to work, it needs to have a Ed-BigData 'reflexive bloc' that works with large flows of education data that users create while learning (Knewton and some MOOC platforms operate today in roughly the same logic). First, these are systems that collect information about productive education trajectories (more broadly education, career and development trajectories), about the impact of any given solutions on advancing user competences, on demand for various types of educational content, on student behavior patters, etc. At the same time, they will play the role of systems that build models of new pedagogical science (in the sense that we discussed this in section 3.5.2). Second, these same systems can work in junction with systems that build individual education trajectories by processing personal user data and issuing recommendations for changing a trajectory and for the possibility to refine courses or game educational scenarios that the user is undergoing. Third, these systems will work as tools for developers by recommending productive solutions for specific audiences and types of educational content.

Of course, the solutions we have listed do not exhaust new education's technological infrastructure, and it is entirely possible that specific functions will be implemented where several components of this infrastructure overlap (ex. the MOOC platform could include a trajectory management system, a content library, and online store for selling this content); however, by relying on the reasoning that we provided in the previous sections, we believe that these tools will emerge in any given form and will be part of the infrastructure, namely they will be universal for the entire education sphere.

### 3.7.4 New financial tools

Creating new tools that allow for financing education is one of the necessary components of the new education model, which is more flexible compared to today. Besides traditional models (paying one's way with savings and student loans, government loans, or an employer paying), in the previous sections we discussed several new models that will be unfurled in the coming years:

1. **Investment model.** As part of this model, education is seen as an investment that provides return on invested funds (if at the beginning the person himself or his employer invested in education, then now it is the investor through the Upstart logic described in

section 3.2.3). To have this model start working, as we already discussed, education must have the status of a service: it must become as accountable as possible, it must be provided with as much objective quality control as possible. This will allow for creating agents that act in the service recipient's interests, in particularly recommendation services (for choosing a provider) and 'education attorneys' (defending students from unscrupulous providers).

To have investment in education be transparent and manageable, the process and effects of education must be as documentable and measurable as possible. Hence, this is where we get demand for the following from both the students themselves and their investors:

(a) Certificates, achievement portfolios, and later competence passports;

(b) An analysis of the contribution from individual educational products to advancing a skill

(c) Education trajectories as the 'right' course assemblies, including proven by 'successful investments' (hence there is demand for the service to analyze big data volumes about education routes and calculating successful worker/businessman trajectories);

(d) The transition to the model of integrated 'education and career' trajectories (since, as we said, a career is a part of the competences obtained, while work in the right places can be no less of an important education process than getting the right course).

As far as the investor is concerned, such tools allow for calculating investment risks in individual people and to build large, balanced portfolios out of a host of students/ professionals. In the future, as we discussed, the model of portfolio investments in talents could become the foundation for new pension funds, where talented professionals work in pensioners' interests who have invested in funds. (Essentially, the investments model is completely applicable in the reverse logic as well: we believe that there could be special-ized pension funds for professionals working in education that grateful students, recog-nizing their teachers/advisors' contribution to their individual success, would contribute money to).

2. **Insurance model.** This model is built on the presupposition that 'being competent' is in essence like 'being healthy.' Competence means being able to adapt to modern society as much as possible, including suitability to a competitive job. Consequently, similarly to medical insurance that compensates expenditures made to rehabilitate one's health in case of illness, 'education insurance' can be fashioned to compensate for expenditures made on overcoming ignorance in case of incompetence.

Several plans for similar insurances can be proposed, including the following:

- The 'education subscription' or 'education ad-hoc' model when the appeal is made to education for making up for current incompetence (roughly the same as going to the doctor when illnesses flare up);

■ The 'ignorance insurance' model (as a supplemental format to the model of investment in education): insurance payment is made if education does not live up to the promised result through an achieved level of competence or obtained position on the career ladder.

3. **The 'mutual aid cashier desk'** is a model that could develop in horizontal education (including in network education) as such education develops (see section 3.3.4), when communities assemble a common fund and order education services to fit the current participant needs (in essence, a number of communities practice such model already, such as Entrepreneurs Organization, a major network of medium-sized business entrepreneurs that conducts regular education conferences and mentor sessions that are financed from its members' annual fees).*

4. **The 'education casino' model** is one that is more light-hearted, but could be realized in several education services. In this situation, education process participants create additional monetary motivation for learning by making bets on their capability to study a subject/shape a skill. If the individual was not able to achieve the stated goal, he loses the bet, while if he notably exceeds his goal, then he wins. An 'education casino' could be carried out as a bet between participants (ex. the person who finishes the course with the best results wins), or as a 'play against the casino' approach' (when participants make contributing bets to the education provider's accounts and receive payment only if they achieve their result, for example when shaping the required skill). Such models are being implemented in other spheres, such as in personal weight control (in particularly, the DietBet startup is based on this idea: it proposes competing for the capability to lose weight at the establish percentage over a limited amount of time).** We will point out that as motivation research shows (Ballentine et al., 2009), monetary motivation is not sustainable and often unproductive (especially when developing unusual skills and creative thinking, as well as in cooperative tasks).*** Therefore, we do not think that this model will become dominant, but it is entirely suitable in some cases.

5. **The 'exchange and accumulation' of reputational capital model.** We believe that in the long term this could become one of the main models, especially given the active transition to 'horizontal education' (in communities of practice, 'family universities,' etc.). It presumes that reputational capital could serve as an indicator for accumulating personal qualities, and could be spent on developing supplemental qualities. A reputation is shaped through assessments that are given by registered achievements (ex. implemented projects, earned money, etc.) and activity participants (including colleagues, mentors, clients, etc.). Education can be obtained, first and foremost, from other bearers of skills, and accumulated 'merit' currency can be used to pay for these bearers' services (see. SABER case in section 2.3.4). The additional accumulation of merits (status, competence, etc.) can happen through taking part in game 'people-less' education (section 3.4.3), where the game process shapes the right knowledge and skills that later on can be conveyed/strengthened and in 'live' education.

* http://www.eonetwork.org/Pages/welcome.aspx

** http://www.forbes.com/sites/alextaub/2013/04/25/dietbet-is-betting-that-losing-weight-is-about-to-get-more-social/

*** Also see Dan Pink's presentation on TED: http://www.ted.com/talks/dan_pink_on_motivation

In addition to these tools meant for the end user, other funding tools can be developed as well. For example, tools that have to do with changing a state funding model for education (ex. introducing personal certificates for paying for services in a competitive market of education providers instead of direct provider financing) and with adjusting a budget structure for major educational institutions (ex. financing education activities through owning shares in graduates' companies). We will partially examine these variations below (in the sections dedicated to strategic recommendations).

## 3.7.5 Education's technical environment and employees: competitors or partners?

Education has always been a sphere where people worked with people, and the adjustment in an organization's model in this sphere can look threatening. Technologicalizing education processes means that many processes that are currently done by individual specialists could very well be done by devices or expert systems. It is clear that many existing positions, with that of the modern-day school 'reproducer' teacher being the first, will lose meaning within the coming decade. Does this mean that the new education will become predominantly people-less, and that the shift in the education paradigm will require large-scale layoffs of teachers and professors?

We believe that this is not the case at all. The new understanding of education as a process that takes place throughout one's life will require creating an enormous new industry that, in terms of the volume of human resources, is many times larger than the existing school and university system. In any case, education is a sphere where people work with people. But people should not turn into machines (be it machines for holding classes or grading tests). On the contrary, in giving up the 'machine aspect to the machine,' people can concentrate on the authentically human aspect: creativity, communication, self-development, etc.* In the long term future, as people leave the spheres of physical and routine intellectual labor, the education field could become one of the dominating types of jobs in next community practices.

*See also http://www.fastcompany.com/1722914/teacher-replacing-tech-friend-or-foe

To have the changes described in the previous sections implemented, a large number of new specialists will be required who are capable of creating and supporting new education formats: in the future, as the economic organization models shift, the education sphere could even become one of the most wide-spread in human activities. In particular, based on our reasoning about which education processes will be subject to the most changes, these should be specialists in the following spheres:

- 'Mixed' education through special education models (online/offline);

- Learning within real projects;

- Learning within playing (an educational component in virtual worlds and augmented reality);

- Learning through wearable biomonitoring devices;

- Managing education and career trajectories;

- Assessment.

Some competences that will be required to develop new solutions in the listed districts and to implement these solutions are indicated below (Table 7). We will point out that only an insignificant part of these competences are being shaped in teacher colleges at pedagogical competence development courses for professors. In the future, it will be required to create new training programs in order to provide the education sphere with the required specialists.

Among other things, the broad use of 'school vice-versa' models can be expected. These models are for creating jobs for teachers not within the education system, but among users of education results, ex. in industries (corporate universities and training sections), in service companies, charitable and non-commercial organizations and institutions working in municipal development. If one accepts the idea (voiced by John Dewey more than 100 years ago, but only now being implemented) that a school must become a part of society, then education specialists must work where education really is taking place: in businesses, social services, theme parks, city streets, etc.

We believe that additional research is necessary on the impact of changes in the education sphere on the labor market, including quantitative assessments of the education sector's capacity as a space that can accept specialists from other sectors.

**Table 7**

# EMERGING OCCUPATIONS FOR THE NEW EDUCATION SPHERE

| NEW EDUCATIONAL ACTIVITIES | SPECIALISTS THAT APPLY NEW SOLUTIONS | SPECIALISTS THAT DEVELOP NEW SOLUTIONS |
|---|---|---|
| 'Blended' learning through online & offline educational modules | • tutors<br>• 'blended' educational program directors | • online and blended pedagogy experts<br>• educational content authors<br>• online and blended learning platform developers |
| Project – based learning and on-job training | • project work facilitators / moderators / directors<br>• project mentors (within business,<br>• government & non-government sector)<br>• supervisors / coordinators of internship & apprenticeship programs, coordinators for business & school / university relations | • designers of project-based educational programs<br>• developers of teamwork collaborative environments |
| Game-based learning | • live non-player characters<br>• chief & assistant game masters (in charge of playing)<br>• game-based teaching faculty that help integrate games into educational process | • gamification experts that help embed games into non-gaming activities<br>• game design masters that develop game scenarios and game mechanics<br>• virtual & augmented reality gaming solution developers<br>• game-based education methodologists |
| Wearable-based learning | • mind fitness experts<br>• instructors that help integrate wearables into educational process | • developers of training programs and supporting software for productive mind-and-body states<br>• new educational hardware designers (based on biofeedback wearables etc.) |
| Education and career tracks management | • personal mentors<br>• experts on marketing of 'branded' educational trajectories<br>• quality control experts for education & career trajectories (role alike 'movie critics') | • educational trajectory designers<br>• big data system developers for trajectory / success factors analytics<br>• education & career 'heroes' (alike 'movie stars')<br>• personal trajectory management platform developers |
| Assessment & evaluation | • independent evaluators & evaluation observers<br>• independent auditors of assessment systems | • assessment / reputation system designers (incl. reputation capital models)<br>• behavior monitoring system designers (incl. game-based monitoring) |

# 4. RECOMMENDATIONS FOR KEY PLAYERS

In the beginning of this book, we promised to describe the possible strategies in the education sphere for businessmen and investors, academic institution administrators, and state regulators. Future education is a field of immense uncertainties and colossal opportunities. Therefore, our recommendations only denote the areas where, as we see it, these opportunities are the most significant — and we will try to explain how it will be possible to take advantage of them.

## 4.1 CONCLUSIONS FOR VENTURE BUSINESS: THE EDUCATION STARTUP SPHERE

The fundamental process taking place right before our eyes is the transformation of the education system (with states and a limited number of private players being the 'custodians') into the education sphere (with the participants being, in addition to major players, members of communities of practice, a host of independent educational projects and individuals willing to pass on their knowledge and experience either full-time or part-time). Education startups are new players that in the coming decade could reshape education markets and set new rules of the game for them.

Technological and cultural transformations (which we talked about in sections 2.2 and 2.3) create a fundamentally new education landscape:

- Education goes beyond a specific time in life and becomes truly 'life-long education' that starts right after being born and ends only when you die;

- Education goes beyond educational institutions and becomes 'education everywhere.' Education components are included in real and leisure activities. Education becomes a part of daily practice that each person should dedicate time to, just as with personal hygiene;

- Any group or individual willing to provide content or educational technologies to interested students can act as education providers (in the future, one of the largest-scale fields will be getting involved in educational activities (see section 3.6.5));

- A number of technological platforms uniting interested students and educational resources act as the custodian of uniform rules of the game for this education market.

If the map of future education we have presented and the trends shaping it are accurate, then enormous (and in essence empty) solution sectors for new education appear, including the following:

- Systemic solutions that create the technological infrastructure of new education (in particularly, those we describe in section 3.6.3);

- New financial and investment tools for the developing education sphere (in particularly, those we describe in section 3.6.4);

- Education solutions for groups that are undervalued receive insufficient attention from traditional education systems, including early independent children, 'modernist' families (section 2.3.5), and 'new old' people and 'extra people' (section 2.3.3);

- New game solutions and virtual worlds designated to develop personal and team skills (including those we describe in section 3.4);

- Solutions that integrate education with the health/fitness industry, and various neuro-technological solutions in education (including those we describe in section 3.7).

Some of the examples provided below (Table 8) could become truly large-scale in the coming decade (it is entirely likely that they will become more famous than Google and Facebook).

**Table 8**

# SEVERAL NEW MARKETS FOR EDUCATION STARTUPS

| SPHERE OF APPLICATION | EXAMPLES OF SOLUTIONS |
|---|---|
| BACKBONE ICT SOLUTIONS | • competency, achievement and reputation tracking systems<br>• education content search engine and/or EdStore<br>• Ed-BigData solutions<br>• education software developer tools<br>• education trajectory design & management (including artificial tutors)<br>• mentor networks<br>• opportunity and talent exchange markets |
| NEW FINANCIAL INSTRUMENTS | • direct investment into education & career trajectories of talented individuals<br>• insurance instruments for talents and their investors<br>• reputation capital instruments, incl. reputation-based educational service exchange<br>• instruments for betting on education & training outcomes |
| EDUCATIONAL SERVICES FOR UNDERESTIMATED CONSUMER GROUPS | • professional training programs for early maturing children<br>• support of career track relaunch for 'New Old' (people 65+ in active physical & mental form)<br>• 'family universities' for family life-long learning and integration |
| VIRTUAL WORLDS FOR GAMES AND EDUCATION | • simulators for prolonged team training<br>• simulators for alienated people & delinquents<br>• games with augmented reality in corporate & urban environment<br>• simulators of risky & hazardous situations<br>• 'playing with values': simulators that facilitate the children's moral development<br>• psychodrama worlds' |
| BRAIN FITNESS AND OBJECTIFICATION | • body-mind state training tools (incl. wearables) & attention management schools<br>• measurement of engagement & learning attained<br>• sensoriums: virtual environments that help recreate sensory experiences and emotions |

We are presuming that a wave of education startups has begun on education markets, and these startups could create the infrastructure for the new education sphere; however, we would like to head off the excess enthusiasm over currently emerging solutions. Excess enthusiasm has emerged in the education sector over the new possibilities of educational high technologies (as an attempt to find answers to the systemic crisis in education);

however, the markets that these startups are focusing on are still derivatives of industrial education. For example, Coursera and EdX are built off the possibilities of leading U.S. universities, while Knewton provides services to train students for standardized 'industrial' tests, such as the GRE and GMAT. At the same time, as we have shown, these projects could shape the rules of the game for the new education sphere. Some of the educational projects now emerging are the crutches that temporarily support the 'breaking' components of the education system (such as, for example, gamification working to increase students' interest in course content). Other educational projects are the 'prostheses' that replace the missing components of the education system (such as, for example, MOOC platforms creating an efficient system for scanning talent across the world for leading universities). Still, all of them are based on the industrial logic. The 'crutches' and 'prostheses' are currently dominating in the portfolios of foundations that invest in education, because the models of their monetization can easily be calculated, while the return on investment in such projects can be quicker; nonetheless, all these solutions by nature are always auxiliary, and therefore it is unlikely that companies such as Facebook can emerge from them. Moreover, it is clear that while society is still being reconstructed and the contours of the next socio-economic structure are still being determined, it is impossible to rely on another logic, because sufficient social demand for this logic has yet to arise. What is most likely is that this demand will be made only when the balance of generations shifts in the 2020s, including with the advent of generation Z into the social elite. This generation itself will be shaped by the first generations of new education projects.

Education startups, which could emerge in developing markets, should be singled out. The super-inexpensive education niche is one possibility in such markets (per the 'bottom of the pyramid' model*). For example, the Kenyan network of schools Bridge International Academies uses the advantages of high technologies to drastically reduce management and teaching expenses, which allows them to provide quality kindergarten and basic school education at a price of no more than five dollars a month**. Education startups in these relatively empty markets could be rather quickly be brought to scale and become national leaders, which could serve as an additional threat to them: the risk of a direct ban (because these services violate the regulator's monopoly) or of nationalization (because they are becoming a critically important component of learning). Several leading Russian education startups, such as Dnevnik.RU, are apprehensive of their fate turning out as such.

Still, the enthusiasm is high, and in the coming years the vogue of education startups awaits us (they are already becoming must-haves for many self-respecting venture funds, along with big data or biotechnology startups). If making a comparison with the web solutions market, then we are at the time when it launched, 1994-95; however, we have to admit that only a few companies will have enough vision and systemic solutions that are suitable for use in the new education system. As a result, by the end of the 2010s it is highly likely that we can expect the bubble to burst, causing a collapse in the original education high-tech market (Figure 9).

* http://www.thebop-strategy.com/

** http://www.bridgeinternationalacademies.com/approach/model/

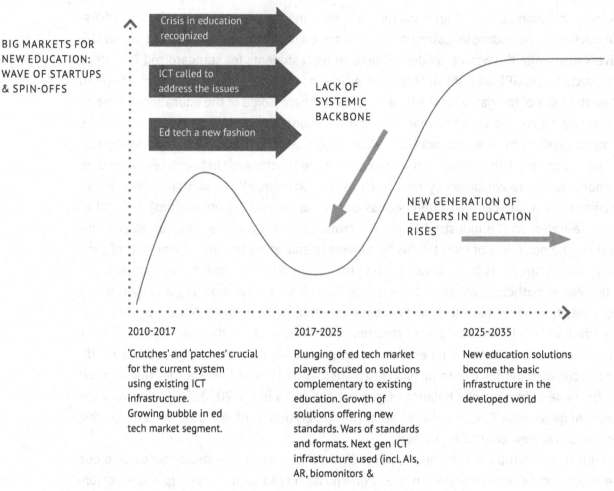

BIG MARKETS FOR
NEW EDUCATION:
WAVE OF STARTUPS
& SPIN-OFFS

Crisis in education
recognized

ICT called to
address the issues

LACK OF
SYSTEMIC
BACKBONE

Ed tech a new fashion

NEW GENERATION OF
LEADERS IN EDUCATION
RISES

**2010-2017**

'Crutches' and 'patches' crucial
for the current system
using existing ICT
infrastructure.
Growing bubble in ed
tech market segment.

**2017-2025**

Plunging of ed tech market
players focused on solutions
complementary to existing
education. Growth of
solutions offering new
standards. Wars of standards
and formats. Next gen ICT
infrastructure used (incl. AIs,
AR, biomonitors &

**2025-2035**

New education solutions
become the basic
infrastructure in the
developed world

**Figure 9** The evolution of the education startup
market: a possible scenario

This scenario could shock the public, while talk about the 'failure' of new education models that did not justify the hopes of the traditional education system and of regulators is entirely possible; however, venture investors are well familiar with the 'double hump' effect, which often affects innovative sectors (Lowenstein, 2004). The sobering era arrives in the wake of early enthusiasm and often dovetails with a negative phase in the economic cycle (and we believe this to be a possible scenario for a new crisis phase in OECD countries at the end of the 2010s, see section 2.4.1). At the same time, the risk of overheating and market collapse is compensated by the possibility of breakthrough, backbone innovations emerging.

While on the path to establishing new systemic standards, it is highly likely that we will encounter a market war between leading education providers. Dominating skill models, ways for assessing and endorsing qualifications, quality management and content diversity methods, etc., could be the subjects of this war. In addition to the virtually inevitable patent conflicts over ways to convey educational content, 'shadow' wars can be expected over content itself, when providers can try to 'intercept' the market by proliferating training systems free of charge or at significantly below what they cost to run. It is very likely that these 'wars' will actively begin to unfurl in the coming decade as the new education market takes shape, while new internal or supranational standards will be established in this sector by the end of 2025.

Moreover, it is hard to say ahead of time, which startups will be able to assert their claim to being the backbone of the system. Such companies endure the bursting bubble stage, a sort of Death Valley, and then later become companies that reshape the market and set the industry standards. Companies that have defined the face of the global economy in the second half of the 20th century, such as Hewlett-Packard, Walt Disney, or McDonald's, emerged during the Great Depression. Amazon, Google, and PayPal passed through the 'crucible' of the dot-com boom, and became synonymous with the Internet. Therefore, we believe that the new education environment will become truly large-scale only in the 2020s, while the 2010s will serve as the time for experiments that will determine the new education market leaders.

## 4.2 CONCLUSIONS FOR EDUCATION INSTITUTION ADMINISTRATORS: LOOKING FOR THE NEW NICHE

*They always say time changes things,*
*but you actually have to change them yourself*
**Andy Warhol**
*The task of a university is the creation of the future.*
**Alfred North Whitehead**

### 4.2.1 Industrial education: ensuring the 'basic capacity'

The arguments presented above could give the false impression that we are for the complex dismantling of the established education system and that we are predicting that this will take place soon, followed by it being replaced by extra-systemic education. In reality, of course, this is not so: the existing education system needs to be radically reformed, but it is functional, and therefore it is more likely that it will undergo gradual reformation from within and be supplemented from the outside than be completely dismantled.

In this sense, the processes in the education system are in some ways similar to what is happening now with electricity, which is seeing the advent of 'smart grids.' The existing energy supply system is tailored to supply large volumes of electricity from big energy production centers (ex. TPP) to large consumption centers (cities and industrial facilities) and have them subsequently distributed within. The energy system emerging now presumes that each energy consumer can fundamentally also be an energy producer, such as solar panels on the roof of a house providing energy for the family, while the excess energy is sent back to the public grid. 'Smart grids' allow connecting small producers together by evening out the energy loads and overflows. Fully implemented 'smart grids' have a number of advantages: they allow decreasing the total cost of energy, employ alternative and small-scale energy, and ensure grid flexibility and durability. It is clear that the cost of industrial energy will increase in the coming decades (including because of increasing environmental safety requirements and the exhaustion of easily accessible energy sources), while the price for new energy will drop (including because of the refinement and proliferation of large-scale solutions). Still, while local production and autonomous homes with roughly zero energy consumption have not become the main solution in arranging the economy and life. The energy system needs large energy providers (ex. nuclear power plants) that can provide the energy system with the 'basic capacity' to meet demand from major and large-scale consumers given day-time and seasonal peaks and drop-offs in consumption. In other words, although electricity is becoming more and more integrated, over the coming energy cycle (30-40 years) it will need industrial facilities that produce large volumes of energy. Therefore, national energy systems will consist of small energy producers combined with major producers (such a model has been adopted, for example, in South Korea, which by 2030 plans on using it as the base for becoming the first country to have transitioned completely to smart grids and green energies).

THE LOGIC OF BASE AND PEAK ENERGY CAPACITIES

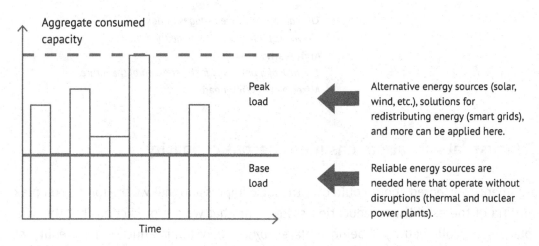

THE LOGIC OF SYSTEMIC AND AUXILIARY EDUCATION OPERATORS

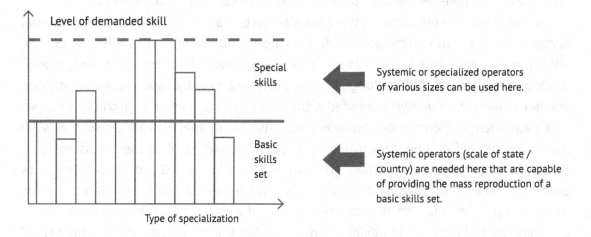

**Figure 10** The power supply system metaphor as applied to education systems

We are purposely using this industrial analogy (Figure 10). 20th century education was built predominantly as a system of large centers that produce specialists according to specific standards that states usually establish. 21st century education could be developed on the basis of network technologies as an allocated system for exchanging skills. With time, each person in such environments will have to find their own unique proposal for the rest of the system's participants; however, a host of specialists with standard qualifications will be needed for the coming generation (20-25 years) to support and develop existing socio-economic systems. In other words, the industrial education system will provide a 'basic capacity' that 'extra-system' projects of new education for still a long time will not be able to provide (including by virtue of social inertia).

Still, as the multitude of education startups develops (some of which in the coming decade will turn into durable formats), the industrial system will forfeit its exclusivity as the education provider. The selection of extra-systemic solutions (both local and transnational) for education in OECD countries already by the 2020s will be sufficient for a person to cover the development trajectory, similar to pre-school, school, and university education, from end to end while not going to kindergarten, school, or university. Moreover, as in the example with energy, the cost of new education will gradually fall (as large-scale solutions and new infrastructure are created), while the cost of industrial education increases and will continue to increase (including because of increasing consumer requirements and increasing competition for talent). In other words, totally new system operators will be emerging on this market, such as major IT companies that will start to see education as one of their key markets (roughly in the same way as 'mobile' health is currently seen).

How the reproduction of the elite will unfurl in this environment is another question, because schools and universities, among others, serve the reproduction of a specific model of social stratification; however, the shift in the socio-economic structure that we discussed in previous sections will mean a shit in the elites as well. In this sense, new education projects (sometimes related to the existing 'elite' academic institutions, and sometimes not) often become spaces where the reproduction of new elites commences (see also section 2.4.4).

The state to a large extent supports the industrial education system because it has a stake in specific educational content: studying the national language, conveying national culture and values, molding civil loyalty and knowledge of the foundations of the state system, and training professional skills that the state requires (ex. an engineering education to strengthen the national economy). How fast new education arrives will stem from the capability of new solutions to carry out for less the functions of the industrial system that the state invests in (a conditional graph of this process is provided below in Figure 11). We believe that the first precedents in transferring the large-scale education process from industrial education providers to network providers will be created in the coming 7-12 years (in the first half of the 2020s).

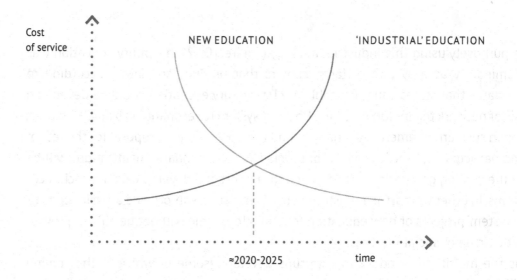

**Figure 11** Fundamental graph for replacing 'old' education with 'new' education

Traditional educational institutions have to understand that the 'time of the easy life' has come to an end. If the school and university education paradigm can change, this has to happen now. Competition for students, professors, content, and funding is becoming truly global, especially in university education. In particularly, most universities in the world in the coming decade will be faced with a challenge: 'Universities for a billion' are pressuring them 'from above' by conveying the content that is the most competitive and that the mass user demands, while 'universities for one' are pressuring them from below by providing customized programs that are fully adapted to the student's individual demands and particularities. Schools will encounter the very same challenge, but in this case from the children's goods and services industry (including the industry of videogames), which will offer school-aged children the opportunity to study in developmental environments and in game worlds. Each school and university will choose the survival strategy that fits them, but this strategy will, no matter what, involve finding a unique quality that cannot be obtained in digital education. Inertia in assimilating new practices or resisting the advent of new pedagogics is a suicidal strategy that is fraught with the loss of competitive advantage in the education sphere. Smart schools and universities will not fight new education, but rather will use it in their own interests.

### 4.2.2 Segmenting the education system and probable strategies within segments

The spread of 'extra-systemic' education providers will mean a growth in competition for resources (students, professors, funding, etc.) in education markets. Existing education systems will be all the more segmented depending on their willingness to adapt to changing demands. If we were to cut up the education system (schools and universities) in the majority of OECD countries in the early 2020s, then it is highly likely that we would see the following groups:

a. Leaders that have mastered the practices of new education and that actively use these practices in their education process, including the following:

- Shaping and retaining a unique competition advantage is stressed — education that can be obtained only within this school or university (access to the bearers of unique skills, idiosyncratic education approaches, the advantages of a unique neighborhood, etc.);

- An end-to-end digital environment that supports the entire education process, the development of courses, interacting with communities, etc.;

- Every student having an individual education trajectory (including a forecasted career trajectory) with the possibility of a full-fledged asynchronized education that at the foundation unites the education process and extra-academic activities, and that has mentors accompany this trajectory (work with mentors as one of the competitive advantages that an institution has);

- A flexible assessment system designated for supporting a student's motivation and shaping a student's self-improvement skills;

- The 'experiment culture': providing the abilities and resources (including time for students and professors) for individual and collective experiments in education, science, art, social activities (accompanying and proliferating successful solutions);

- A flexible architecture of educational institutions that allows for implementing a large number of education formats for individuals and groups (see section 4.2.3);

- A strong community within and around the academic institution (that acts as a network producer — see section 3.3.1), supporting horizontal education within this community (including strong connections with the local community, businesses, government, etc.);

- Joint academic processes with students' families and those representing real activities (businesses, social movements, and professional communities).

These solutions have been implemented in the world's leading educational institutions, which shows that, for example, the top U.S. universities will retain their positions as leaders; nonetheless, should this model be successfully implemented, then new players are entirely capable of becoming leaders as well, including from developing countries.

Moreover, some 'grandees' are able to afford not going down the path of assimilating new education practices and assume that their brand power will preserve their status as leaders, just as in the preceding decades or centuries: it is clear that Eton, Oxbridge, Ivy

League schools, and several other universities in the top 20 essentially can afford to not change, and at the same time retain their status as leaders. In reality, however, it is the existing leaders who are starting to actively back transforming universities. First, this is because the do not want to lose their strong positions by mistake. Second, this is because they have the resources to develop and promote new education platforms. Thanks to leading universities being the first to assimilate new education technologies and often make them a part of their education practices (such as with 'university for a billion' solutions), the divide between them and 'average' universities is becoming virtually insurmountable, turning the former into key global producers of scientific knowledge, centers where the global scientific elite concentrate, and centers for training the global political and business elite.*

b. The mass segment is designated for implementing a combination of solutions from traditional and new pedagogics that ensure conveying both standard and outside-the-box content (Figure 12). Standard content will be conveyed through technological solutions (online courses and simulators), while non-standard solutions will be conveyed through social interaction and joint practice.

* We presume that a conditional 'Global Ivy League' will definitively take shape in the coming 10-20 years out of the world's 20 leading universities that are year after year rated as the best universities and that remain head and shoulders above other universities around the world.

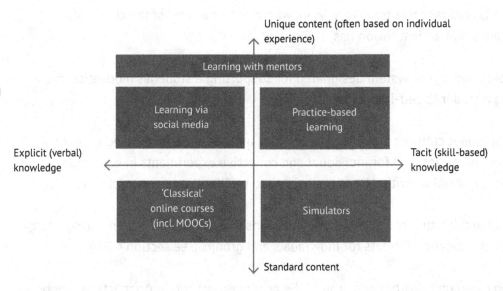

Figure 12 The main formats of new pedagogy for mass education

The mass segment strategy will partially imitate leaders' solutions (while accounting for resource and competence limitations), including the following:

- The unique advantage is in the 'niche' strategy: either concentrating on a territory's needs (school or university will become the center of social life for the local community), or concentrating on serving the goals of a sector of industry or the economy;

- Pseudo-individual trajectories (selected from a set of 'branded' trajectories) that have individual components, but are also a common content 'nucleus,' while education remains to a large extent synchronized (namely, 'courses' or 'classes' are retained, since this lowers administration expenditures);

- Learning — predominantly in teams working on creative projects with support from advisors;

- 'Mixed' pedagogics using a significant amount of online courses and games purchased for a class/course/entire school or university (a 'flipped' school or university model, including in cooperation with leading MOOC platforms);

- Using social network resources to support the education process with external competences;

- Partnership programs with other institutes that develop student mobility, introduce the student to different country and global cultures, and the ability to work in various contexts;

- Investments in mechanisms for long-term student loyalty, such as the following:

- Intangible motivation for young talent through working with group identity (ex. a unique culture or an academic institution's reputation);

- Long-term contract affiliation (ex. consolidating the obligations to serve some time working at one's school or university in exchange for free education);

- Working with graduate communities (offering supplemental learning services, engaging in internal education programs as experts or professors, engaging in funding academic institution programs, participating in graduates' startups, etc.).

Moreover, learning entrepreneurial skills and thinking should become a mass component of training in schools and (especially) universities in the coming years. Universities essentially must transition to project-oriented learning and gradually turn into spaces for entrepreneurial experiments, into 'startup factories.' This means that an individual zone should be created for startups both in the architectural sense (see below) and in the sense of planning education capacity. For example, university startup acceleration programs must become a part of education training for both engineers and students of the humanities. In addition to this, universities' own students and graduates investing in startups (including indirect investing, when in exchange for cutting tuition, the student upon entering the academic institution signs an obligation to assign the university shares in companies that he will found during or after his education) should be a part of universities' financial model (and possibly in several schools). In other words, it is wise for universities to develop their own competences in venture portfolio management or to do this in cooperation with venture funds.

b. Finally, there will be the 'tail' of educational institutions that perform functional goals from both the state and society's position:

b1. Institutes that provide fast training for professional or public purposes are in essence a combination of 'collective user centers' and academic centers (colleges, further training centers, etc.) where training programs can quickly develop. The main advantage of such centers is their flexibility and quickness in shifting education programs: they do not have any traditions or any special self-identification, but they are willing to adapt to the changing demands of local labor markets. Therefore, various simulators (including in augmented reality) and solutions for super-fast learning are the foundation of training, while centers themselves act as the 'gravitational centers' and meeting place for interested employers and potential employees. What is most likely of all is that many professional educational institutions will develop in this direction.

b2. Institutes serving a predominantly or exclusively social safety function (ex. schools in poor regions oftentimes with the main goal of keeping students away from street crime when their parents are at work). This social burden from the industrial education system could remain for a long time. Most likely, such institutes will have a strategy that includes the following:

- Creating an architecture and IT environment designated to ensure student safety and control;

- Predominantly digital education, including in virtual worlds and working with curators to resolve complex tasks and personal issues;

- Special social adaptation programs for troubled students, including in partnership with social movements.

## 4.2.3 New education architecture and education's place in the urban space

Another issue that we cannot ignore involves the requirements for organizing an academic space for future schools and universities, and the correlation of schools and universities with the urban environment surrounding them. If digital technologies transfer us to virtual worlds, while augmented reality will allow refining any physical spaces at our discretion, then is it worth even addressing any requirements or, as futurologists say, there will be enough 2x2 meter large rooms for accommodating access capsules in virtual worlds?

1. **Education architecture.** At the end of the 20th century, education architecture was one of the most important experimental objects: as Winston Churchill once said, 'We shape our buildings: thereafter, they shape us.' In the end, now educational institutions, including

schools, universities, museums, and libraries have become one of the most interesting objects in urban space; however, we can already observe a library crisis happening around the world: libraries are no longer needed as material repositories (excluding repositories for unique books), because readers can get virtually any material in digital format. As a result, libraries are starting to redefine their purposes. For example, they are becoming cultural centers, places for young people to socialize, co-working spaces, business incubators, etc. (Peterson, 2013).

We aspired to show in the previous parts (two and three) that digital education reforms 'live' education but does not nullify it. Telepresence, sensoria and developed virtual worlds will be able to make the online experience almost as rich as the offline experience (and it is hard to say where the line can be drawn between virtuality and reality), but it will be 'almost' the same for a good while longer yet. Places for joint practice, creativity, meditation, experiments, and games are still needed, and far from all these activities can be digitized, not to mention that it is not worth digitizing them. What requirements, however, should be made for these spaces?

It is evident that the architecture must, first and foremost, be based on the perceptions of what activities will take place within an educational institution. Since education itself is becoming all the more a field for experimenting (and we do not know for certain what types of activities will emerge and what type will vanish), the architecture must provide as much flexibility as possible for conducting these experiments. Buildings that are simple to rebuild, easily and quickly modifiable interior spaces (ex. using interior partition walls), and mobile furniture all must serve the ability to assemble any size room for any type of work. In particularly, if universities want to take advantage of the 'wave of technological startups' (section 2.3.1), then they need to envisage an empty space where the activities of new laboratories and high technology companies can be based. It is fundamentally important to not plan the entire territory of a campus (leaving free places) and to create as many freely transforming areas as possible within the existing campus. For universities that are tightly built into the space of old cities, this could require additional redevelopment efforts.

Of course, in some cases premises could have additional requirements: for example, if reference is being made to natural science laboratories or production floors, then the modular principle works well here. One of the formats that is becoming all the less functionable is the amphitheater, famous since antiquity. It was good in the 4th century B.C. to hear guru speakers, but now they are almost unsuitable for joint work or for moving freely. At the same time, insulated premises are absolutely necessary for small groups and individual work (moreover, this is very important to ensure simple regulations for using (and rebuilding) premises within an educational institution at the request of professors and the students themselves.* The mobility of the architecture and the education processes must be supported by the mobility of administrative regulations).

Second, education space has to easily provide for 'mixed' types of work. For example, large screens, including interactive ones, for joint work with remote audiences and groups, ubiquitous access points, possibilities to quickly connect different types of electronic devices. Equipment for augmented reality is absolutely necessary, because the augmented reality resource allows for continually increasing premises polyfunctionality (when several groups can simultaneously use the same space for various scenarios).

* http://www.acui.org/uploaded-Files/_PUBLISHED_CONTENT/About_ACUI/Association_News/2012/SummitReport05172012.pdf

Third, there should be enough places for relaxation, socializing, and cultural exchanges within an educational institution. Learning is all the more taking place not only (and not so much) within formal lectures, but also during a friendly chat or an unexpected meeting with an advisor over lunch. Serendipity is in human life; to have the circumstances for serendipity to happen more often, there need to be specially created serendipity places located at the crossroads of the most intensive human and informational flows. If education on campus takes places 24 hours a day (namely if the asynchronized learning principle is implemented), then an educational institution's campus must provide every possibility for those who wish to spend 24 hours a day there, to study, to create, and play during the day, evening, and middle of the night (namely there should be cafes, relaxation rooms, fitness rooms, and other infrastructure that is open around the clock, at least automatically).

* Although there are several examples of successful architectural solutions for the 21st century–see the following detailed OECD study: http://www.oecd.org/education/innovation-education/centreforeffectivelearningenvironmentscele/designingforeducationcompendiumofexemplaryeducationalfacilities2011.htm

The models of such architecture already exist, but they are not first and foremost university campuses,* but rather the offices of leading IT companies, such as Google, Facebook, and Amazon.** In particularly, these campuses have modulation, the ability to freely and creatively use various spaces for new projects, the ability to organize allocated work, and the ability to freely socialize and exchange ideas. They also are space that is highly connected on the inside, which allows for moving all around campus without going outside. Above (section 2.1.2) we were saying that the education sphere needs, first and foremost, to learn from the IT sector, while organizing the working space is one of the things that needs to be learned before anything else.

**2. Education in the urban environment.** Educational institutions since antiquity have been one of the centers that attract attention in a city, and often have entirely redefined their rhythms (such as student cities like Oxford, Bologna, Paris, Boston or Tomsk); however, with time many universities (and especially schools) have retreated within their own borders, their education processes have become unsynchronized with what is going on in the surrounding environment. More than a century ago, J. Dewey wrote about the need to blur the lines between schools and society around them (Dewey, 1907), but this call was not heeded.

** http://www.telegraph.co.uk/technology/picture-galleries/9461561/Inside-Googles-quirky-new-London-headquarters.html?frame=2303595 http://online.wsj.com/news/articles/SB10001424052702304371504577402702156152694 http://news.cnet.com/8301-1023_3-57585602-93/amazon-proposes-a-colossal-biospherelike-seattle-campus/

Now, education can no longer ignore this call. Some leading universities are already becoming 'agents for changing the world' with global ambitions, but such universities cannot be and should not be many. The surround urban or regional environment for the majority of schools and universities should become the subject of their attention. Through both academic processes and engaging active citizens in various spaces, academic institutions can become the centers of local development

This chance to change the city space by working with education processes could be mutually interesting for the administrations of academic institutions and for cities. Of course, the risk is mutual as well. The university is in the city, while the city becomes the experimental object at the university, for example, to be able to launch a space rocket from a barren piece of land or to hold a theatrical parade on a central city street. If the cultural and economic limitations of the city itself do not allow this to be done, then the opportunities for developing education become drastically limited. The choice of both the city and the academic institution (universities to a greater extent and schools to a lesser extent) is to find this mutual, long-term interest, because only cities that are willing to encourage risk will have the energy for cultural and economic development (Florida, 2005).

It is entirely possible that not all schools and universities will retain their role in the 2020s and beyond. As network-linked services grow, the real space's role will decline and the space will become denser, while far from all academic institutions will be able to become local development leaders (and thus, preserve their meaningfulness). It is likely that many cities by the middle of the 2020s will face the task of redeveloping part of their educational and cultural institutions (as has already been mentioned with libraries, as well as movie theaters) that are no longer needed. As is roughly the same as with how old industrial facilities in large cities that are gradually turning into loft apartments and offices, old academic facilities could become spaces for any other activities: they are entirely suitable as residential accommodations as well, while some of them could be absorbed by the new entertainment industry (ex. by growing 'big games,' which we wrote about in section 3.4.3).

## 4.3 REPERCUSSIONS FOR REGULATORS

*The future isn't something hidden in a corner.*
*The future is something we build in the present.*
**Paulo Freire**, Education as the Practice of Freedom

*When you cannot do what you want, want what you can do*
**Leonardo da Vinci**

The area of government education policies is a serious field of study, to which dozens of monographs have been dedicated, and we do not expect to voice a totally new opinion in this area. Moreover, we are inclined to agree with José Ortega y Gasset, who wrote: 'the school as a natural state institute depends much more on the public atmosphere than on the artificial pedagogical atmosphere within its walls.' He also wrote that the best education systems 'are impossible to adopt, because they are only one of the parts of a whole (Ortega y Gasset, 1991). Education policy is closely linked to state policy as a whole, and good education systems can exist only within a country's appropriate economic, political, and cultural environment.

We can, nonetheless, discuss the general principles, by which not so much current policy is built (which is pointless to talk about, because such policy is always dependent on a country's domestic situation), as much the 'policy for the future' that guarantees a country a strategic advantage in the education sphere. Moreover, since we believe that most OECD countries follow models similar to those described below, our recommendations concern more quickly developing countries that are currently expanding (and are already partially reorganizing) their education model (Figure 12).

We believe that regulators' main challenge is in no way to reform existing educational institutions to adapt them to new goals, but rather to create an environment in the country that permits a new, efficient education to emerge that corresponds to the level and objectives of a country's development. It is entirely possible that the level of required changes for educational institutions modeled after industrial templates is so high that it is easier to leave them alone than to try and redo them. As organizational researchers Michael Hannan and John Freeman (Hannan, Freeman, 1984) believe, the shift of organizational forms that dominate in an industry or sector usually takes place not through regeneration, but rather through replacing such forms with new players created while accounting for the changed environment. As a result, the model for developing education through creating greenfield projects is more promising than the model for reorganizing brownfield projects.* On the other hand, history is aware of a host of examples of such regeneration in many different industries, including in education: for example, one of Europe's oldest universities, Cambridge University, was at first a scholastic school, then became a Humboldt-style research university, and now is Great Britain's most successful laboratory for producing technological startups.**

* http://www. skolkovo.ru/public/ ru/press/news/ item/3892-2013-10-10-15/

** http://www. theguardian.com/ technology/2013/ dec/01/ cambridge-university-inter-net-tech-startup

### 1. **Industrial education policies.**

The scenario we describe for the spread of new education is one involving the gradual displacement and replacement of industrial education solutions with 'mixed' education solutions using new technologies. Within this logic, industrial education should retain its purpose for supporting the basic level of education in the coming 10-15 years at the least. Moreover, industrial education institutes could become 'development agents' in states' interest, namely places were changes to the local economy and socio-cultural environment are created. Finally, they can serve as platforms where experiments are conducted on new educational approaches. As a result, the following could be the political priorities in relation to existing national education systems:

a. Support funding designated to maintain the level of quality of basic education given the needed overhauls and additions to educational content that reflect technological and social changes (including knowing native and foreign languages, mathematics, programming, perceptions of the natural and scientific worldview, and assimilating 21st century skills);***

*** http://www.p21. org/overview/ skills-framework

b. Precise investments that tackle the following challenges:

- Shaping leading institutes that are capable of being members of the global education elite (since investments in such projects are very high, any quickly developing country can afford to take on at least one or several such projects);

- Creating one or several large 'breakthrough' projects (products with a high rate of replicability and high export potential) in the field of professional training and general education using education high technologies (modeled after the Advanced Research Projects Agency for Education (ARPA-ED) — see below), including training programs for successful industrial and innovation clusters, training programs for big science projects, etc.;

- Reorganizing some of the leading national universities (or integrated school university complexes) into regional development centers.

c. The challenge of reconstructing the economy to adapt it to the new technological structure (section 2.2.12.3.1), including resolving the issue of 'extra' people who will transition to new areas of employment (section 2.3.3), will be one of the main challenges for the industrial education system in the coming years. Longer cycles for training programs to shift compared with technology shift cycles are a systemic problem of the education system. As a result, projects for developing industrial education must, in particularly, do the following:

- Ensure dialog between the education and industrial spheres, including jointly discussing the prospects for industry development and adaption to the future (and not only current) needs of the economy for skills while accounting for technological and social changes (Luksha et al., 2014);

- Tear down the barriers for adapting to an industry's needs for professional education, including proliferating dual education and super-fast professional training models, jointly developing professional standards together with employer associations and implementing education programs based on them, and independent industry certification or employer certification;

- Drastically expand the opportunities for student internships at businesses in the real economy and for trying out various professions — not only for students and young professionals, but also for school children (all the way up to primary school students) — and create an environment where school children assimilate 1-2 working professions through basic training;

- Develop programs to support self-employment (including business education, mentorship programs for startups and non-commercial projects, creating impulses and infrastructure for youth entrepreneurship, etc.).

National regulators need to draw up their own position and policy regarding leading MOOC platforms. Although national educational institutes in developing countries could perceive these platforms as a threat, and they could start lobbying for restrictions on MOOC resource access for local students, imposing such bans is unlikely to be a foreword-thinking solution. This is because this would deprive the national workforce of opportunities to have better educational content and this would give local education players the illusion of temporary security (when they can pay less attention to their own competitiveness). Free MOOC access, however, in the long term could have negative repercussions for national labor markets (we discussed this issue in section 3.1.3). The best that regulators in this situation can do is create an environment for mutually beneficial partnership between MOOC platforms and national education systems and integrate such partnerships together with the many countries' national talent learning support programs at the world's leading universities.

Furthermore, regulators need to be ready for when global competition on the education market will grow, and this competition for most countries will become the already mentioned 'Queen of Hearts race,' when investments need to be increased in the national education system just to retain that system's competitive level. On the backdrop of the leaders in this race who have left the others in the dust, getting return on investment in overhauling existing industrial education projects and creating new such projects will become all the more difficult.

### 2. New education policies.

New education promises to be ready to assume the purposes that industrial education serves and to provide additional services that industrial education does not, all the while being willing to do this for less and with greater success. If this is indeed the case, then the best that regulators can do is not get in the way of this natural replacement happening, while also making it as productive as possible as far as society's interests are concerned.

First, a significant part of new education will be implemented as various technological startups (section 4.1). If a country has an environment that makes technological entrepreneurship an attractive business to be in (including having venture finance mechanisms, the infrastructure for technopark and business incubators, and effective property protection regulations, including for intellectual property), then this creates great prerequisites for developing new education projects. What is significant is that a country should simultaneously possess a pedagogical, entrepreneurial, and programmer culture, which make it possible to develop new education for far from all quickly developing countries (but allows entirely for countries such as India, China, Russia, Turkey, and a few other South East Asian countries to do this). As a result, if these prerequisites are fulfilled, then regulators can help the development of new education by creating 'education incubators' (interaction platforms between teachers, programmers, and businesspeople through incubators, startup accelerators, etc.) and by providing financial and fiscal support for launching education startups (including by introducing tax breaks and organizing target venture funds through public-private partnerships).

The second extremely important issue concerns the fact that education is capable of having a direct impact on people's physical and mental health, and of shaping their future behavior. This problem is especially acute in regards to child education, since children more rarely have the established corresponding psychological defense mechanisms, and since they are more susceptible to new content. As a result, shaping the new education sphere must be accompanied by drawing up the physical and psychological safety requirements for education products (especially in relation to products based on neurotechnologies, which we discussed in section 3.7). It is very important to adhere to a balance between protecting consumer interests and creating an environment for developing the new education sphere. This is important in order to preserve enough interest for new project initiators, while cutting those that are obviously harmful. The U.S. child education products industry's experience shows that developed professional communities — where developers, producers, independent psychology and pedagogy experts, and consumer representatives are in contact with each other — are the best solution here.*

* For example, the Juvenile Products Manufacturers Association's model: http://jpma.org/content/about/about-jpma

3. **General policies for the education sphere.**

If a country sees both industrial education projects and new education projects develop, then the regulator's main challenge is to create equal rules to the game that will allow the best qualities of existing and new approaches to be on display, and make way for shaping a balanced system for them to be cross-linked. In other words, the regulator must ensure as much social efficiency as possible while adhering to national and end-user interests.

First, a country must have equal access rights to key resources for various educational institutes: access to students, budget growth, grants and subsidies, etc. Excess preferences for traditional institutes, including state institutions, should be avoided, because this causes the competitiveness of new projects to decline drastically.

Second, there need to be ways to define a person's achievements throughout his life, as well as support for individual education trajectories. This will allow for choosing between 'systemic' and 'new' education providers.

Third, special work needs to be done on cross-linking existing (traditional, systemic) solutions with emerging new solutions. For example, schools and universities should be encouraged to use learning mechanisms in social networks, individual education trajectory management tools, online learning resources, etc.

Fourth, the quality of educational innovations seriously improve, if educational product producers are capable of operating not only domestically, but also abroad. Since most developing countries have high-technology export support programs, such programs can be implemented for exporting education services, including education technology solutions.

Finally, there need to be changes for new education forms to emerge through supporting research and development experiments in the education field. In particularly, specialized grants are needed to create new educational technologies. A fine model here comes from an ARPA-ED project,* which the Obama administration and the U.S. Congress initiated in 2012-13 to search for breakthrough technological solutions (such as personal 'digital mentors' available 24/7; education courses that improve as their students use them; education simulators that have the attractiveness of videogames and are able to retain student's high level of engagement for a long period of time) for radically overhauling the education system. The ARPA-ED initiative emerged to a large extent in response to China's extremely efficient assimilation of the industrial education model, which requires looking for an asymmetrical response in new technological education (the second important motivation was the evident necessity to keep the state-of-art skills and knowledge of American military forces). Moreover, the opportunities to experiment within the education system itself need to be expanded. In particularly, approaches can be applied here that 'learning organizations' (see section 3.3.1) implement, such as Google, Toyota, and Apple. Namely, this involves allocating time for activities that fundamentally are not related to the current routine and that encourage those willing to try, make mistakes, and try again.

*  http://www.ed.gov/ technology/arpa-ed

4. **Interstate and transnational policies.**

As we discussed above (in particularly, in section 3.1.3), creating mechanisms for the new, truly transnational education market to regulate itself will be one of the key international regulation issues in the coming years. Large-scale online education technologies are a double-edged sword: on the one hand, they allow for creating the environment to develop national and local education systems, while on the other hand, they can destroy this environment while also wrecking the needed diversity of human cultures. Therefore, we believe that the issue of how this architecture for coordinating education and personnel markets will be developed is one of the highest priority issues in the coming years. This issue concerns not only the relations between 'universities for a billion' and traditional education systems, but also just how transparent and fair the talent overflow mechanisms will be established between countries (foreseeing the emergence of 'global talent vaccuum cleaners', we discussed two possible mechanisms: The World Education and Personnel Organization, which regulators talent overflow rules and resolves disputed issues, and the Kyoto Education Protocol, which presupposes compensation payments to countries that produce talent from the countries that benefit from such talent).

Moreover, we presume that new supranational solutions, playing the role of 'harmonizers' of the world's education systems, will emerge for the education infrastructure when a global education infrastructure is created. International competence models that were founded by industry professional communities and that determine the basic requirements for specialist skills and knowledge in these industries could become one of these solutions. Furthermore, global testing systems that allow for verifying a specialist's knowledge and skill level, and for granting such specialist more opportunities for professional self-fulfillment in various countries and regions, could be created on the basis of international professional associations. Such work is being done together with leading MOOC platforms that could gradually evolve toward global certification systems that assist the development of the international talent market.

Another important issue concerns creating the opportunities for accelerated growth in the education sphere for developing countries. Despite us having indicated at the beginning of this Report the drawbacks in the dominating paradigm of catching up in international education policy, overall we believe that this is the right approach; however, we also believe that trying to reconstruct the school and university education model, used in industrially develop countries, in developing countries would first and foremost require investing a lot more than what these countries can afford at the moment. Second, this would consolidate their lagging behind developed countries, since they would imitate education models that are quickly going out of date rather than search for new solutions. Following the manner of Nicholas Negroponte (MIT Media Lab) and Sugata Mitra (Newcastle University), we believe that the education divide between developing countries, including underdeveloped countries, and economically developed countries could be surmounted through actively using new education formats.

Providing users (children and adults) with simple laptops and tablets, the ability to recharge (including mechanically), the corresponding foreseen programs and (when possible) minimal Internet access could provide users with modern education tools. Moreover, it could not only provide such users with the chance to be more efficient in resolving pressing issues (for example becoming familiar with more modern land farming and plant care methods, building autonomous power plants, etc.), but also raise education to a level where it will be able to become part of a more highly developed education system. Therefore, as part of the One Laptop Per Child (OLPC) project, 2.5 million XO-1 laptops (standard models being worth around 100 dollars) have already been supplied to developing countries. The OLPC project has proven to be highly effective, including specially conducted experiment where residents of African villages were given only laptops without any instructions, and they assimilated the majority of these laptops' possibilities in just a few days, learning reading skills and even basic programming.*

Such projects in the future could be supplemented with a number of resources designated for users from developing and underdeveloped countries: for example, instructions for organizing basic industrial production or for building more efficient and reliable homes out of makeshift materials (modeled after the Reaction Housing System).** If knowledge is power, then access to new knowledge could help overcome hunger, epidemics, and poverty much better than direct humanitarian aid. Education using network-linked and digital technologies — by nature extremely inexpensive — will allow all the more people to get involved in the global economy and culture. Moreover, it is developing and underdeveloped countries that could become the new education innovations laboratories, where the most socially and economically efficient solutions could originate (Leadbeater, Wong, 2010). Moreover, these solutions could be conveyed all across the world, including to developed countries, enriching their pedagogical practice. What is more, educated people from these countries having access to the Internet will enrich human culture with new ideas and give our society fundamentally new products, because a resource insufficiency disciplines the mind, forces to appreciate what you have, and invent what is truly needed.

* http://blog.laptop.org/

** http://www.reaction-housingsystem.com

| 'INDUSTRIAL MODEL' EDUCATION POLICIES | NEW EDUCATION POLICIES |
|---|---|
| • Sufficient funding to maintain the existing quality level<br>• Focused investments<br>    • Creation of leading institutions,<br>    • Setting up 'megaprojects' to facilitate a breakthrough,<br>    • Transforming universities into educational centers for regional<br>    growth and development<br>• Rebuilding economy to accommodate waves of new technologies (also solving the problem of the 'new unemployed')<br>    • Supporting dialog between education and industry regarding future skills needs<br>    • Removing barriers that impede adaptation to industry requirements<br>    • Creation of programs to support self-employment<br>• Organization of partnerships between MOOC-platforms and national education systems | • Creation of Ed Tech incubators for educators, programmers, and entrepreneurs (in the form of incubators, startup accelerators etc.)<br>• Financial and fiscal support for startups in education, incl.:<br>    • Preferential tax regimes<br>    • Establishment of specialized Ed Tech venture capital funds in PPP format<br>• Development of standards for physiological and mental safety of educational products (involving communities of educators, healthcare specialists, psychologists, and parents) – with gradual shift towards self-regulated standards of New Education |

| GENERAL POLICIES |
|---|

• Equal rights for all educational providers to access key resources: students, development budgets, grants, subsidies etc.
• Possibility of tracking and recording individual's achievements throughout his/her life and support of individual educational trajectories. (This will allow to choose between 'industrial model' and 'new education' providers.)
• Special initiatives that help 'stitching' old and new education practices
• Support of educational services export (incl. hi-tech solutions)
• Support of research and experimentation in educational sphere (target grants to support development of educational technologies, creating new possibilities for experimentation inside the system )

| TRANSBOUNDARY / INTERNATIONAL POLICIES |
|---|

• Promotion of inexpensive education technologies in developing countries (e.g. OLPC model)
• Identification and global replication of educational practiced from developing countries (e.g. 'learning from extremes' model)
• Establishment of global certification systems and global simulators for skill testing
• Uniform rules of international talent market functioning: W(E)TO or Talent 'Kyoto Protocol'

**Figure 13.** Key types of education policies to support transformation of education systems

*A sage goes about his business preferring inaction*
*Teaches without the use of words*
*Invokes change without summoning it*
*Creates without that which has been created*
*Impels without putting forth effort*
*Takes no pride in what is accomplished.*
**Tao Te Ching**

# 5. CONCLUSION

One of the authors of this text at one time had the chance to discuss the ancient Chinese symbol yin yang. As we know, yin yang symbolizes two basic contrary forces, one of which (yin) is light, clear, organized and male, while the other (yang) is dark, latent, chaotic, and female. These two forces in yin yang (or tai chi) spill over into each other. When one spreads, the other shrinks. When one blossoms, the other germinates, all the while pointing to the cycles of change that are inherent to nature, man, and society. This symbol, the author said, has an internal contradiction at its base. Such a dynamic is possible only when the system has a third element that forces yin and yang to lose their equilibrium, move in a cycle and mutually engender each other* (in reality, this intuition is not accidental: China and Korea have another wide-spread, less well-known version of this same symbol that has three elements).

    A significant number of publications about future education describe the process of the changing education sphere as a battle of two forces, a sort of 'battle between good and evil,' that pits 'new' education, supported by new technologies and designated to transform society, against 'industrial' education, which aspires to retain the status-quo of educational institutions (Figure 13).

    In fact, we can see a forming social consensus: major media, children's goods and health-care businesses, various ICT players, progressive academic institutions (ex. top universities launching their own MOOC platforms), revolutionaries within the school and university system, and from independent NGOs all present the new education system project. The new generation of parents, willing to assert a conscious and outside-the-box demand for training their children, echo them, as do some governments that see education as a tool for conveying their agenda in the world. On the other hand, the vast majority of teachers and professors within the education system take an extremely conservative position, perceiving any innovations as a threat to the stability of their status (it should be said it is the academic and teacher lobby that often becomes the main stopper in transformation of education, blocking many of education reform initiatives and curriculum revisions in schools and

* Roughly like with a pendulum that has a gravitational pull acting on weight, the suspension retaining the weight, and a certain third force that disrupts the pendulum's initial equilibrium.

universities). Conservatives from the academic elite support them, as do many people from organized religion and conservative families that oppose new education because they see it as an encroachment on the foundations of social order, the danger of losing basic skills necessary for each member of society, technological dumbing down, etc. These arguments are well known, and there is no point in repeating them. The struggle between two camps is taking place not so much between itself, as much for swaying major education customers capable of tipping the scales in favor of one of the sides: the political elites, education designers in developing countries, and finally, employers.

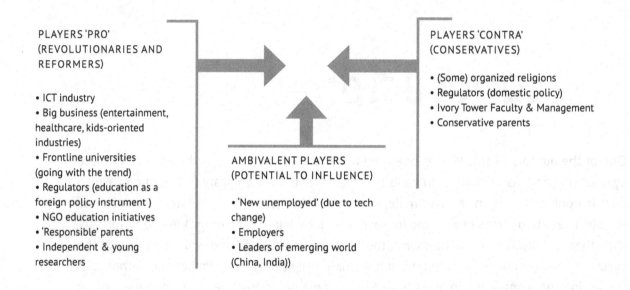

**PLAYERS 'PRO'**
**(REVOLUTIONARIES AND REFORMERS)**

- ICT industry
- Big business (entertainment, healthcare, kids-oriented industries)
- Frontline universities (going with the trend)
- Regulators (education as a foreign policy instrument )
- NGO education initiatives
- 'Responsible' parents
- Independent & young researchers

**PLAYERS 'CONTRA'**
**(CONSERVATIVES)**

- (Some) organized religions
- Regulators (domestic policy)
- Ivory Tower Faculty & Management
- Conservative parents

**AMBIVALENT PLAYERS**
**(POTENTIAL TO INFLUENCE)**

- 'New unemployed' (due to tech change)
- Employers
- Leaders of emerging world (China, India))

**Figure 13** Force fields in new education

In reality, the dramatic struggle for future education is making far from its first twist: we will recall the school and university system reorganization projects in the early 1970s, before this in the 1930s, before this in the 1910s, etc. Each of these projects was able to achieve a systemic shift, but none of them shook the foundations of the education system. This is exactly why the texts of Dewey, Ortega y Gasset, Illich or Freire are such fresh and modern reads, even though they were written dozens of years ago.

There are in fact three, and not two, forces in the struggle for future education, and each of them by nature is absolutely constructive:

1. **Social conservation:** Education as a process of accumulating and conveying collective/social memory as a way to retain social norms and patterns. The conservation logic gives the priority to the pattern, standard, repeating routine, 'archive management' − this was how education in the family has been built since antiquity; this was how the first schools of scribes were framed; this is how the Confucian education system or European schools for training monks were shaped. This principle concentrates on the past. It is typical even for

those who believe their first experience to be the benchmark by following early imprinting models*, and it does not try to be critical of this experience. This principle's message is the sacredness of the past, following the canon.

2. **Social pragmatism:** Education as a tool for overcoming current social challenges. Pragmatism is an unmistakable source of renewal and change, because oftentimes it is perceptions from the past and conserved by education that get in the way of surmounting current challenges. There is often the trend of imagining pragmatism as a new phenomenon in the education sphere. In reality, that was the case a lifetime ago. The rise of the current industrial education system, for that matter, stemmed from purely pragmatic objectives: Prussian King Frederick II in 1763 was the first to introduce mandatory secondary-level education for all children ages 5 to 13 as a way to have more efficient control over his subjects; other monarchs would soon follow his example. Pragmatism blurs the lines between education and public life, crosses over onto the territory of traditional educational institutions (be it a university or the family), and provides education with an important, albeit subjected role: for example, as a tool for conveying state priorities (here we should recall the especially efficient 'education machine' built in the Soviet Union) or the method for increasing labor productivity. This principle is concentrated on the present. This principle's message is that practice is the criterion of truth.

3. **Social progressivism:** education as a zone for 'breaking through into the future.' If education is a process where society assimilates norms, rules, and values, then many reformers, revolutionaries, and prophets eventually get the desire to 'reset' the existing norms and values by teaching people (often adults) new meanings and perceptions. The source for the emergence of these meanings is a separate issue that we will not begin to discuss here. What is significant is that these meanings usually are linked to images of the 'best' person and the 'best' society, while the reformers bearing them strive to personify these meanings in their own lives, make them the foundation of their own existence. Of course, there cannot be many of these phenomena, but it is these phenomena that highlight the exclusive role of education in public life and transforming civilization. Each progressives leaves their footprint, albeit it a small one, in education. It is worth mentioning not only widely known progressives, such as John Dewey, Maria Montessori, Anton Makarenko, Lev Vygotsky, Paulo Freire or Jiddu Krishnamurti, but also the host of education innovators and experimenters from all over the world who search for new models of formal and non-systemic education for children and adults. In the end, it was the great figures in human history— Christ, Socrates, Buddha, Confucius, Moses or Muhammad—who were first and foremost the teachers, and only then they were tsars, warriors, merchants or travellers. The message of the principle of progressivism is self-awareness, unleashing one's best qualities. This principle is meant for the future:

Any real progress in education combines these principles. Referring to ideal proportions here is likely pointless: like the philosophical stone, the ideal recipe for education will never be found; however, as with medieval alchemy, the side effects from searching for this ideal are much more important.

*Similar to how in K. Lawerence's famous experiments, only the hatched goslings perceived the researcher's rubber boots as their 'mom' and followed them wherever they went.

What is important is that the landscape we describe for future education—the first contours of which we presented in this Report—will be shaped by groups playing for these principles. By following only one of these (ex. the thesis that education must become practically oriented) within the design of systemic education solutions, policies or principles of a global education architecture, we risk losing the very meaning of the education process as continuously linking the present, past, and future.

When discussing the future of education and the new version of social projects related to it, we need supporting points, while mass technologies and widely used institutes are becoming those supporting points; however, we as people are moved not only by technologies and institutional regulations (although in the modern technocivilization we constantly are inclined to forget about this). The main source of renewal is the restoration of man, a person's expressed discontent with the status quo. The need for revolution is tied to it being impossible to support the current order. A schism festers within apparent tranquility, because renewal happens only through opposition. Our common goal is to preserve this tension, to retain the dividing process in its entirety, to not put ourselves to sleep with pseudo-consensuses, hold dialog between irreconcilable positions, because this is the only way we will be able to surmount systemic crises of civilization and complete the transition to a new quality.

The future of education cannot be predicted, but it can be created, together. Foresight is a way to draw the future closer to the present and assemble it here and now.

# BIBLIOGRAPHY

LIST OF SOURCES USED

Ackerman J. (2010) "Plastic Surf: The Unhealthful Afterlife of Toys and Packaging". **Scientific American**, August 10, 2010

Altbach P., Reisberg L., Rumbley L. (2009) **Trends in Global Higher Education: Tracking an Academic Revolution**, UNESCO.

Arbesman, S. (2012) **The Half-life of Facts: Why Everything We Know Has an Expiration Date**. Penguin, New York.

Armstrong K. (2010) **Twelve steps to compassionate life**. Anchor.

Ashby E. (1967) **Reflections on Technology in Education.** Haifa, Israel Institute of Technology.

Bakhurst D., Padden C. (1991) "The Meshcheryakov Experiment: Soviet work on the education of blind-deaf children". **Learning & Instruction** 1: 201-215.

Ballentine A., McKenzie N., Wysocki A., Kepner K. (2009) **The role of monetary and non-monetary incentives in the workplace as influenced by career stage**. University of Florida.

Barber M., Donnelly K., Rizvi S. (2012) **Oceans of Innovation: the Atlantic, the Pacific, Global Leadership and the Future of Education**. Institute for Public Policy Research.

Bateson G. (1972) **Steps to an ecology of mind**. The University of Chicago Press, Chicago.

Bell D. (1973) **The coming of post-industrial society: A venture of social forecasting**. Basic Books, NY.

Berners-Lee T., Hendler J., Lassila O. (2001) "The Semantic Web". **Scientific American**, May 2001.

Block N., Proctor T. (2009) **Scouting Frontiers: Youth and the Scout Movement's First Century**. Cambridge Scholars Publishing.

Boyd R., Richerson P. (2009) Culture and the evolution of human cooperation. **Philos Trans R Soc Lond B Biol Sci**. 364(1533): 3281–3288.

Brenn-White M., van Rest E. (2012), **English-Taught Master's Programs in Europe: New Findings on Supply and Demand**. The Institute of International Education.

Brin D. (1998) **The Transparent Society.** Perseus Books, Cambridge, MA, USA.

Budgeon S., Roseneil S. (eds.) (2004) "Beyond the Conventional Family". Special Issue. **Current Sociology** 52.

Capra F. (1982) **The Turning Point. Science, Society and the Rising Culture**, Simon &Schuster, NY.

Chesbrough H. (2003) **Open Innovation**, Harvard Business School Press, Boston.

Cock C., Fitchett J., Mangan J. (2005) "Constructing the New Economy: A Discursive Perspective". **British Journal of Management**, 16: 37-49.

Cohen B. (2006) "Urbanization in developing countries: Current trends, future projections, and key challenges for sustainability". **Technology in Society** 28: 63–80.

Colander D., Föllmer H., Haas A., Goldberg M., Juselius K., Kirman A., Lux T., Sloth B. (2009) "The Financial Crisis and the Systemic Failure of Academic Economics", **Kiel Working Paper** 1489, Kiel Institute for the World Economy, Kiel, Germany.

Corcoran E. (2010) "The 'Gamification' Of Education", **Forbes**, 29 October 2010.

Csíkszentmihályi, M. (1996) Creativity: **Flow and the Psychology of Discovery and Invention.** Harper Perennial, NY.

Curtsinger J. (2007) "Genes, Aging, and Prospects for Extended Life Span". **Minnesota Medicine**, October 2007.

Davenport S., Cummings S., Daellenbach U., Campbell C. (2013) "Problemsourcing : Local Open Innovation for R & D Organizations". **Technology Innovation Management Review**, March: 14–20.

Despommier D. (2009) "Growing Skyscrapers: The Rise of Vertical Farms". **Scientific American**, November 2009.

Deterding et al. (2011) "Gamification. Using game-design elements in non-gaming contexts", PART 2 **Proceedings of the 2011 annual conference extended abstracts on Human factors in computing systems**, ACM.

Dewey J. (1907) "The School and Social Progress." Chapter 1 in **The School and Society**. Chicago: University of Chicago Press: 19-44. URL: http://www.brocku.ca/MeadProject/Dewey/Dewey_1907/Dewey_1907a.html

Diamandis P., Kotler S. (2012) Abundance: **The future is better than you think.** Free Press.

Doidge N. (2007) **The Brain That Changes Itself: Stories of Personal Triumph from the Frontiers of Brain Science**. Penguin Books, NY.

Dyson F. (1999) **The Sun, the Genome, and the Internet**. Oxford University Press, Oxford.

Enkel E., Gassmann O., Chesbrough H. (2009) "Open R&D and open innovation: exploring the phenomenon". **R&D Management** 39 (4): 311-316.

Erikson E. (1959) **Identity and the Life Cycle**. New York: International Universities Press

Florida R. (2005) **Cities and the Creative Class**. Routledge.

de Freitas, S., and Liarokapis, F. (2011) "Serious Games: A New Paradigm for Education?". In **Serious Games and Edutainment Applications**. By Ma M., Oikonomou A., Jain L. (eds.): 9-23.

Frost & Sullivan (2010) **Next Generation Biofuels: Strategic Portfolio Management** (Technical Insights), Frost & Sullivan.

Fung A., Wright E. (2003) **Deepening Democracy**. Verso, NY.

Gantz J., Reinsel D. (2011) Extracting Value from Chaos, **IDC IVIEW**.

Gilmore J., Pine J. (2007) **Authenticity: what consumers really want**. Harvard Business School Press.

Gould S.J. (1997) "Nonoverlapping Magisteria". **Natural History** 106: 16-22.

Hakimi P. et al. (2007) "Overexpression of the Cytosolic Form of Phosphoenolpyruvate Carboxykinase (GTP) in Skeletal Muscle Repatterns Energy Metabolism in the Mouse", **The Journal of Biological Chemistry,** 282(45):32844-55 (see full details at: http://www.ncbi.nlm.nih.gov/pubmed/17716967)

Hall J. (2010) "The Reindustrialization of America". **American Thinker**, 10 July.

Hamel G. (2007) **The Future of Management**, Harvard Business Review Press, Boston.

Hannan M., Freeman J. (1984) "Structural inertia and organizational change". **American sociological review**, pp. 149-164.

Harden N. (2013) "The End of the University as We Know It". **The American Interest**, 2013 January/February issue.

Hayek F. (1976) **Denationalization of Money – The Argument Refined**. The Institute of Economic Affairs, London.

Hey T., Tansley S., Tolle K. (eds.) (2009) **The Fourth Paradigm: Data-Intensive Scientific Discovery. Microsoft Research**. Also available at: http://research.microsoft.com/en-us/collaboration/fourthparadigm/

Howe N., Strauss W. (1991) Generations: **The History of America's Future, 1584 to 2069**, William Morrow & Company, NY.

Hunt T. (2009) **The Whuffie Factor: Using the Power of Social Networks to Build Your Business**. Random House.

Ijsselsteijn W., Nap H., de Kort Y., Poels K. (2007) "Digital game design for elderly users". **Proceedings of the 2007 conference on Future Play**. ACM.

Illich I. (1971) **Deschooling Society**. Calder & Boyars, NY.

Intergovernmental Panel on Climate Change (2013) **Climate Change 2013**: The Physical Science Basis, IPCC Secretariat, Geneva.

Jünger F. (1949) **The failure of technology: perfection without purpose**, H. Regnery, Chicago.

Kaplan J., Pocharski M. (2010) **Growth Capitals: Megacity Growth Strategy**. Monitor Group Report.

Katzenbach J., Smith D. (2006) **The Wisdom of Teams: Creating the High-Performance Organization**, HarperBusiness, NY.

Klein G., Snowden D., Pin C.L. (2010) Anticipatory thinking. **Informed by Knowledge: Expert Performance in Complex Situations**, 235.

Kopeikina L. (2005) **The Right Decision Every Time: How to Reach Perfect Clarity on Tough Decisions**. FT Press.

Lakhani K., Boudreau K., Loh P., Backstrom L., Baldwin C., Lonstein E., Guinan E. (2013) "Prize-based contests can provide solutions to computational biology problems", **Nature biotechnology**, 31(2): 108-111.

Lathrop D., Ruma, L. (2010) **Open Government: Collaboration, Transparency, and Participation in Practice**, O'Reilly Media, Sebastopol, CA.

Lave J., Wenger E. (1991) **Situated Learning: Legitimate Peripheral Participation (Learning in Doing: Social, Cognitive and Computational Perspectives)**. Cambridge University Press, Cambridge, UK.

Leadbeater C., Wong A. (2010) **Learning from the Extremes**. Cisco. Available at: http://www.charlesleadbeater.net/cms/xstandard/LearningfromExtremes_WhitePaper.pdf

Lem S. (2013) **Summa technologiae**, University of Minnesota Press, Minneapolis.

Lockard C. (2012) "The Asian Resurgence in World History Perspective", **World History Connected**, February.

Lowenstein R. (2004) **Origins of the Crash: The Great Bubble and Its Undoing**. Penguin Books.

Luksha P., Afanasyev M., Sudakov D. (eds.) (2014) **Using Technology Foresights for Identifying Future Skills Needs**. Proceedings of SKOLKOVO-ILO 2013 Workshop. MSU SKOLKOVO, Moscow.

Lynch C. (2009) **Jim Gray's fourth paradigm and the construction of the scientific record**. URL: http://research.microsoft.com/en-us/collaboration/fourthparadigm/4th_paradigm_book_part4_lynch.pdf

Manyika J., Chui M., Bughin J., Dobbs R., Bisson P., Marrs A. (2013) Disruptive technologies: **Advances that will transform life, business, and the global economy**, McKinsey Global Institute, May 2013.

Marmer M., Herrmann B., Berman R., Easley C., Blank S., Bishara F. (2011) **Startup Genome Report 01. A new framework for understanding why startups succeed**.

Martin B. (2001) **Technology Foresight In A Rapidly Globalizing Economy**, United Nations Industrial Development Organization (UNIDO).

Martin J. (2007) **The Meaning of the 21st Century: A Vital Blueprint for Ensuring Our Future**. Riverhead Trade.

Maslow A. (1943) "A Theory of Human Motivation", **Psychological Review**, 50(4): 370-396.

Maurer H., Balke T., Kappe F., Kulathuramaiyer N., Weber S., Zaka B. (2007) **Report on dangers and opportunities posed by large search engines, particularly Google**. Institute for Information Systems and Computer Media, Graz University of Technology URL: http://www.iicm.tugraz.at/iicm_papers/dangers_google.pdf

McCleary R. (2013) "Protestantism and Human Capital in Guatemala and the Republic of Korea". Asian Development Bank Economics Working Paper Series, No.332. URL: http://papers.ssrn.com/sol3/papers.cfm?abstract_id=2239556

McDermott R. (1999) "Nurturing Three Dimensional Communities of Practice: How to get the most out of human networks", **Knowledge Management Review**, Fall edition.

McGonigal J. (2011) **The reality is broken: Why Games Make Us Better and How They Can Change the World**. The Penguin Press, NY.

Meadows D., Randers J., Meadows D. (2004) **Limits to Growth, The 30-Year Update**. Chelsea Green Publishing Company.

Meshcheryakov, A. (1979) **Awakening to life — Forming Behaviour and the Mind in Deaf-Blind Children**. (Transl. by K. Judelson). Progress Publishers, Moscow.

Mestad A., Myrdal R., Dingsøyr T., Dybå T. (2007) "Building a Learning Organization: Three Phases of Communities of Practice in a Software Consulting Company", **IEEE, Proceedings of the 40th Annual Hawaii International Conference on System Sciences (HICSS'07)**, URL: http://www.computer.org/csdl/proceedings/hicss/2007/2755/00/27550189a.pdf

Millstein R. (2006) "Natural Selection as a Population-Level Causal Process". **The British Journal for the Philosophy of Science** 57(4): 627-653.

Naisbitt J. (1988) Megatrends: **Ten New Directions Transforming Our Lives**. Grand Central Publishing.

National Intelligence Council (2010) **Global Governance 2025: At a Critical Juncture**. Washington, DC.

National Intelligence Council (2012) **Global Trends 2030: Alternative Worlds.** Washington, DC.

Nikolaus K. (2013) 'Self-Organizing Factories', **Pictures of the Future Magazine**, Spring 2013.

OECD (2011) Pensions at a Glance 2011: **Retirement-income Systems in OECD and G20 Countries,** OECD Publishing.

Ortega y Gasset J. (1991) **Mission of the University (Foundations of Higher Education)**. Transaction Publishers.

Pastrana E. (2010). "Optogenetics: Controlling cell function with light". **Nature Methods** 8: 24.

Peirce C (1931) **Pragmatism and Pramaticism**, volume V of The Collected Papers.

Perrenoud P. (2001) "The key to social fields: competencies of an autonomous actor." In: Rychen D., Hersh S. (eds.) **Defining and selecting key competencies.** Göttingen, Hogrefe & Huber Publishers.

Peterson A. (2013) "The digital age is forcing libraries to change. Here's what that looks like". **The Washington Post**, 7 August.

Reynolds C.W. (1987). "Flocks, herds and schools: A distributed behavioral model". **Computer Graphics** 21 (4): 25–34.

Robinson K. (2011) Out of Our Minds: Learning to be Creative. Wiley, NY.

Robinson K., Aronica L. (2009) **The Element: How Finding Your Passion Changes Everything**. Penguin Books, NY.

Rose S. (1993) **The Making of Memory: From Molecules to Mind**. Anchor Books, NY.

Scharmer O. (2009) **Theory U: Leading from the future as it emerges**. Berrett-Koehler, San Francisco.

Schweitzer, A. (1987) **The philosophy of civilization**. Prometheus Books.

Shernoff D. (2002) "Flow States and Student Engagement in the Classroom", **American Sports Institute**
URL: http://www.amersports.org/library/reports/8.html

Shirky C. (2008) **Here Comes Everybody: The Power of Organizing Without Organizations**, Penguin Press, London.

Small G., Vorgan G. (2008) **iBrain: Surviving the Technological Alteration of the Modern Mind**, Harper Collins, NY.

Small G., Moody T., Siddarth P., Bookheimer S. (2009) "Your Brain on Google: Patterns of Cerebral Activation during Internet Searching". **American Journal of Geriatric Psychiatry** 17(2): 116-126.

Stephenson N. (1995) **The Diamond Age: Or, A Young Lady's Illustrated Primer**. Bantam Spectra.

Summerskill B. (2000) "Playtime as Kidults Grow Up at Last", **The Observer**, 23 July.

Sutarto A., Abdul Wahab M., Mat Zin N. (2010) "Heart Rate Variability (HRV) biofeedback: A new training approach for operator's performance enhancement". **Journal of Industrial Engineering & Management**, 3(1): 176-198.

Szirmai A., Naudé W., Alcorta L. (2013) **Pathways to Industrialization in the Twenty-First Century: New Challenges and Emerging Paradigms**. Oxford Scholarship.

Tamburri R. (2013) "Universities open campuses in foreign countries, with mixed results", **University Affairs**, 9 January.

Turchin V., Joslyn C. (1989) Cybernetic Manifesto. URL: http://pespmc1.vub.ac.be/MANIFESTO.html

UN-Habitat (2012) **Sustainable Urbanization in Asia: A Sourcebook for Local Governments**, United Nations Human Settlements Programme.

Varela F., Thompson E., Rosch E. (1992) **The Embodied Mind: Cognitive Science and Human Experience**. The MIT Press, Boston.

Vinge V. (2006) **Rainbows End**. Tor Science Fiction.

Waddington D. (2012) "A Parallel World for the World Bank: A Case Study of Urgent: Evoke". **Educational theory** 62 (4), 427-447.

Wahba M., Bridwell L. (1976) "Maslow Reconsidered: A Review of Research on the Need Hierarchy Theory". **Organizational Behavior & Human Performance**, 15: 212-240.

Walker R. (2010) **After the Globe, Before the World**, Routledge, NY.

Weinberg S. (2012) 'The Crisis of Big Science', **The New York Review of Books**, 10 May.
URL: http://www.nybooks.com/articles/archives/2012/may/10/crisis-big-science/

Wilson R., Boyle P., Yu L., Barnes L., Schneider J., Bennett D. (2013) "Life-span cognitive activity, neuropathologic burden, and cognitive aging". **Neurology** 10.1212.

Wolff C. (2009) "IRS flexible working survey 2009: availability, take-up and impact", **IRS Employment Review** No. 921

Yoo K.H, Filandrianos E., Taghados S., Park S. (2013) "Non-Invasive Brain-to-Brain Interface (BBI): Establishing Functional Links between Two Brains", **PLOS One**, 3 April.

Żurawicki L. (2010) **Neuromarketing: Exploring the Brain of the Consumer**. New York: Springer-Verlag.

## SOME RESEARCH FROM THE PAST DECADE ON THE FUTURE OF EDUCATION SYSTEMS AND SKILL ANTICIPATION

AcMedSci (2012) **Human enhancement and the future of work**. Report from a joint workshop hosted by the Academy of Medical Sciences, the British Academy, the Royal Academy of Engineering and the Royal Society. November 2012
URL: http://www.acmedsci.ac.uk/viewFile/publicationDownloads/135228646747.pdf

ActionCanada (2013) **FutureTense: Adapting Canadian Education Systems for the 21st Century**.
URL: http://www.actioncanada.ca/en/wp-content/uploads/2013/02/TF2-Report_Future-Tense_EN.pdf

Arima A. (2003) **The Future of Higher Education in Japan**. United Nations University Public Lecture.
URL: http://sciencewithoutborders.international.ac.uk/media/4741/the%20future%20of%20higher%20education%20in%20japan.pdf

Aslanian C., Giles N.G. (2008) **Hindsight, Insight, Foresight: Understanding Adult Learning Trends to Predict Future Opportunities**. EducationDynamics.
URL: http://www.educationdynamics.com/CMSPages/GetFile.aspx?guid=119845f5-ed25-4597-a32e-9761e930d300

Ayad A. (2014) "Education Foresight". Imperial College London.
URL: http://www.imperialtechforesight.com/future-visions/87/vision/ed-foresight.html

Barber M., Mourshed M. (2009) **Shaping the Future: How Good Education Systems Can Become Great in the Decade Ahead**. Report on the International Education Roundtable, Singapore.
URL: http://www.mckinsey.com/locations/southeastasia/knowledge/Education_Roundtable.pdf

British Council (2014) Understanding India: The future of higher education and opportunities for international cooperation. February 2014.
URL: http://www.britishcouncil.org/sites/britishcouncil.uk2/files/understanding_india_report.pdf

British Council (2012) **The shape of things to come: higher education global trends and emerging opportunities to 2020**.
URL: http://www.britishcouncil.org/sites/britishcouncil.uk2/files/the_shape_of_things_to_come_-_higher_education_global_trends_and_emerging_opportunities_to_2020.pdf

Butcher J. (2014) "A Vision for Education and the Future of Learning", Policy Report, Goldwater Institute, No.267, 20 February

CCL (2011) **What is the Future of Learning in Canada?** Canadian Council on Learning.
URL: http://www.ccl-cca.ca/pdfs/CEOCorner/2010-10-11WhatistheFutureofLearninginCanada.pdf

CCN (2010) **Talking the Future 2010-2020: Languages in Education**. CLIL Cascade Network (CCN): University of Jyväskylä, Finland, March 2010

CEDEFOP (2009) **Future skill supply in Europe**. Luxembourg: Office for Official Publications of the European Communities.
URL: http://www.cedefop.europa.eu/EN/Files/4086_en.pdf

Collins A., Halverson R. (2009) **Rethinking education in the age of technology: The digital revolution and schooling in America**. New York: Teachers College Press

Council of Graduate Schools and Educational Testing Service. (2010) **The Path Forward: The Future of Graduate Education in the United States. Report from the Commission on the Future of Graduate Education in the United States**. Princeton, NJ: Educational Testing Service
URL: http://www.fgereport.org/rsc/pdf/CFGE_report.pdf

Davidson C., Goldberg D.T. (2009) **The Future of Learning Institutions in a Digital Age.** MIT Press
URL: http://mitpress.mit.edu/sites/default/files/titles/free_download/9780262513593_Future_of_Learning.pdf

Dawe G., Jucker R., Martin S. (2005) **Sustainable Development in Higher Education: Current Practice and Future Developments**. A report for The Higher Education Academy
URL: http://thesite.eu/sustdevinHEfinalreport.pdf

Eckel P. (2008) **Collective Foresight: Organizing for the Future**. American Council on Education.
URL: http://www.learningace.com/doc/383692/800b041680140b7b45e59dda8e995b86/thinking-future-tennessee

Economist Intelligence Unit (2008) **The future of higher education: How technology will shape learning**. Sponsored by the New Media Consortium
URL: http://www.nmc.org/pdf/Future-of-Higher-Ed-(NMC).pdf

Ernst & Young (2012) **University of the future. A thousand year old industry on the cusp of profound change**.
URL: http://www.ey.com/Publication/vwLUAssets/University_of_the_future/$FILE/University_of_the_future_2012.pdf

European Science Foundation (2008) Higher Education Looking Forward: An Agenda for Future Research.
URL: http://www.esf.org/fileadmin/Public_documents/Publications/HELF_01.pdf

Foresight Mental Capital and Wellbeing Project (2008). **Final Project report — Executive summary**. The Government Office for Science, London
URL: https://www.gov.uk/government/uploads/system/uploads/attachment_data/file/292453/mental-capital-wellbeing-summary.pdf

FutureLab (2010) Education futures, teachers and technology. London.
URL: http://www2.futurelab.org.uk/resources/documents/other_research_reports/Education_futures.pdf

GBN & Cisco (2010) **The Evolving Internet. Driving Forces, Uncertainties, and Four Scenarios to 2025**. Report jointly prepared by Cisco and GBN.
URL: http://newsroom.cisco.com/dlls/2010/ekits/Evolving_Internet_GBN_Cisco_2010_Aug.pdf

Green Building Council of Australia (2013) **The future of Australian education — Sustainable places for learning**.
http://www.gbca.org.au/uploads/167/34983/Green_Schools_report_2013_Final_for_web.pdf

Havas A. (2009) "Universities and the emerging new players: building futures for higher education". **Technology Analysis & Strategic Management**, 21(3): 425–443

Hazelkorn E. (2012) "Higher Education's Future: A new global order?" Presentation at EAIR Conference, Stavanger, Norway, September 2012.
URL: http://www.javeriana.edu.co/puj/viceadm/telescopi/wp-content/uploads/EAIR-Satvanger-Hazelkorn-Higher-Educations-Futures.pdf

Iiyoshi T., Kumar M.S.V. (2008) **Opening Up Education. The Collective Advancement of Education through Open Technology, Open Content, and Open Knowledge**. MIT Press.
URL: https://mitpress.mit.edu/sites/default/files/titles/content/9780262515016_Open_Access_Edition.pdf

Institute for the Future (2014) **From Educational Institutions to Learning Flows. Mapping the Future of Learning**.
URL: http://www.iftf.org/uploads/media/SR-1580-IFTF_Future_of_Learning_01.pdf

Institute for the Future (2010) **Future Work Skills 2020**.
URL: http://www.iftf.org/uploads/media/SR-1382A_UPRI_future_work_skills_sm.pdf

Institute for the Future (2008) **Knowledge Tools of The Future**.
URL: http://www.iftf.org/uploads/media/SR-1179_FutKnow.pdf

IPPR Commission on the Future of Higher Education (2013) **A Critical Path. Securing the Future of Higher Education in England**.
URL: http://www.ippr.org/assets/media/images/media/files/publication/2013/06/critical-path-securing-future-higher-education_June2013_10847.pdf

JRC (2011) **The Future of Learning: Preparing for Change**. European Commission Joint Research Centre — Institute for Prospective Technological Studies.
URL: http://www.gencat.cat/salut/ccfcps/html/ca/dir3612/docs/thefuturelearning.pdf

JRC (2010) **The Future of Learning: European Teachers' Visions**. Report on a foresight consultation at the 2010 eTwinning Conference, Seville, 5-7 February 2010.
URL: http://ftp.jrc.es/EURdoc/JRC59775_TN.pdf

KnowledgeWorks Foundation. 2025 Forecast: Recombinant Education: Regenerating the Learning Ecosystem.
URL: http://www.futureofed.org/forecast/

Kubler J., Sayers N. (2010) **Higher Education Futures: Key Themes And Implications For Leadership And Management**. Leadership Foundation for Higher Education.
URL: http://www.lfhe.ac.uk/filemanager/root/site_assets/research_resources/research/series_2/S2-4.1%20Kubler%20&%20Sayers%20-%20Higher%20Education%20Futures.pdf

Long M. (2013) The future of learning. A report sharing the Harvard Graduate School of Education Future of Learning Course.
URL: http://www.stjohnscollege.co.za/pdfs/Margot%20Long_Harvard%20Report%202013.pdf

Lönnblad J., Vartiainen M. (2012) **Future Competences — Competences for New Ways of Working**. University of Turku
URL: http://futurex.utu.fi/julkaisut_Future_Competences.pdf

Manyika J., Lund S., Auguste B., Ramaswamy S. (2012) **Help wanted: The future of work in advanced economies**. McKinsey Global Institute Discussion Paper, March 2012
URL: http://www.mckinsey.com/~/media/McKinsey/dotcom/Insights%20and%20pubs/MGI/Research/Labor%20Markets/Help%20wanted%20-%20The%20future%20of%20work%20in%20advanced%20economies/Help_wanted_future_of_work_full_report.ashx

Malone T. (2004) **The Future of Work How the New Order of Business Will Shape Your Organization, Your Management Style, and Your Life**. Harvard Business School Press.

MIT (2013) Future of MIT Education. Taskforce Preliminary Report.
URL: http://web.mit.edu/future-report/TaskForceOnFutureOfMITEducation_PrelimReport.pdf

NEA (2012) **Transforming Teaching: Connecting Professional responsibility with student learning**.
URL: http://www.nea.org/assets/docs/Transformingteaching2012.pdf

OECD (2008) **The Future of the Family to 2030. A Scoping Report**. OECD International Futures Programme, Paris.

Perkins D. (2013) **Future of Learning. Educating for the unknown**. Harvard Graduate School of Education. Boston, MA

Pew Research Center (2012) **The future impact of the Internet on higher education**. URL: http://www.pewinternet.org/files/old-media/Files/Reports/2012/PIP_Future_of_Higher_Ed.pdf

PricewaterhouseCoopers (2007) **Managing tomorrow's people. The future of work to 2020**. URL: http://www.pwc.com/gx/en/managing-tomorrows-people/future-of-work/pdf/mtp-future-of-work.pdf

Prime Minister's Commission on Japan's Goals in the 21st Century (2000) The Frontier Within: Individual Empowerment and Better Governance in the New Millennium. URL: http://www.kantei.go.jp/jp/21century/report/pdfs/

RIT (2012) **The Future of Teaching and Learning in Higher Education**. Report by the Rochester Institute of Technology Taskforce. URL: https://www.rit.edu/provost/sites/rit.edu.provost/files/future_of_teaching_and_learning_reportv13.pdf

Roland Berger Strategy Consultants. **Trend Compendium 2030: Global Knowledge Society**. URL: http://www.rolandberger.com/expertise/trend_compendium_2030/global_knowledge_society.html

Rudd P., Rickinson M., Benefield P. (2004) **Mapping work on the future of teaching and learning. Report for the General Teaching Council**. URL: http://www.nfer.ac.uk/publications/FTL01/FTL01.pdf

Rudd J., Davia C., Sullivan P. (2009) **Education for a Smarter Planet: The Future of Learning. CIO Report on Enabling Technologies**. IBM Redguide. URL: http://www.redbooks.ibm.com/redpapers/pdfs/redp4564.pdf

Saveri A., Chwierut M. (2009) **The Future of Learning Agents and Disruptive Innovation**. RL: http://andreasaveri.com/wp-content/uploads/2009/03/sr-1160kwf_learning_agents.pdf

Schuller T., Watson D. (2009) **Learning Through Life. Inquiry into the Future for Lifelong Learning**. National Institute for Adult Continuing Education.

Shuler C., Winters N., West M. (2013) **The Future of Mobile Learning. Implications for Policy Makers and Planners**. UNESCO. URL: http://unesdoc.unesco.org/images/0021/002196/219637e.pdf

Stoyanov S., Hoogveld B., Kirschner P. (2010) **Mapping Major Changes to Education and Training in 2025**. European Commission Joint Research Centre – Institute for Prospective Technological Studies. URL: http://ftp.jrc.es/EURdoc/JRC59079_TN.pdf

STRATA-ETAN (2002) **Higher Education and Research for the Era: Current Trends and Challenges for the Near Future**. STRATA-ETAN Expert Group On Foresight For The Development Of Higher Education/Research Relations. URL: ftp://ftp.cordis.europa.eu/pub/foresight/docs/hleg_final25102002_en.pdf

Thornburg D. (1997) 2020 **Visions for the Future of Education.**
URL: http://www.tcpd.org/Thornburg/Handouts/2020visions.html

UK Commission for Employment and Skills (2014) **The Future of Work: Jobs and skills in 2030.**
URL: http://www.z-punkt.de/uploads/media/the-future-of-work-evidence-report.pdf

UNECE (2011) **Learning for the future: Competences in Education for Sustainable Development.** Steering Committee meeting for ESD, 7 and 8 April 2011, Geneva
URL: http://www.unece.org/fileadmin/DAM/env/esd/01_Typo3site/ExpertGroupCompetences.pdf

UNITE Group (2014) Living and Learning in 2034. A Higher Education Futures Project.
URL: http://www.unite-group.co.uk/binaries/744/587/living-learning-in-2034_final.pdf

Universities UK (2012) **Futures For Higher Education: Analysing Trends.**
URL: http://www.universitiesuk.ac.uk/highereducation/Documents/2012/FuturesForHigherEducation.pdf

Winthrop R., Bulloch G., Bhatt P., Wood A. (2013) **Investment in global education. A strategic imperative for business.** Brookings Institution. September 2013

RF Group (2013) Foresight 'Education-2030.'
URL: http://www.asi.ru/molprof/foresight/12254

ACGI (2013) Road map for developing the children's goods and services industry

Social program 'Childhood' (2010) Foresight 'Childhood-2030.
URL: http://detstvo2030.ru/dorojnaya-karta/

# THE TEAM OF CONTRIBUTORS AND ACKNOWLEDGEMENTS

Re-Engineering Futures Group (www.refuture.me) 2010-2014 (CreativeCommons)
Authors: Pavel Luksha and Dmitry Peskov
The following people contributed to preparing the Report texts: Maxim Afanyasev, Aleksei Gusev, Katerina Luksha, Tatyana Makarova, Ivan Smagin, Timur Shchoukine
Co-authors of material used in the report: moderators and session participants
Education foresight at Educamp 2010,
Foresight Steamboat 2012,
Competence Foresight 2012,
Global Education Foresight 2013,
Foresight Fleet 2013
Foresight NeuroWeb 2013


## The following are acknowledged for their support significant contribution to creating the map of the global education futures:

Agency for Strategic Initiatives
Association of Childrens Goods Industry
Center for Strategic Research 'North-West'
Cisco
Intel / Project Harmony International
Junior Academy of Sciences 'Intellect Buduschego'
Konstruirovanie Buduschego Group
Konstruktory Soobschestv Praktiki Group
Metaver Group
Progressor Consortium
Russian Community of Managers
Russian Ministry of Education and Science
Russian Venture Company
SBERINVEST Asset Management
Skolkovo Institute of Science & Technology
SKOLKOVO Moscow School of Management
SOLING Education Bureau

Printed in the United States
By Bookmasters